WOLVERINE: LOGAN. Contains material originally published in magazine form as LOGAN #1-3. First printing 2008. ISBN# 978-0-7851-3425-1. Published by MARVEL PUBLISHING, INC., a subsidiary of MARVEL ENTERTAINMENT, INC. OFFICE OF PUBLICATION: 417 5th Avenue, New York, NY 10016. Copyright © 2008 Marvel Characters, Inc. All rights reserved. $19.99 per copy in the U.S. and $21.00 in Canada (GST #R127032852); Canadian Agreement #40668537. All characters featured in this issue and the distinctive names and likenesses thereof, and all related indicia are trademarks of Marvel Characters, Inc. No similarity between any of the names, characters, persons, and/or institutions in this magazine with those of any living or dead person or institution is intended, and any such similarity which may exist is purely coincidental. **Printed in the U.S.A.** ALAN FINE, CEO Marvel Toys & Publishing Divisions and CMO Marvel Characters, Inc.; DAVID GABRIEL, SVP of Publishing Sales & Circulation; DAVID BOGART, SVP of Business Affairs & Talent Management; MICHAEL PASCIULLO, VP of Merchandising & Communications; JIM O'KEEFE, VP of Operations & Logistics; DAN CARR, Executive Director of Publishing Technology; JUSTIN F. GABRIE, Director of Editorial Operations; SUSAN CRESPI, Editorial Operations Manager; OMAR OTIEKU, Production Manager; STAN LEE, Chairman Emeritus. For information regarding advertising in Marvel Comics or on Marvel.com, please contact Mitch Dane, Advertising Director, at mdane@marvel.com. For Marvel subscription inquiries, please call 800-217-9158.

10 9 8 7 6 5 4 3 2 1

WRITER
Brian K. Vaughan

ARTIST
Eduardo Risso

COLORS: Dean White

LETTERS: Virtual Calligraphy's Joe Caramagna

ASSISTANT EDITOR: Daniel Ketchum

EDITOR: Axel Alonso

COLLECTION EDITOR: Jennifer Grünwald

ASSISTANT EDITORS: Jody LeHeup, Cory Levine & John Denning

EDITOR, SPECIAL PROJECTS: Mark D. Beazley

SENIOR EDITOR, SPECIAL PROJECTS: Jeff Youngquist

SENIOR VICE PRESIDENT OF SALES: David Gabriel

BOOK DESIGNER: Spring Hoteling

EDITOR IN CHIEF: Joe Quesada

PUBLISHER: Dan Buckley

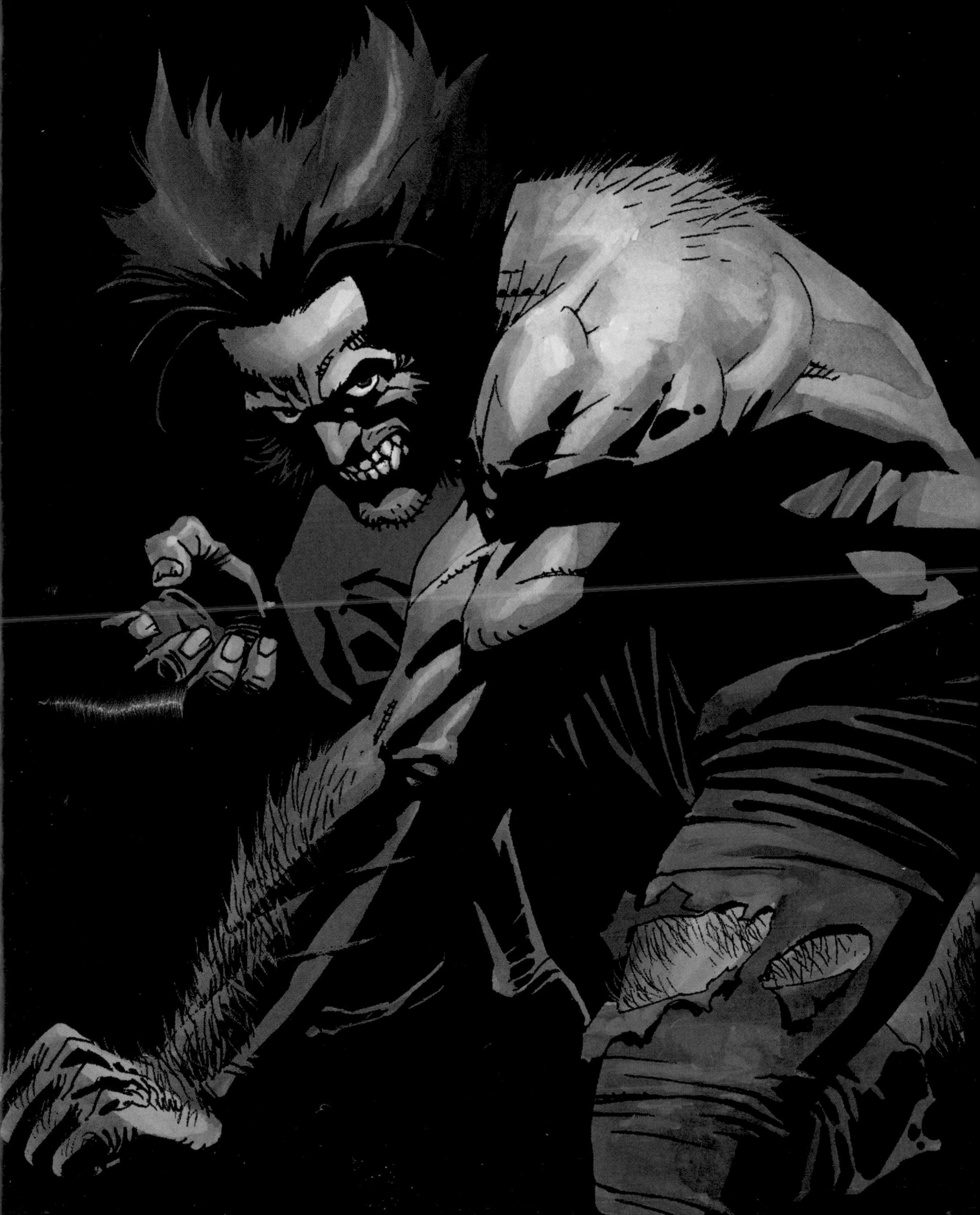

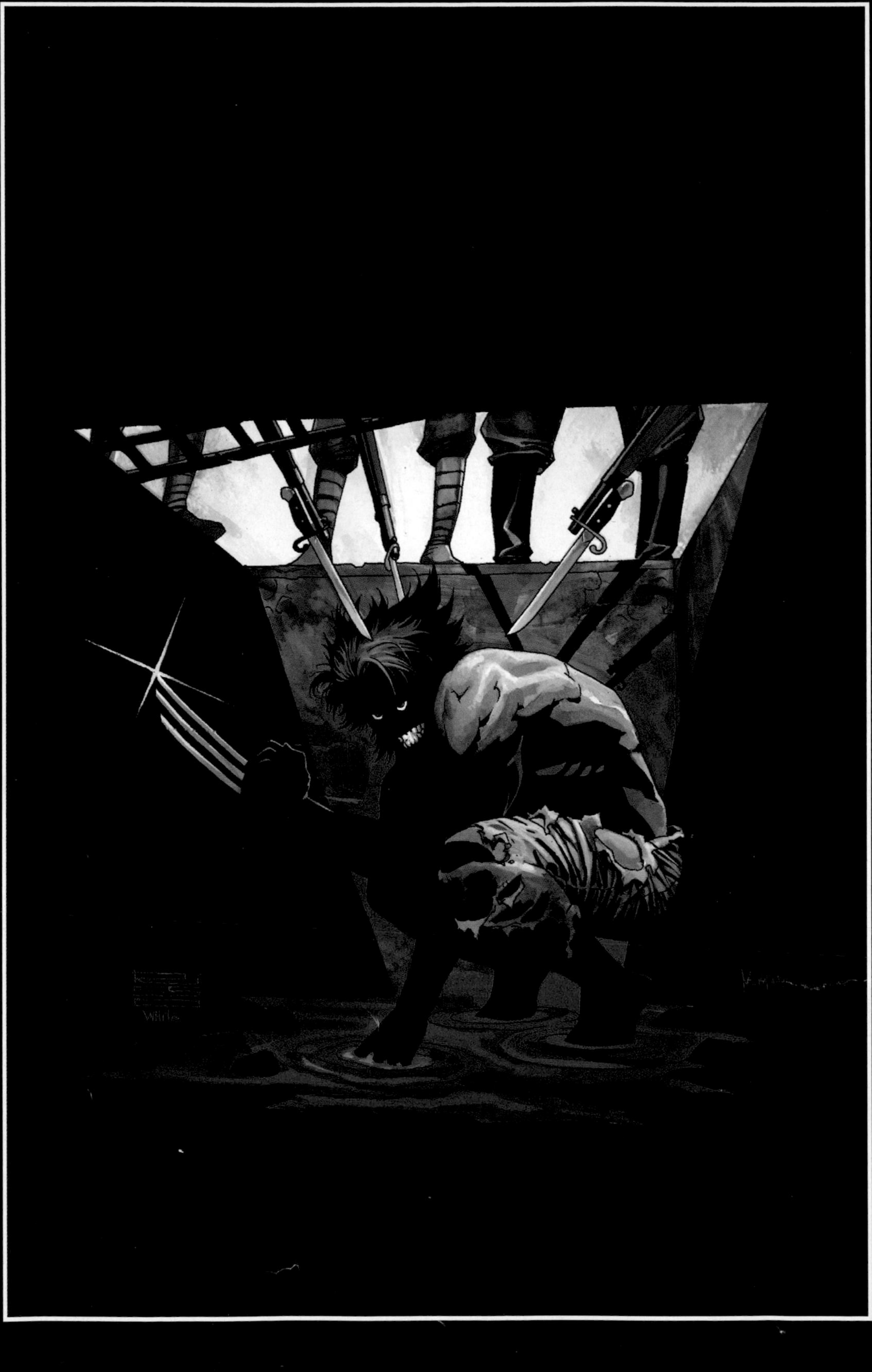

issue number one

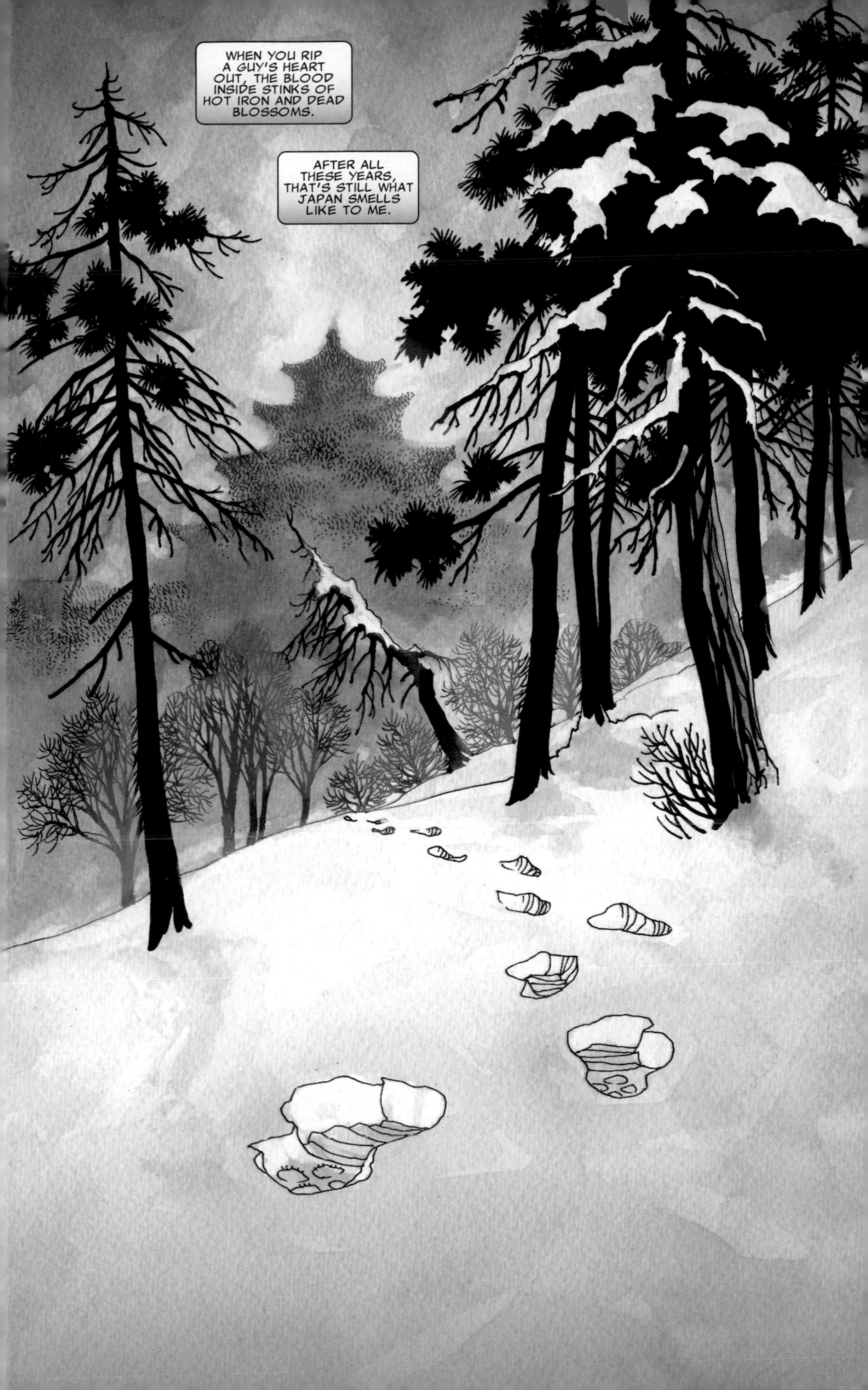
WHEN YOU RIP A GUY'S HEART OUT, THE BLOOD INSIDE STINKS OF HOT IRON AND DEAD BLOSSOMS.
AFTER ALL THESE YEARS, THAT'S STILL WHAT JAPAN SMELLS LIKE TO ME.

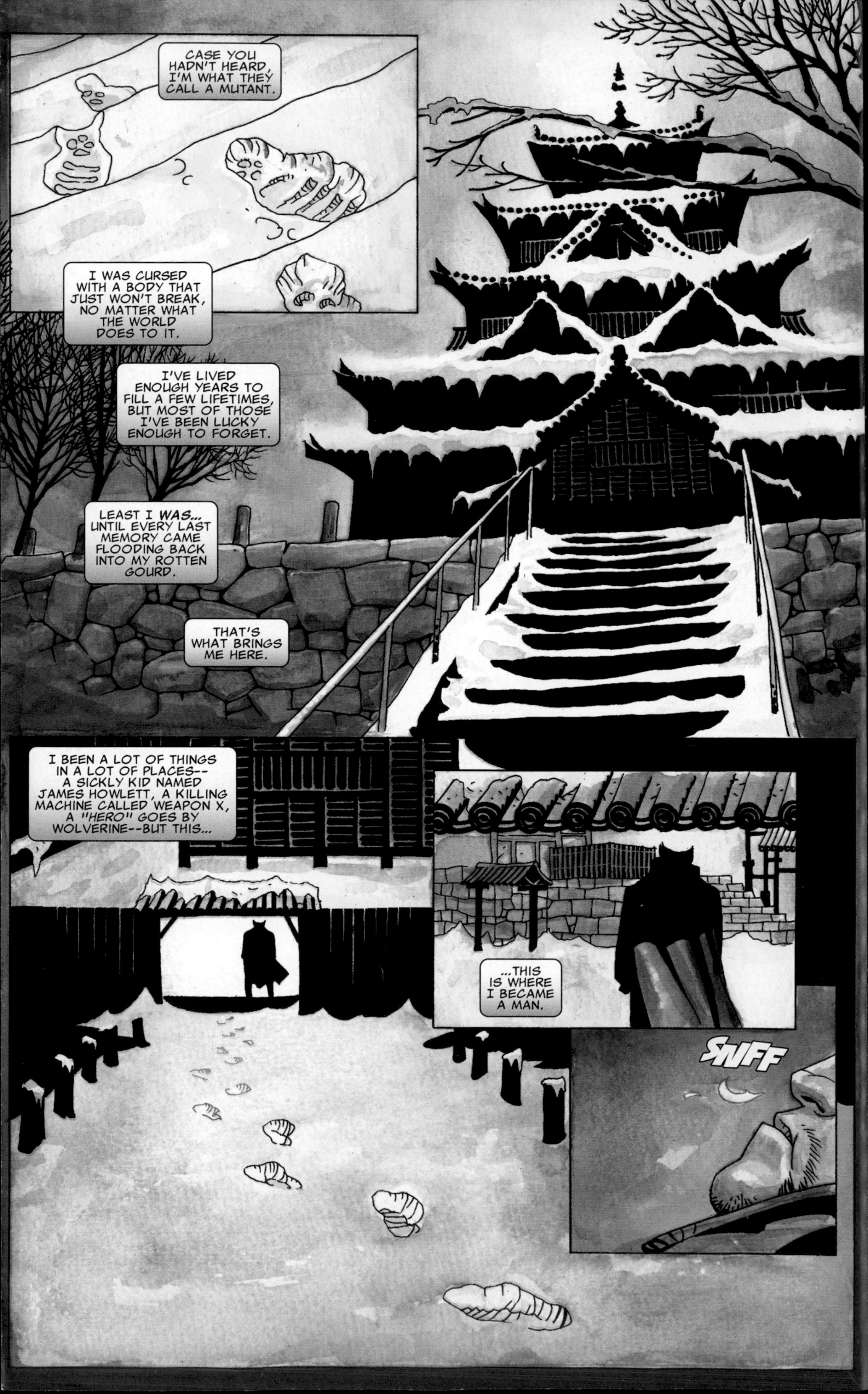

CASE YOU HADN'T HEARD, I'M WHAT THEY CALL A MUTANT.
I WAS CURSED WITH A BODY THAT JUST WON'T BREAK, NO MATTER WHAT THE WORLD DOES TO IT.
I'VE LIVED ENOUGH YEARS TO FILL A FEW LIFETIMES, BUT MOST OF THOSE I'VE BEEN LUCKY ENOUGH TO FORGET.
LEAST I *WAS*... UNTIL EVERY LAST MEMORY CAME FLOODING BACK INTO MY ROTTEN GOURD.
THAT'S WHAT BRINGS ME HERE.
I BEEN A LOT OF THINGS IN A LOT OF PLACES-- A SICKLY KID NAMED JAMES HOWLETT, A KILLING MACHINE CALLED WEAPON X, A "HERO" GOES BY WOLVERINE--BUT THIS...
...THIS IS WHERE I BECAME A MAN.
SNFF

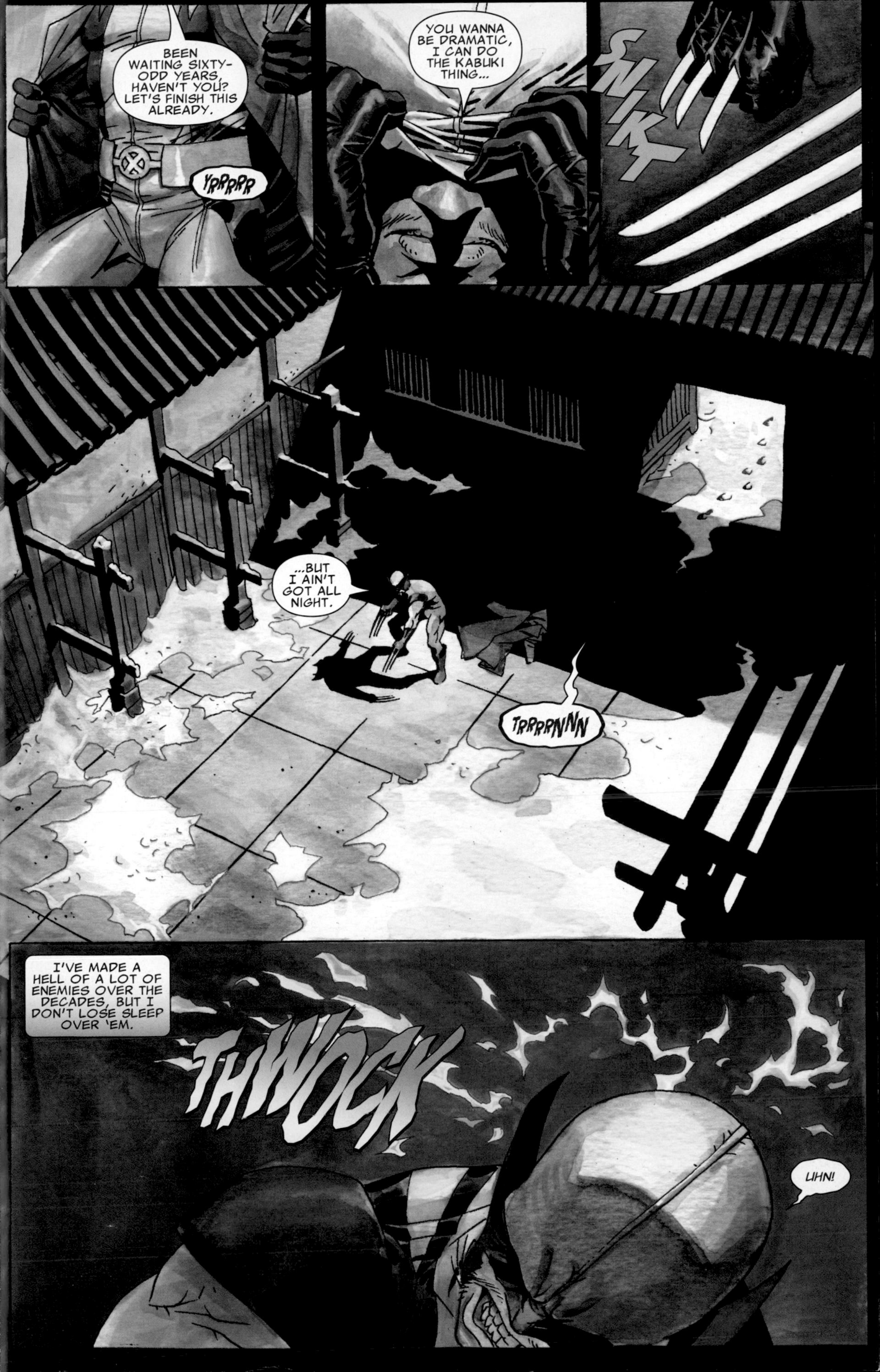
BEEN WAITING SIXTY-ODD YEARS, HAVEN'T YOU? LET'S FINISH THIS ALREADY.
YRRRRR
YOU WANNA BE DRAMATIC, I CAN DO THE KABUKI THING...
SNIKT
...BUT I AIN'T GOT ALL NIGHT.
TRRRRNNN
I'VE MADE A HELL OF A LOT OF ENEMIES OVER THE DECADES, BUT I DON'T LOSE SLEEP OVER 'EM.
THWOCK
UHN!

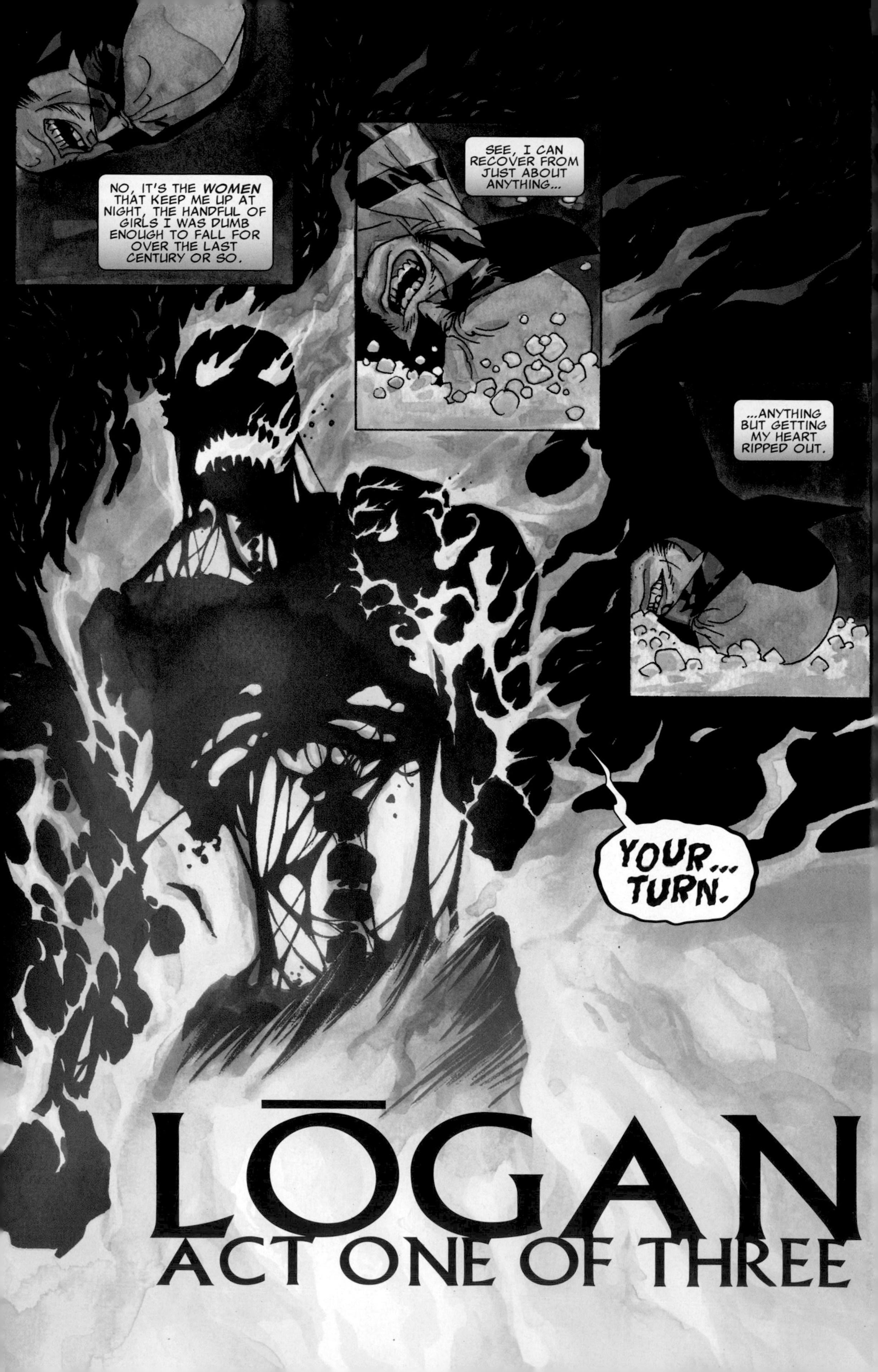
NO, IT'S THE WOMEN THAT KEEP ME UP AT NIGHT, THE HANDFUL OF GIRLS I WAS DUMB ENOUGH TO FALL FOR OVER THE LAST CENTURY OR SO.
SEE, I CAN RECOVER FROM JUST ABOUT ANYTHING...
...ANYTHING BUT GETTING MY HEART RIPPED OUT.
YOUR... TURN.
LŌGAN
ACT ONE OF THREE

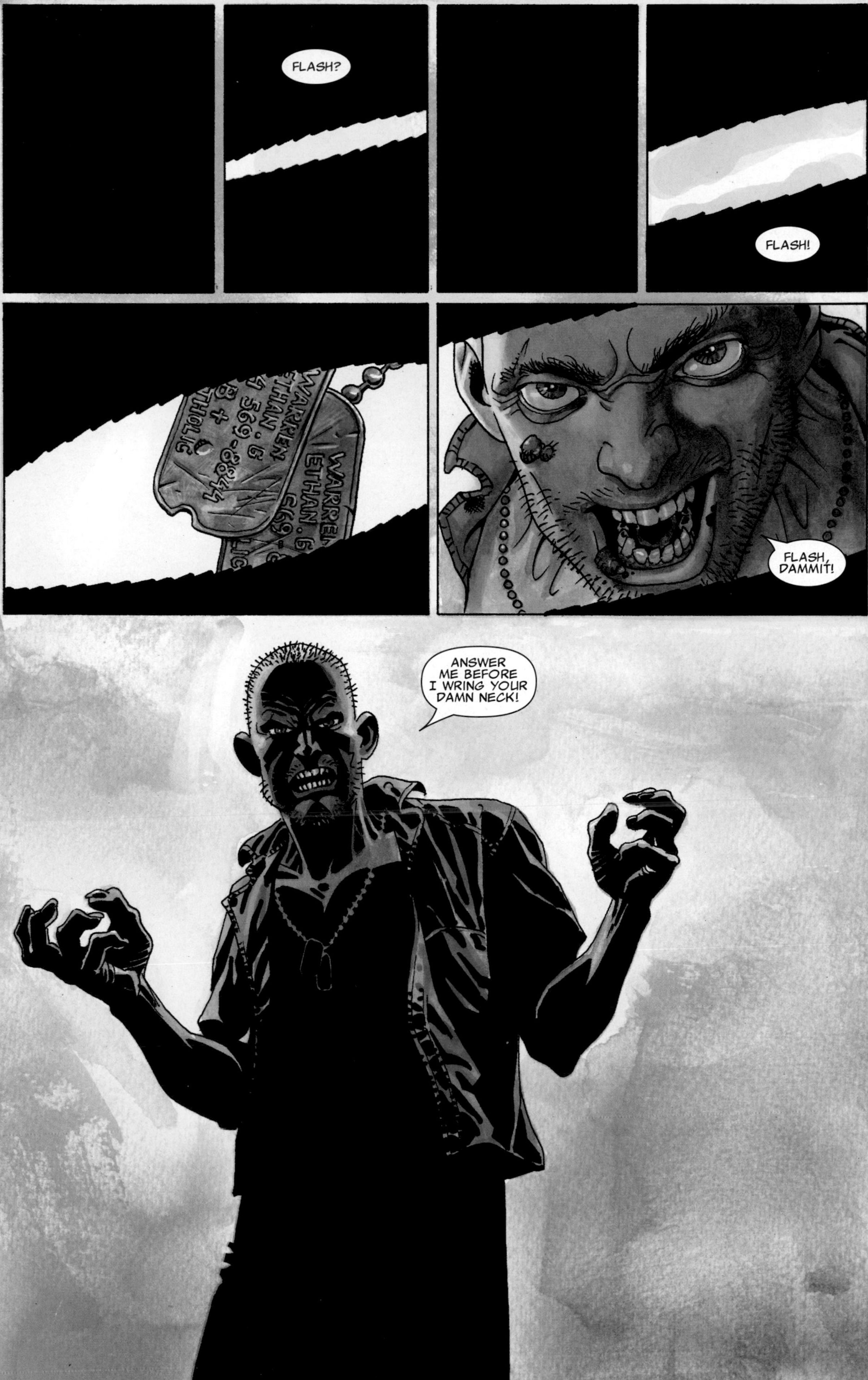
FLASH?
FLASH!
FLASH, DAMMIT!
ANSWER ME BEFORE I WRING YOUR DAMN NECK!

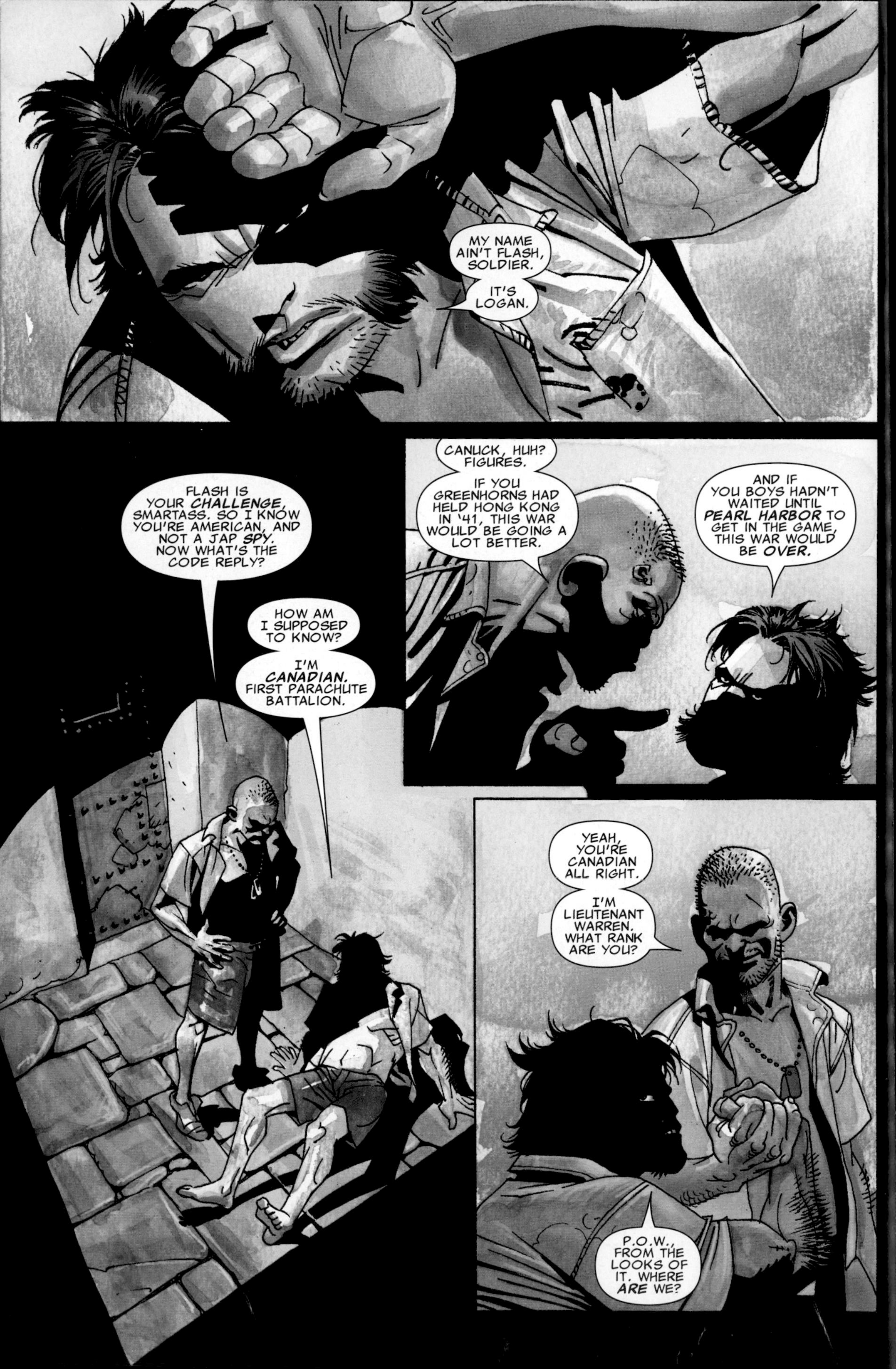
MY NAME AIN'T FLASH, SOLDIER.
IT'S LOGAN.
FLASH IS YOUR CHALLENGE, SMARTASS. SO I KNOW YOU'RE AMERICAN, AND NOT A JAP SPY. NOW WHAT'S THE CODE REPLY?
HOW AM I SUPPOSED TO KNOW?
I'M CANADIAN. FIRST PARACHUTE BATTALION.
CANUCK, HUH? FIGURES.
IF YOU GREENHORNS HAD HELD HONG KONG IN '41, THIS WAR WOULD BE GOING A LOT BETTER.
AND IF YOU BOYS HADN'T WAITED UNTIL PEARL HARBOR TO GET IN THE GAME, THIS WAR WOULD BE OVER.
YEAH, YOU'RE CANADIAN ALL RIGHT.
I'M LIEUTENANT WARREN. WHAT RANK ARE YOU?
P.O.W., FROM THE LOOKS OF IT. WHERE ARE WE?

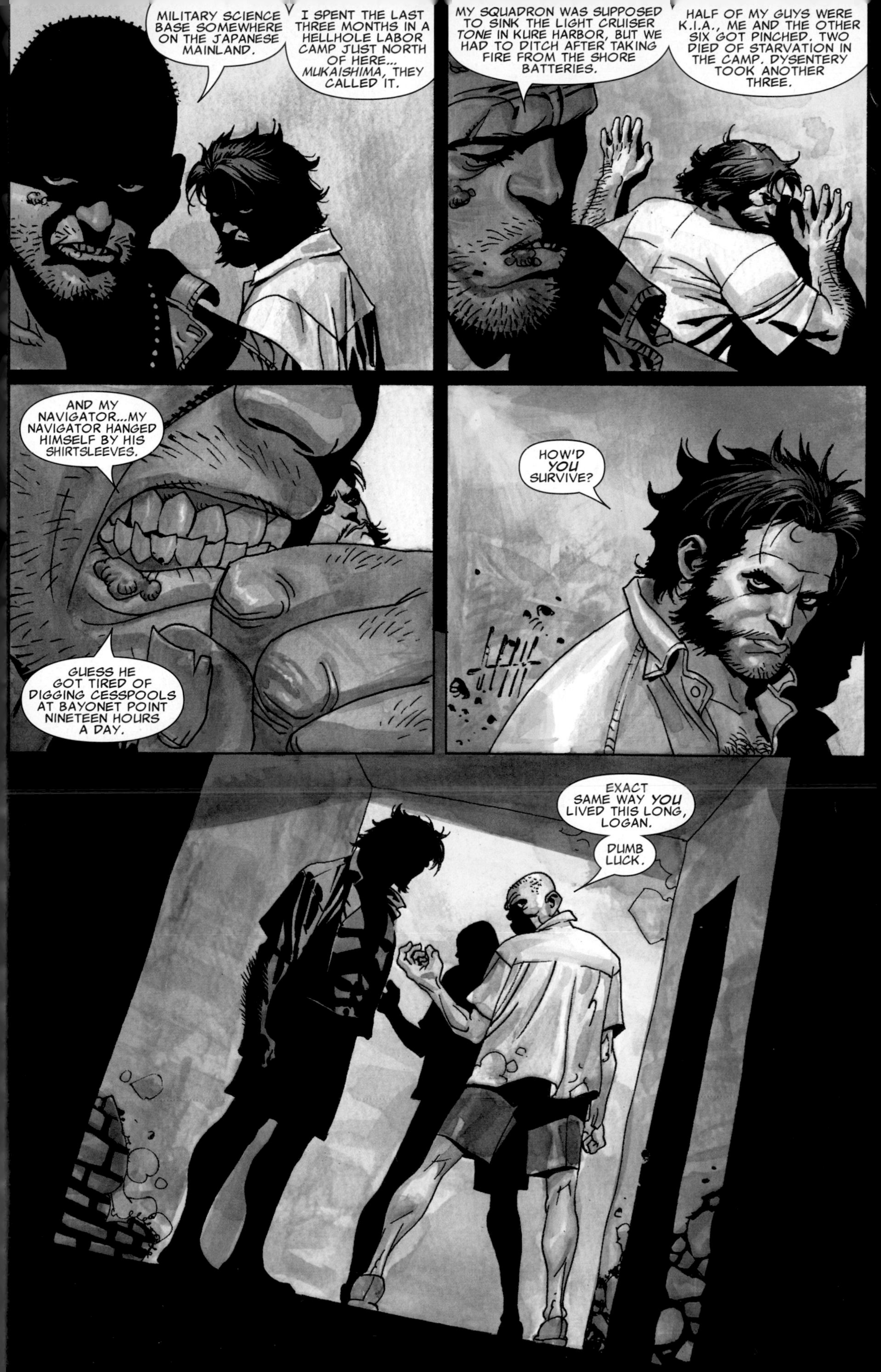
MILITARY SCIENCE BASE SOMEWHERE ON THE JAPANESE MAINLAND.
I SPENT THE LAST THREE MONTHS IN A HELLHOLE LABOR CAMP JUST NORTH OF HERE... MUKAISHIMA, THEY CALLED IT.
MY SQUADRON WAS SUPPOSED TO SINK THE LIGHT CRUISER TONE IN KURE HARBOR, BUT WE HAD TO DITCH AFTER TAKING FIRE FROM THE SHORE BATTERIES.
HALF OF MY GUYS WERE K.I.A., ME AND THE OTHER SIX GOT PINCHED. TWO DIED OF STARVATION IN THE CAMP. DYSENTERY TOOK ANOTHER THREE.
AND MY NAVIGATOR...MY NAVIGATOR HANGED HIMSELF BY HIS SHIRTSLEEVES.
GUESS HE GOT TIRED OF DIGGING CESSPOOLS AT BAYONET POINT NINETEEN HOURS A DAY.
HOW'D YOU SURVIVE?
EXACT SAME WAY YOU LIVED THIS LONG, LOGAN.
DUMB LUCK.

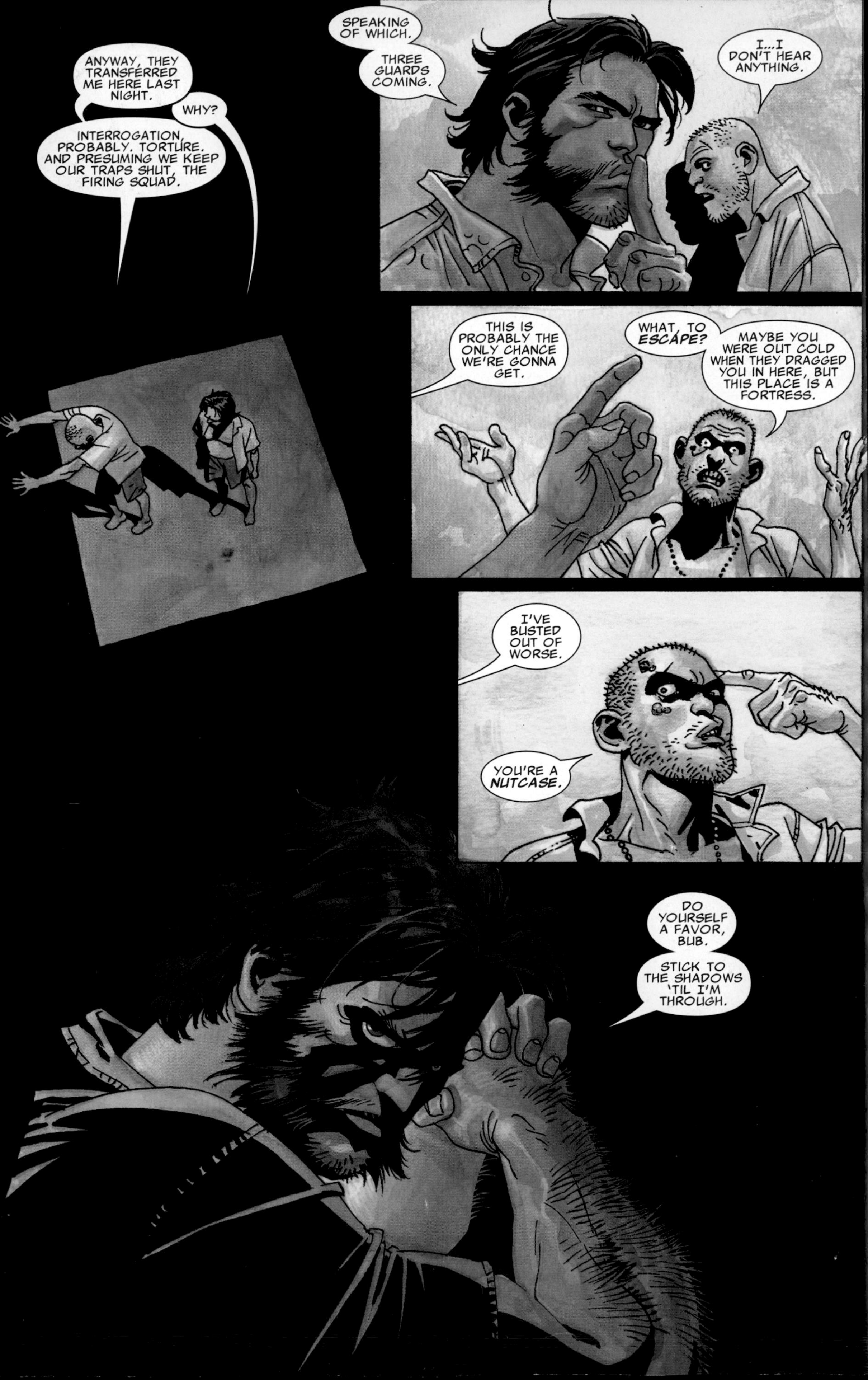
ANYWAY, THEY TRANSFERRED ME HERE LAST NIGHT.
WHY?
INTERROGATION, PROBABLY. TORTURE. AND PRESUMING WE KEEP OUR TRAPS SHUT, THE FIRING SQUAD.
SPEAKING OF WHICH.
THREE GUARDS COMING.
I...I DON'T HEAR ANYTHING.
THIS IS PROBABLY THE ONLY CHANCE WE'RE GONNA GET.
WHAT, TO ESCAPE?
MAYBE YOU WERE OUT COLD WHEN THEY DRAGGED YOU IN HERE, BUT THIS PLACE IS A FORTRESS.
I'VE BUSTED OUT OF WORSE.
YOU'RE A NUTCASE.
DO YOURSELF A FAVOR, BUB.
STICK TO THE SHADOWS 'TIL I'M THROUGH.

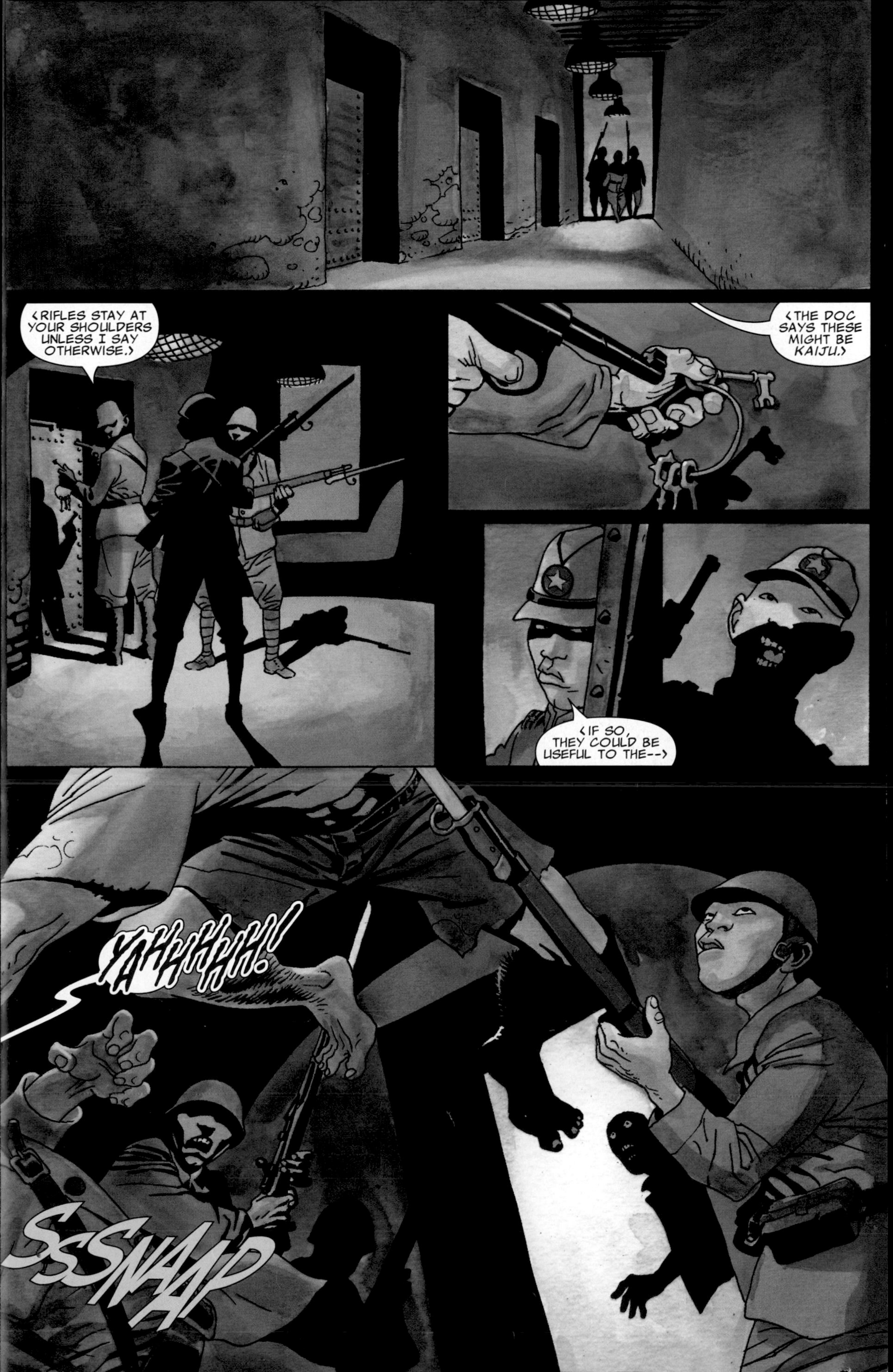
‹RIFLES STAY AT YOUR SHOULDERS UNLESS I SAY OTHERWISE.›
‹THE DOC SAYS THESE MIGHT BE KAIJU.›
‹IF SO, THEY COULD BE USEFUL TO THE--›
YAHHHHH!
SSSNAAP

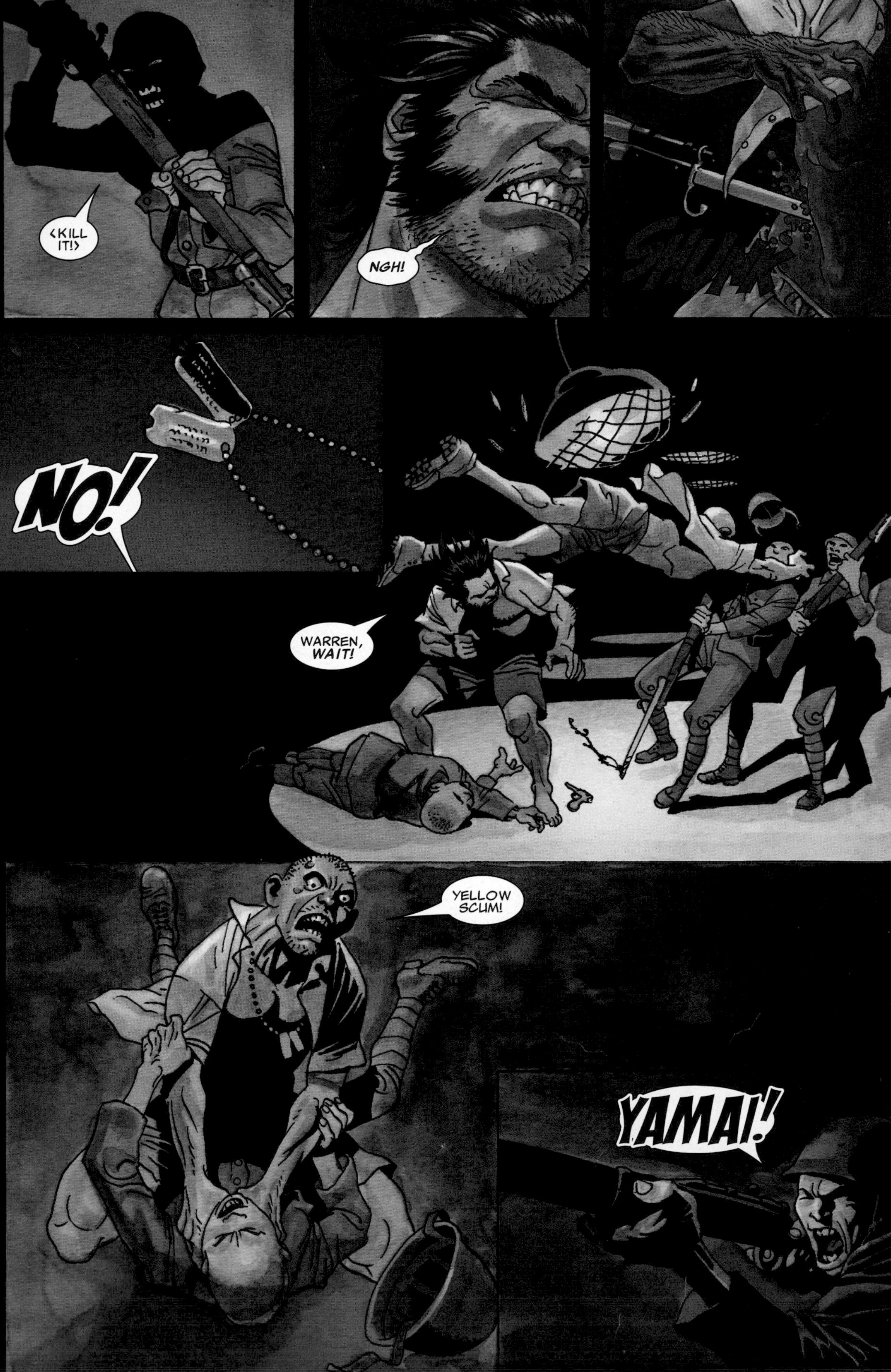

<KILL IT!>
NGH!
SHUNK
NO!
WARREN, WAIT!
YELLOW SCUM!
YAMAI!

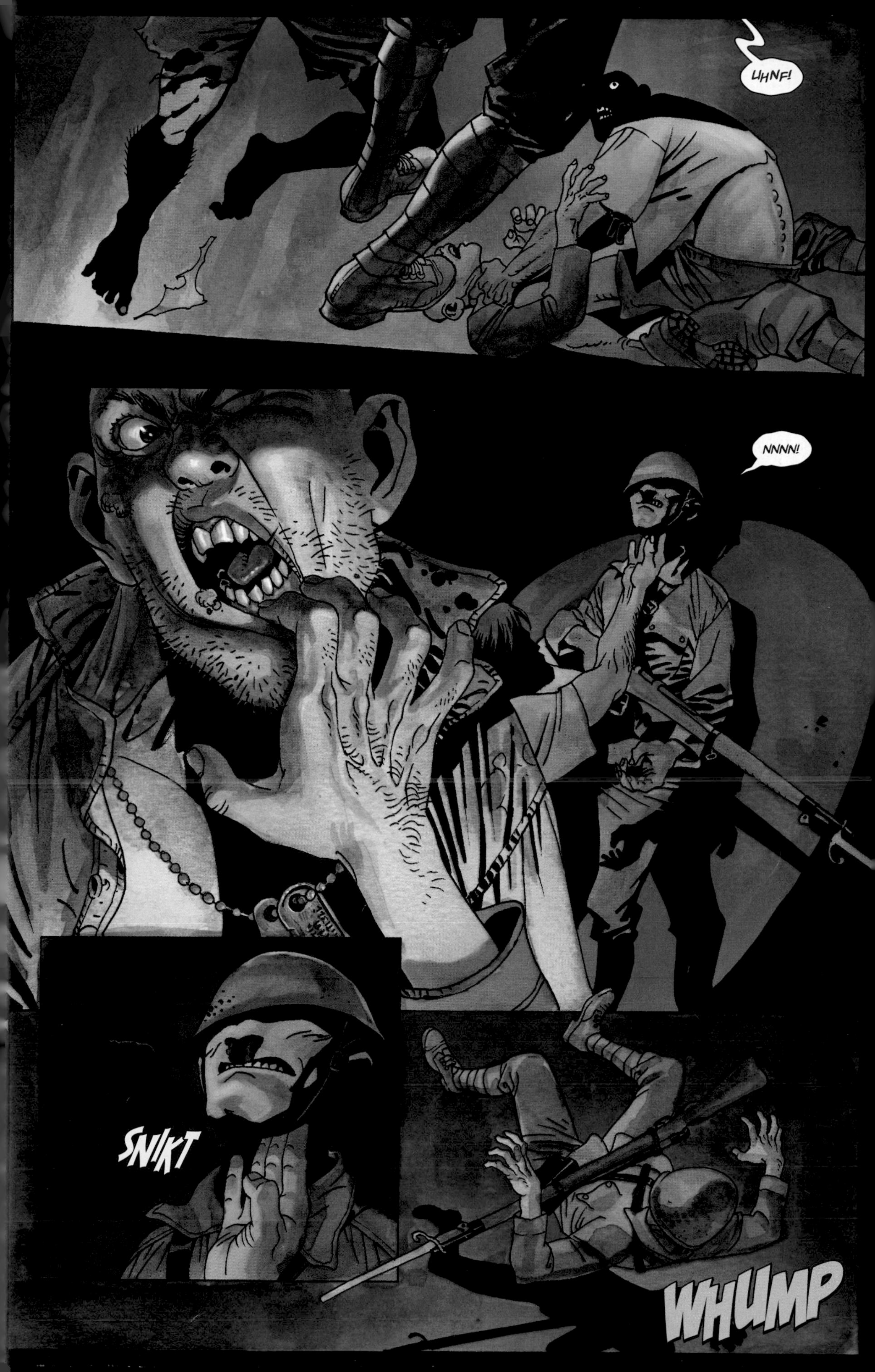
UHNF!
NNNN!
SNIKT
WHUMP

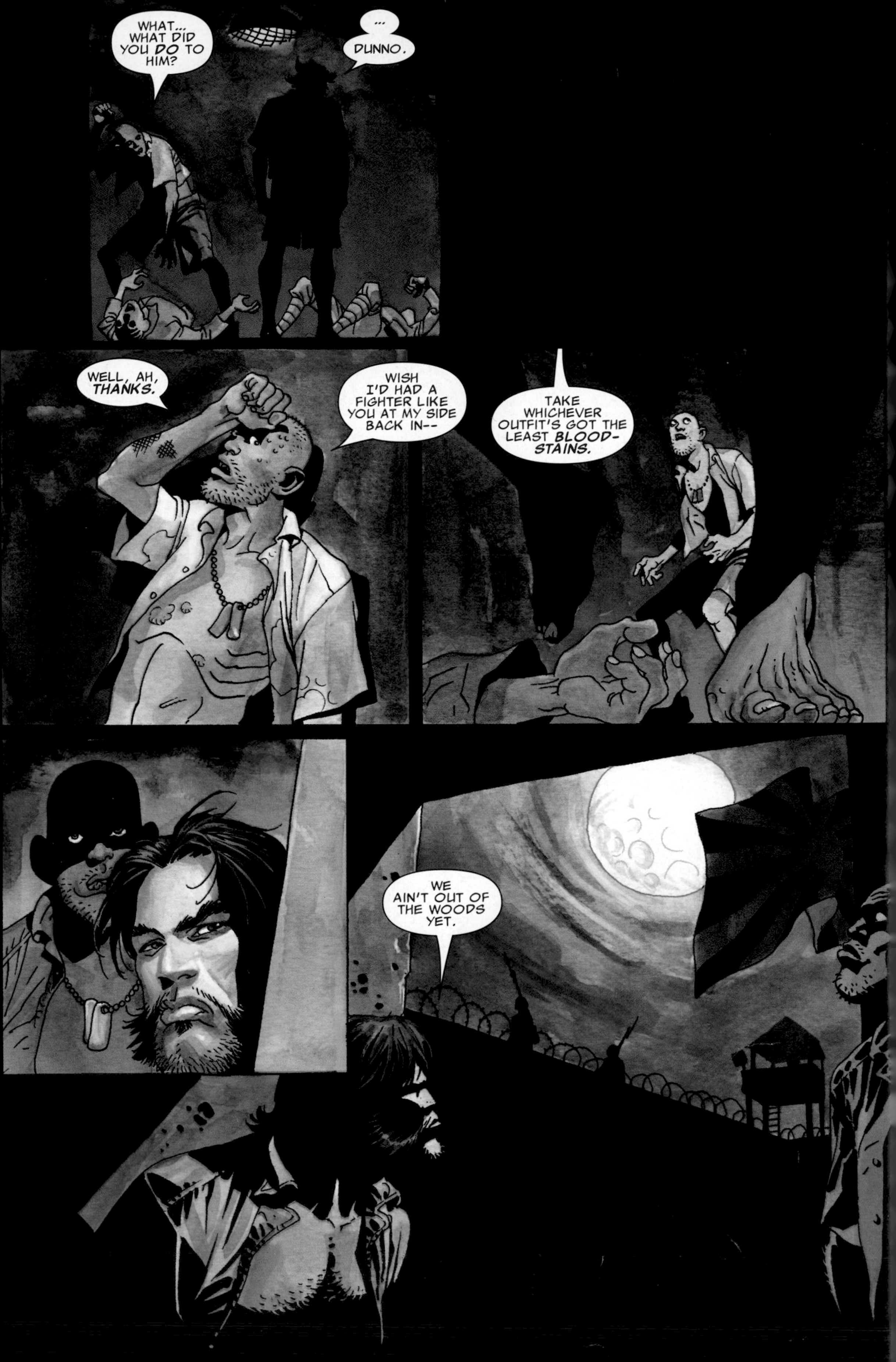
WHAT... WHAT DID YOU *DO* TO HIM?
...
DUNNO.
WELL, AH, ***THANKS.***
WISH I'D HAD A FIGHTER LIKE YOU AT MY SIDE BACK IN--
TAKE WHICHEVER OUTFIT'S GOT THE LEAST ***BLOOD-STAINS.***
WE AIN'T OUT OF THE WOODS YET.

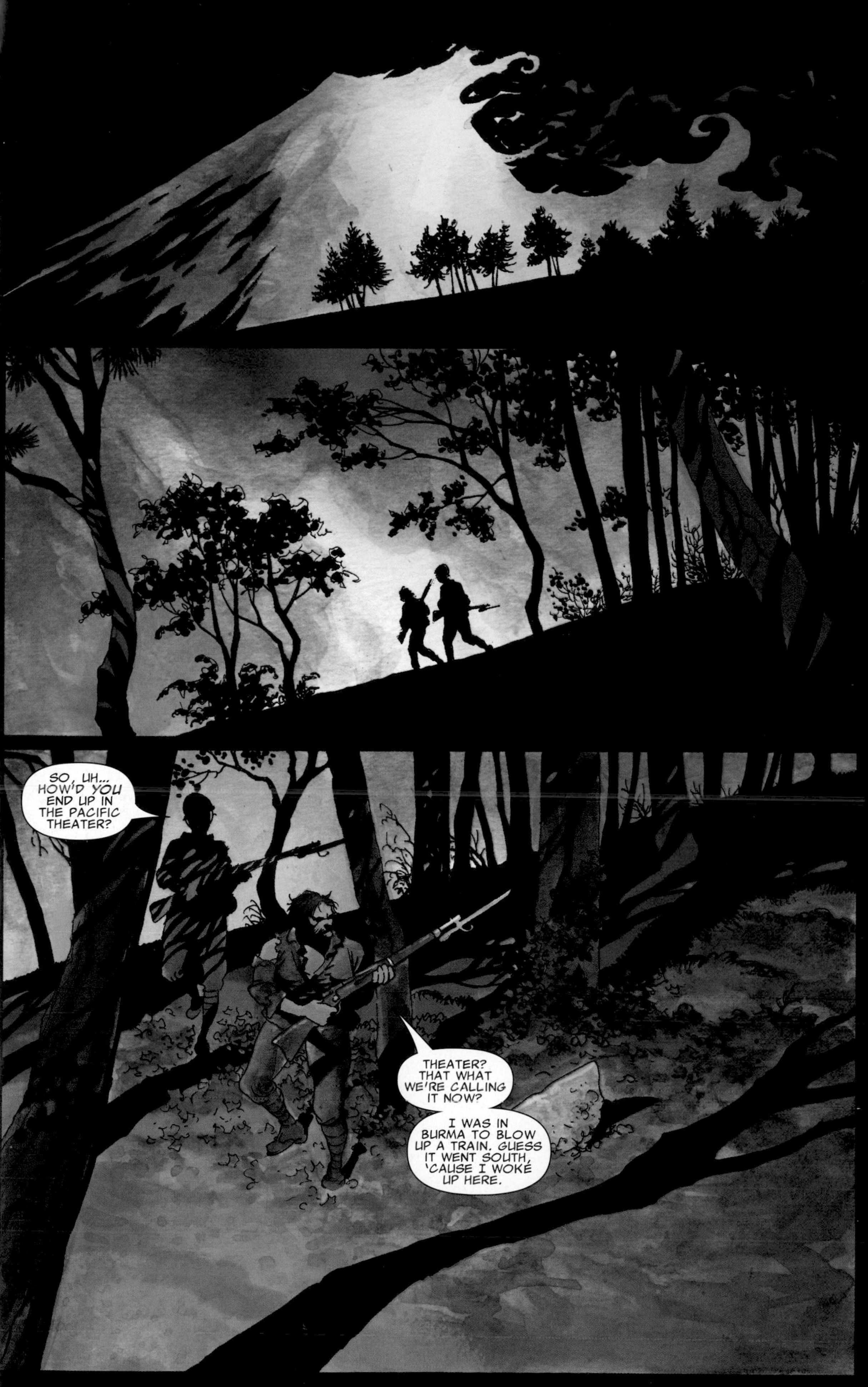
SO, UH... HOW'D YOU END UP IN THE PACIFIC THEATER?
THEATER? THAT WHAT WE'RE CALLING IT NOW?
I WAS IN BURMA TO BLOW UP A TRAIN. GUESS IT WENT SOUTH, 'CAUSE I WOKE UP HERE.

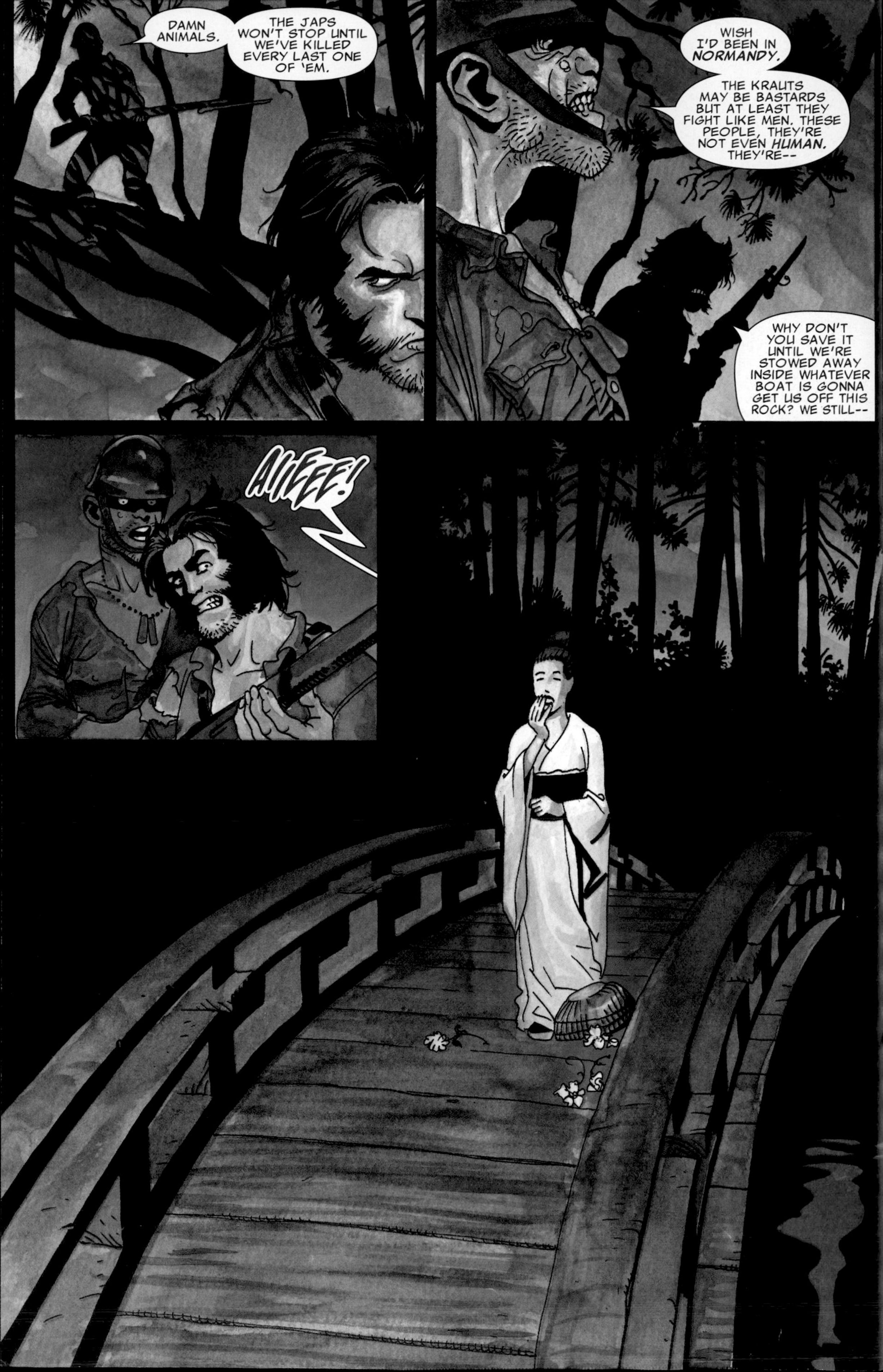
DAMN ANIMALS.
THE JAPS WON'T STOP UNTIL WE'VE KILLED EVERY LAST ONE OF 'EM.
WISH I'D BEEN IN *NORMANDY.*
THE KRAUTS MAY BE BASTARDS BUT AT LEAST THEY FIGHT LIKE MEN. THESE PEOPLE, THEY'RE NOT EVEN *HUMAN.* THEY'RE--
WHY DON'T YOU SAVE IT UNTIL WE'RE STOWED AWAY INSIDE WHATEVER BOAT IS GONNA GET US OFF THIS ROCK? WE STILL--
AIIEEE!

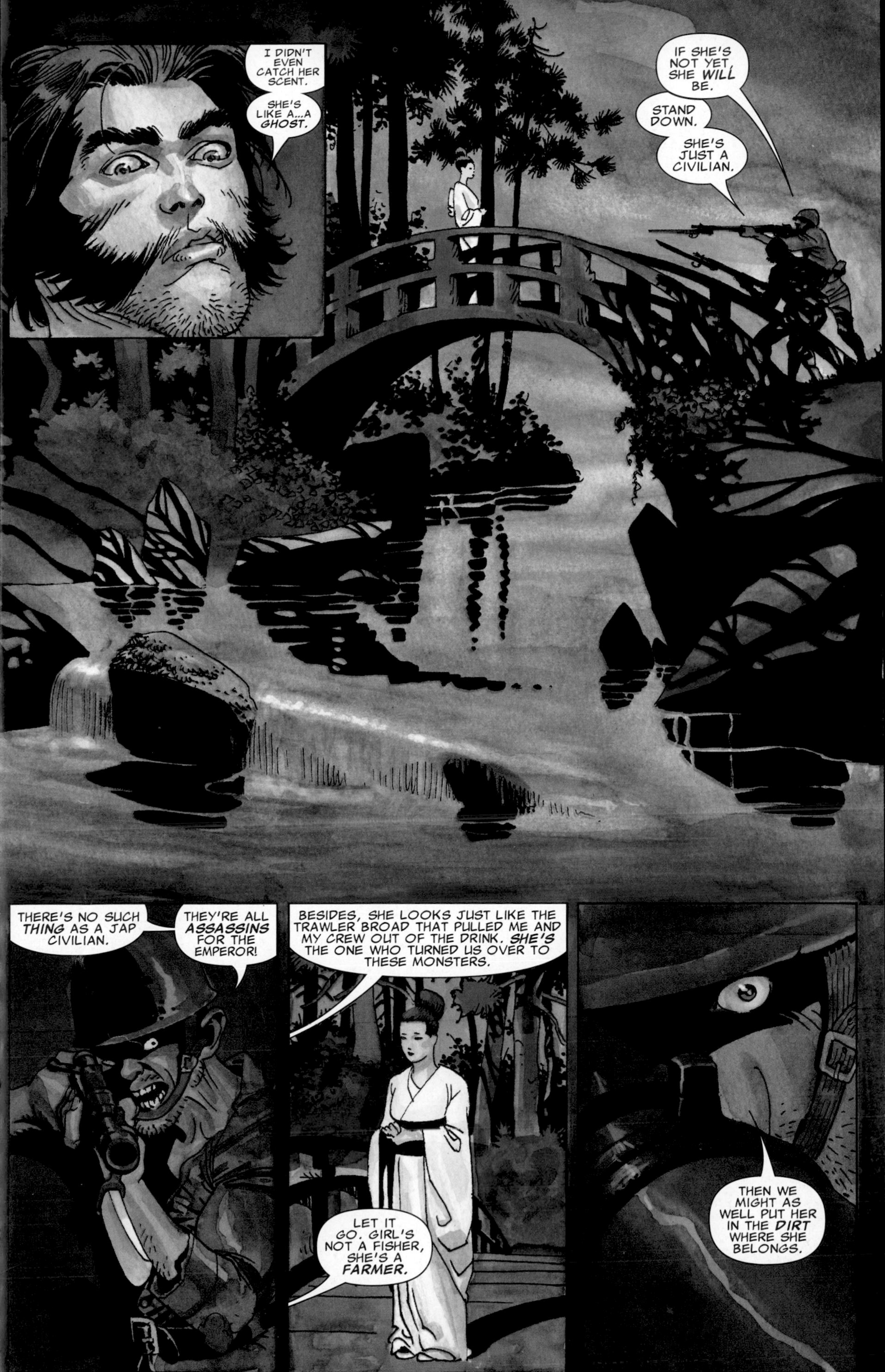
I DIDN'T EVEN CATCH HER SCENT.
SHE'S LIKE A...A *GHOST.*
IF SHE'S NOT YET, SHE *WILL* BE.
STAND DOWN.
SHE'S JUST A CIVILIAN.
THERE'S NO SUCH *THING* AS A JAP CIVILIAN.
THEY'RE ALL *ASSASSINS* FOR THE EMPEROR!
BESIDES, SHE LOOKS JUST LIKE THE TRAWLER BROAD THAT PULLED ME AND MY CREW OUT OF THE DRINK. *SHE'S* THE ONE WHO TURNED US OVER TO THESE MONSTERS.
LET IT GO. GIRL'S NOT A FISHER, SHE'S A *FARMER.*
THEN WE MIGHT AS WELL PUT HER IN THE *DIRT* WHERE SHE BELONGS.

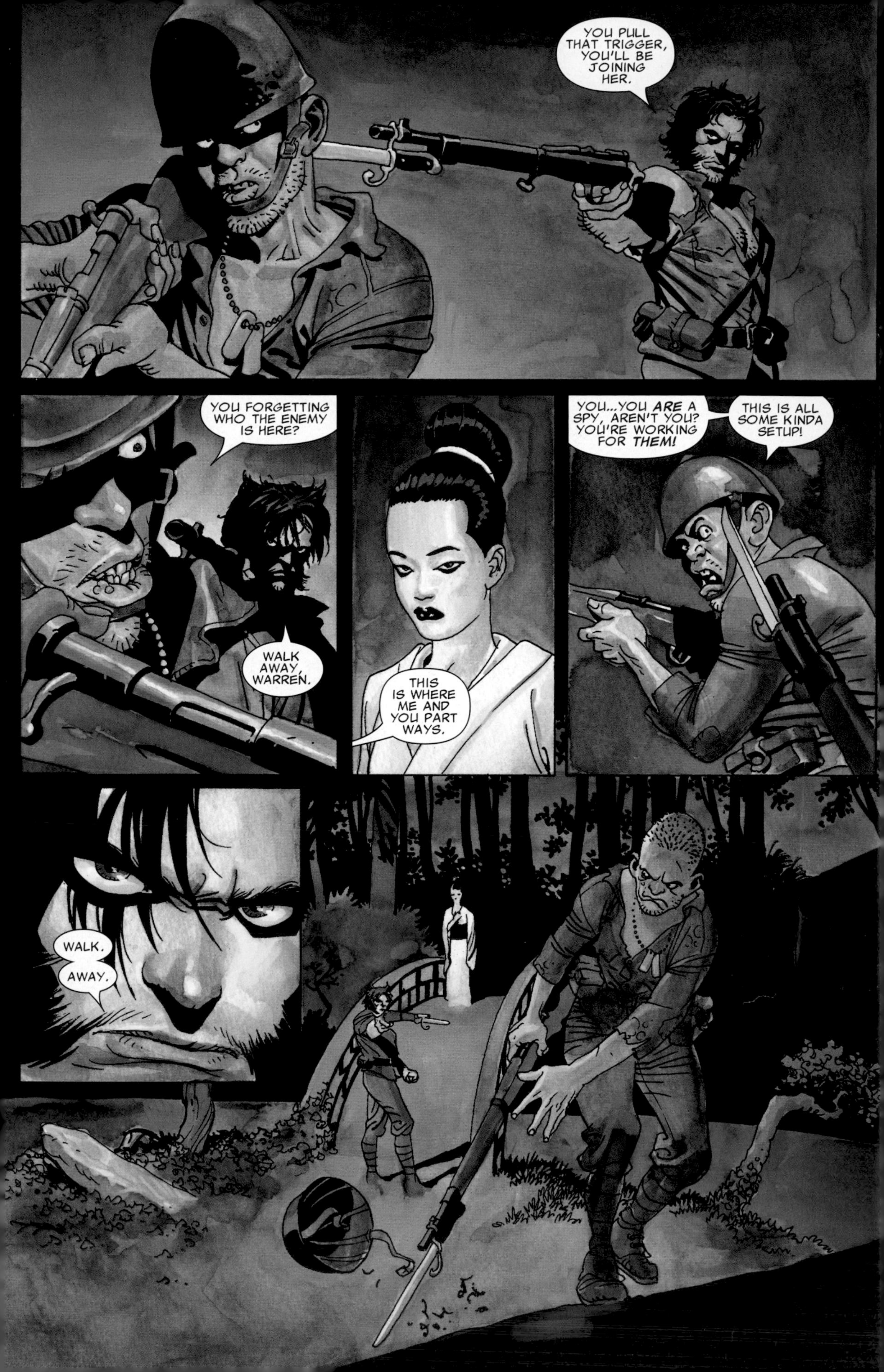
YOU PULL THAT TRIGGER, YOU'LL BE JOINING HER.
YOU FORGETTING WHO THE ENEMY IS HERE?
WALK AWAY, WARREN.
THIS IS WHERE ME AND YOU PART WAYS.
YOU...YOU ARE A SPY, AREN'T YOU? YOU'RE WORKING FOR THEM!
THIS IS ALL SOME KINDA SETUP!
WALK.
AWAY.

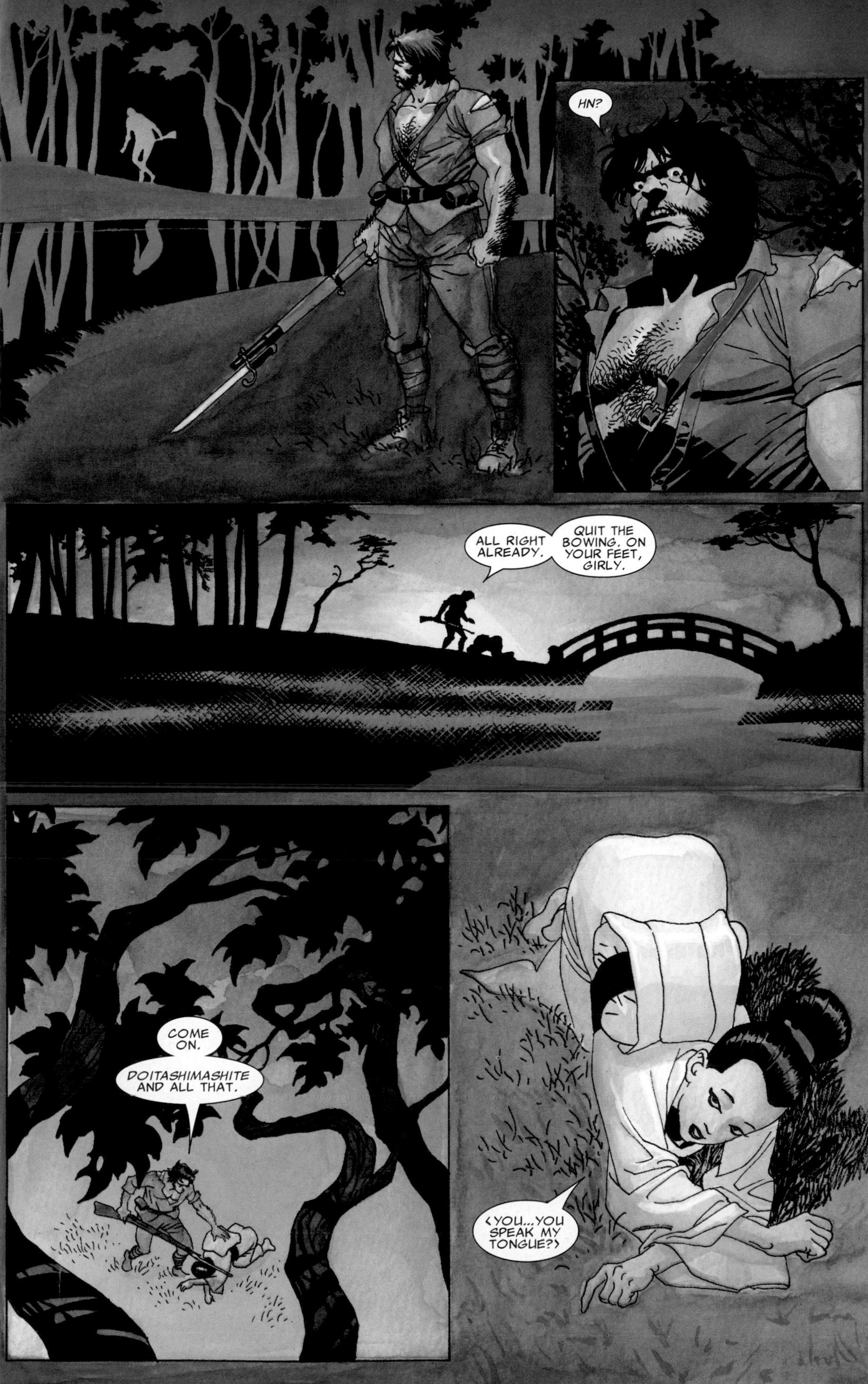
HN?
ALL RIGHT ALREADY.
QUIT THE BOWING. ON YOUR FEET, GIRLY.
COME ON.
DOITASHIMASHITE AND ALL THAT.
<YOU...YOU SPEAK MY TONGUE?>

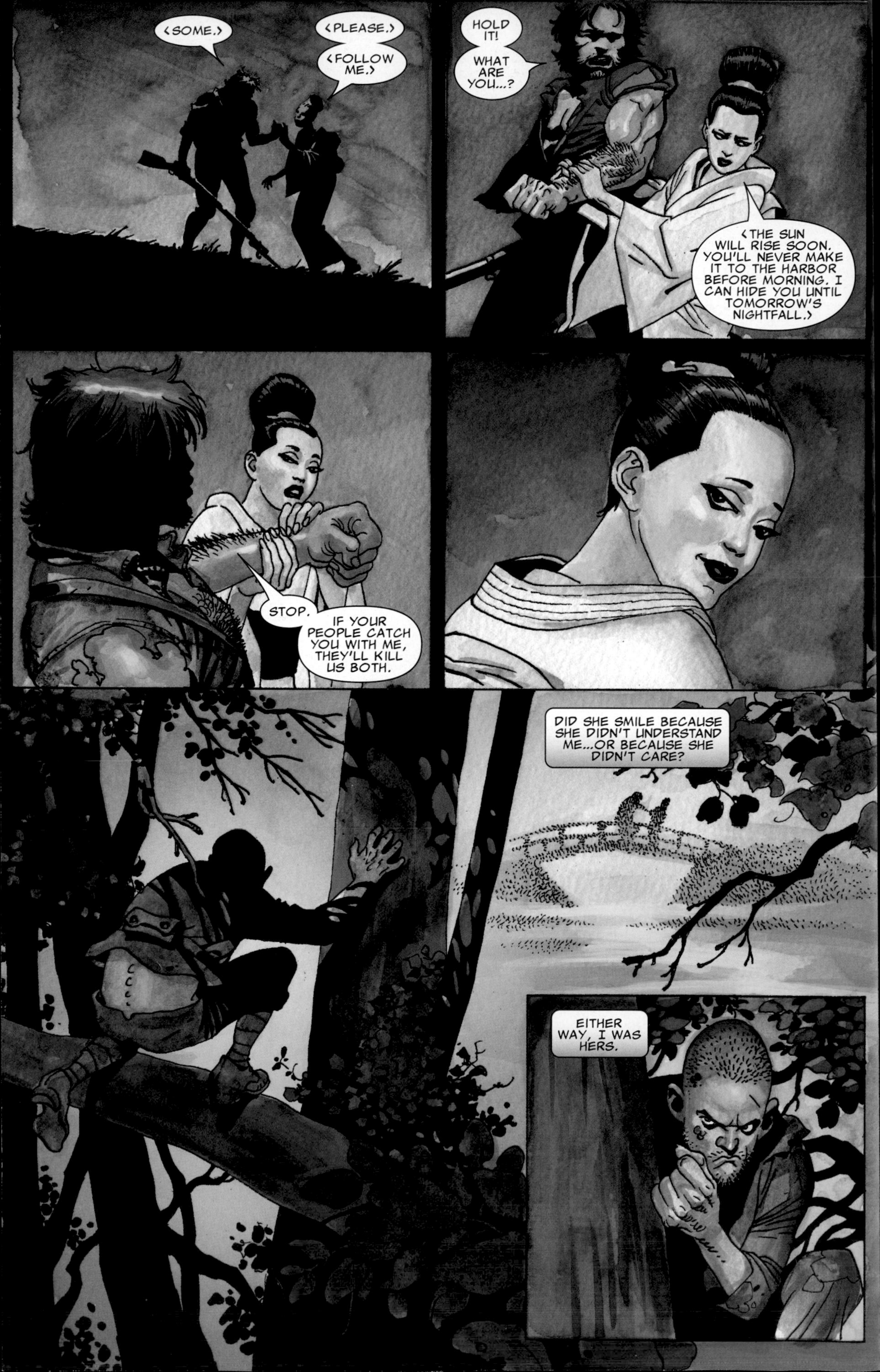

‹SOME.›
‹PLEASE.›
‹FOLLOW ME.›
HOLD IT!
WHAT ARE YOU...?
‹THE SUN WILL RISE SOON. YOU'LL NEVER MAKE IT TO THE HARBOR BEFORE MORNING. I CAN HIDE YOU UNTIL TOMORROW'S NIGHTFALL.›
STOP.
IF YOUR PEOPLE CATCH YOU WITH ME, THEY'LL KILL US BOTH.
DID SHE SMILE BECAUSE SHE DIDN'T UNDERSTAND ME...OR BECAUSE SHE DIDN'T CARE?
EITHER WAY, I WAS HERS.

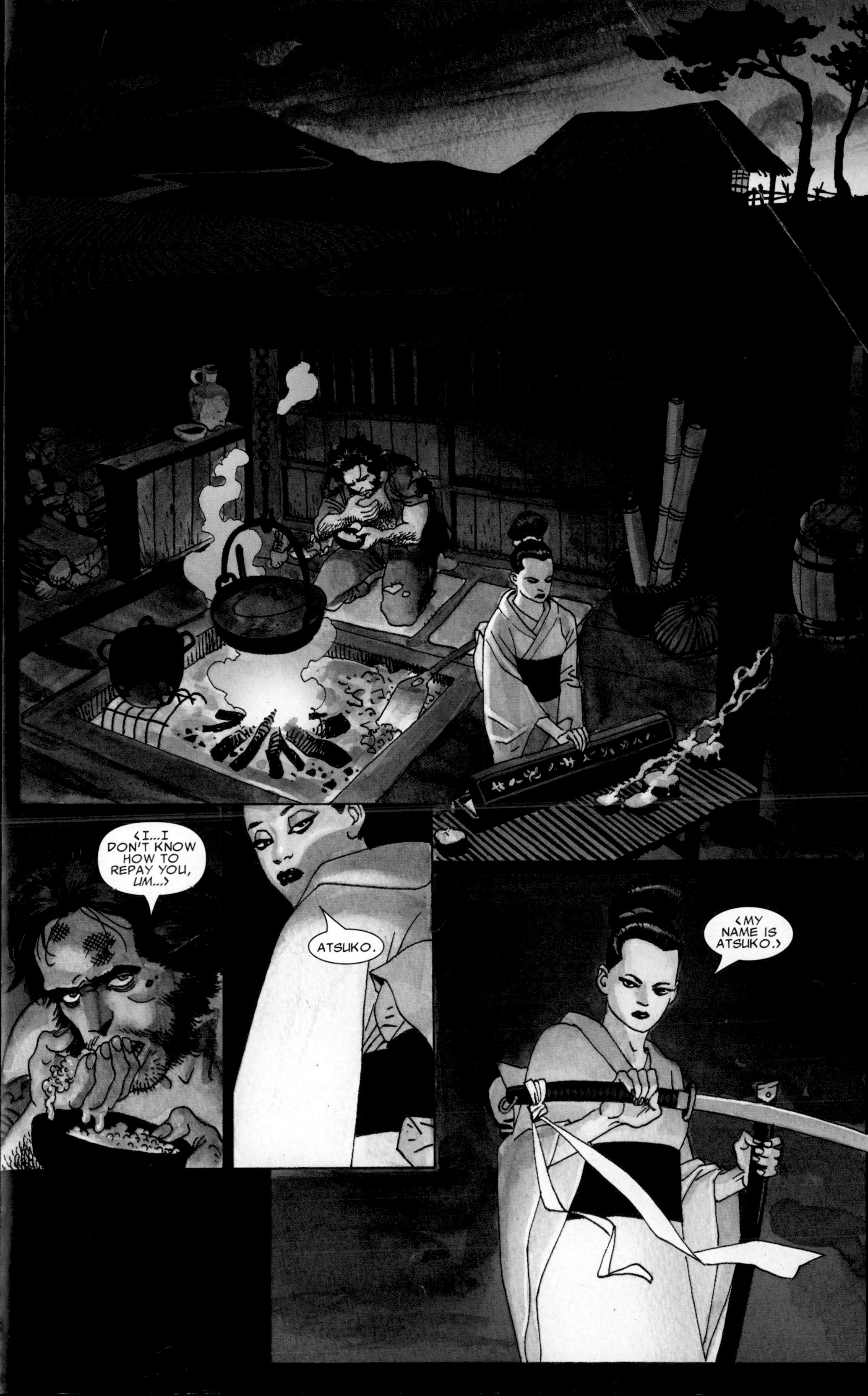
‹I...I DON'T KNOW HOW TO REPAY YOU, UM...›
ATSUKO.
‹MY NAME IS ATSUKO.›

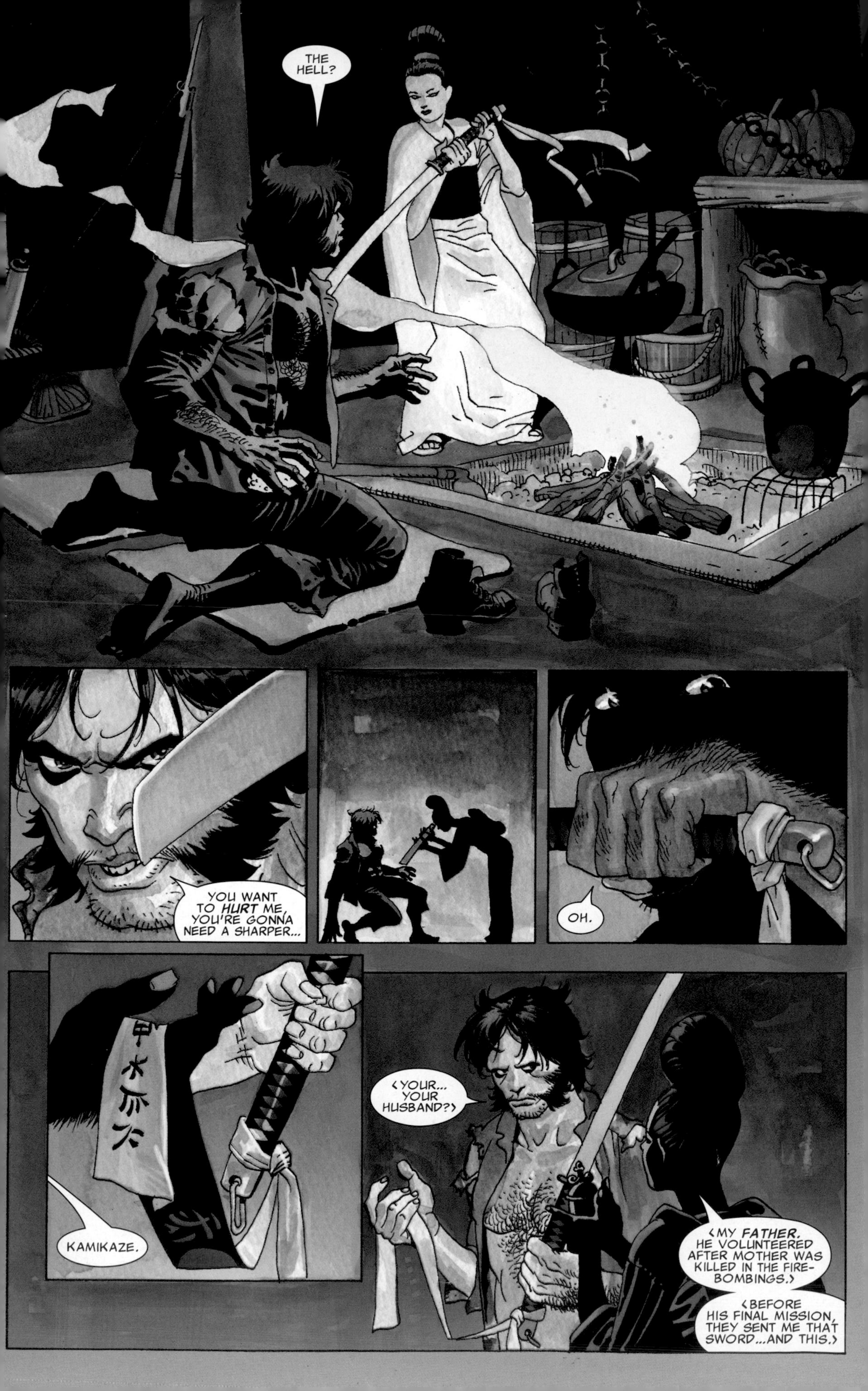
THE HELL?
YOU WANT TO HURT ME YOU'RE GONNA NEED A SHARPER...
OH.
KAMIKAZE.
‹YOUR... YOUR HUSBAND?›
‹MY FATHER. HE VOLUNTEERED AFTER MOTHER WAS KILLED IN THE FIRE-BOMBINGS.›
‹BEFORE HIS FINAL MISSION, THEY SENT ME THAT SWORD...AND THIS.›

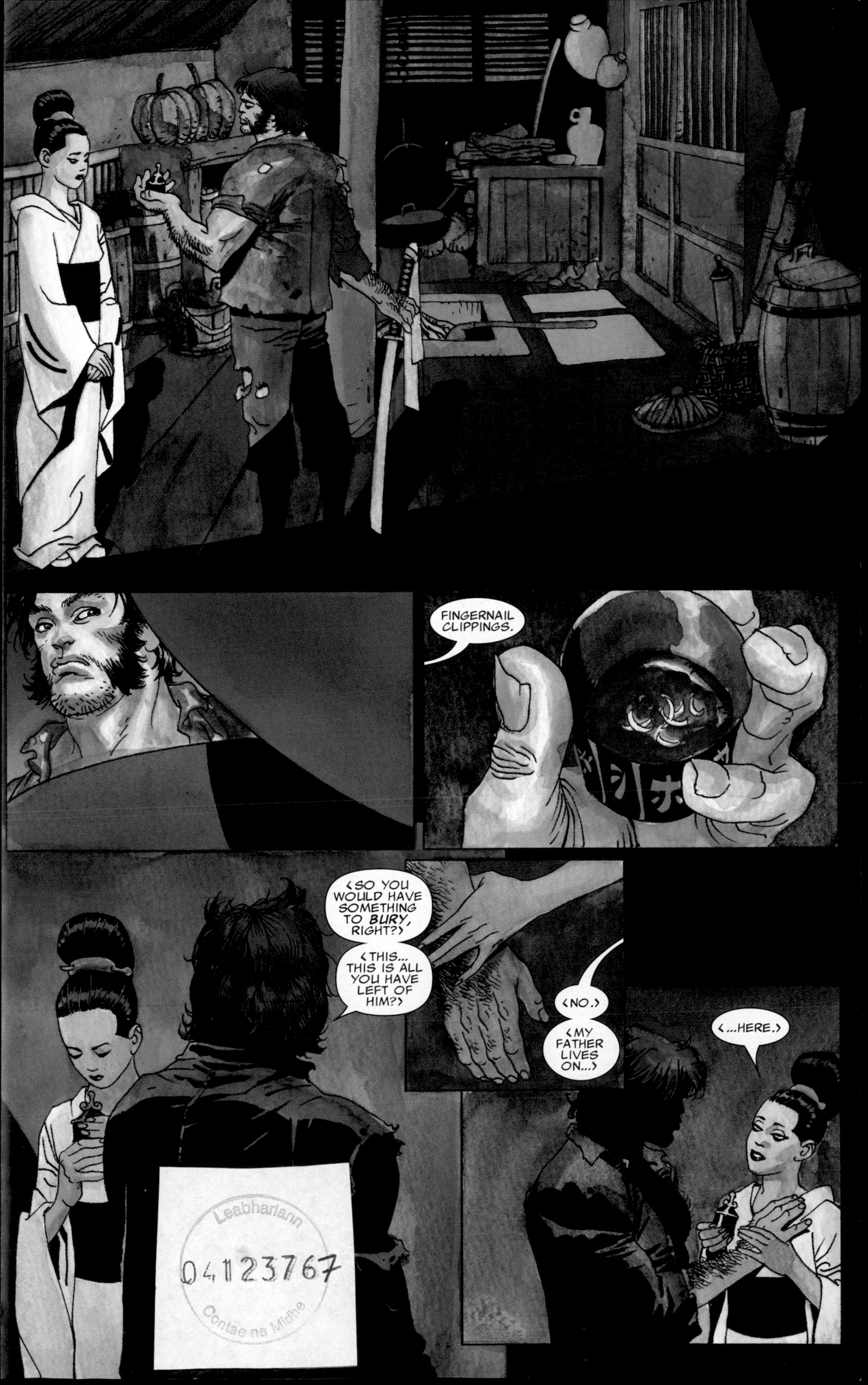
FINGERNAIL CLIPPINGS.
‹SO YOU WOULD HAVE SOMETHING TO BURY, RIGHT?›
‹THIS... THIS IS ALL YOU HAVE LEFT OF HIM?›
‹NO.›
‹MY FATHER LIVES ON...›
‹...HERE.›

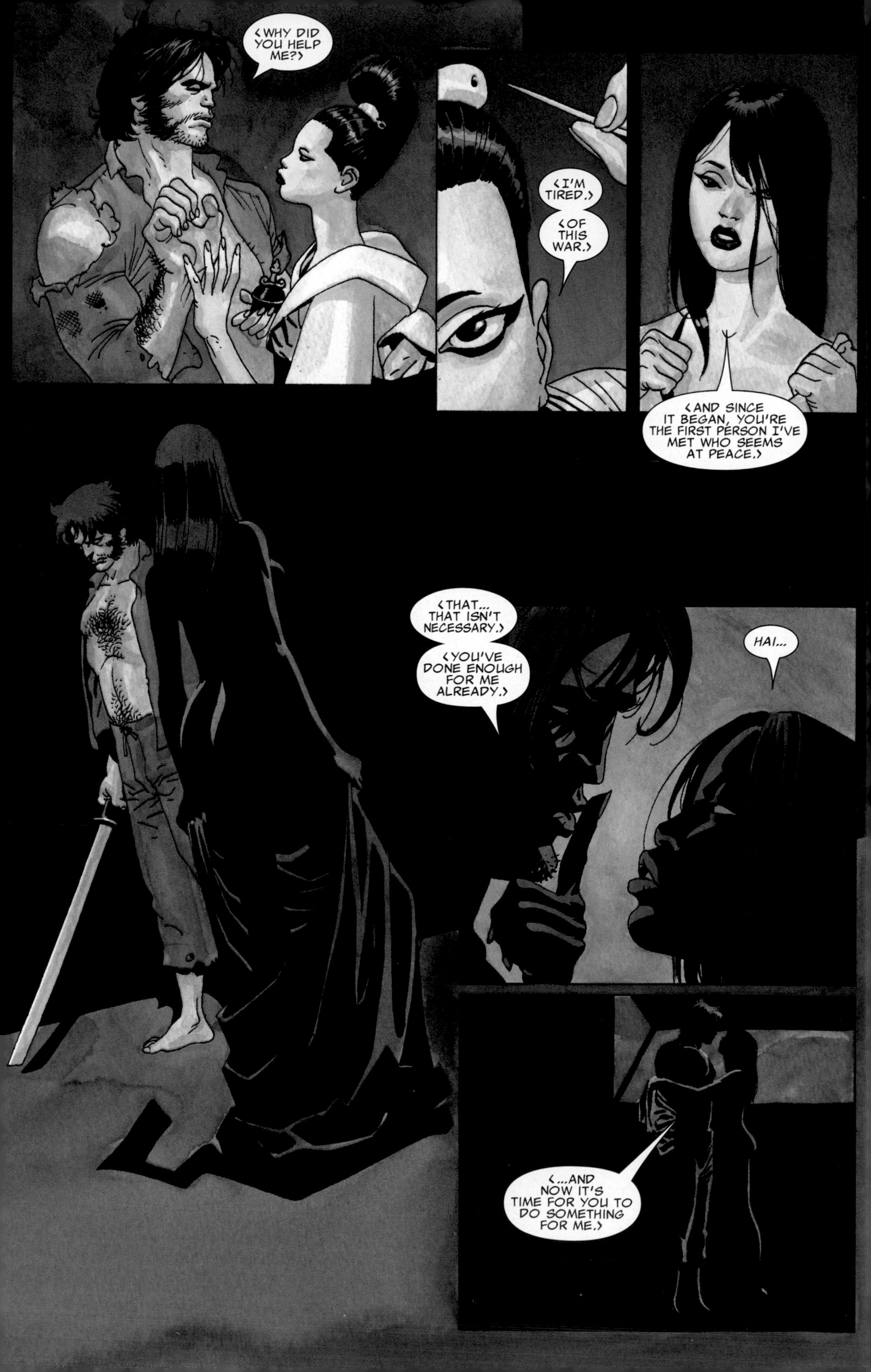
‹WHY DID YOU HELP ME?›
‹I'M TIRED.›
‹OF THIS WAR.›
‹AND SINCE IT BEGAN, YOU'RE THE FIRST PERSON I'VE MET WHO SEEMS AT PEACE.›
‹THAT... THAT ISN'T NECESSARY.›
‹YOU'VE DONE ENOUGH FOR ME ALREADY.›
HAI...
‹...AND NOW IT'S TIME FOR YOU TO DO SOMETHING FOR ME.›

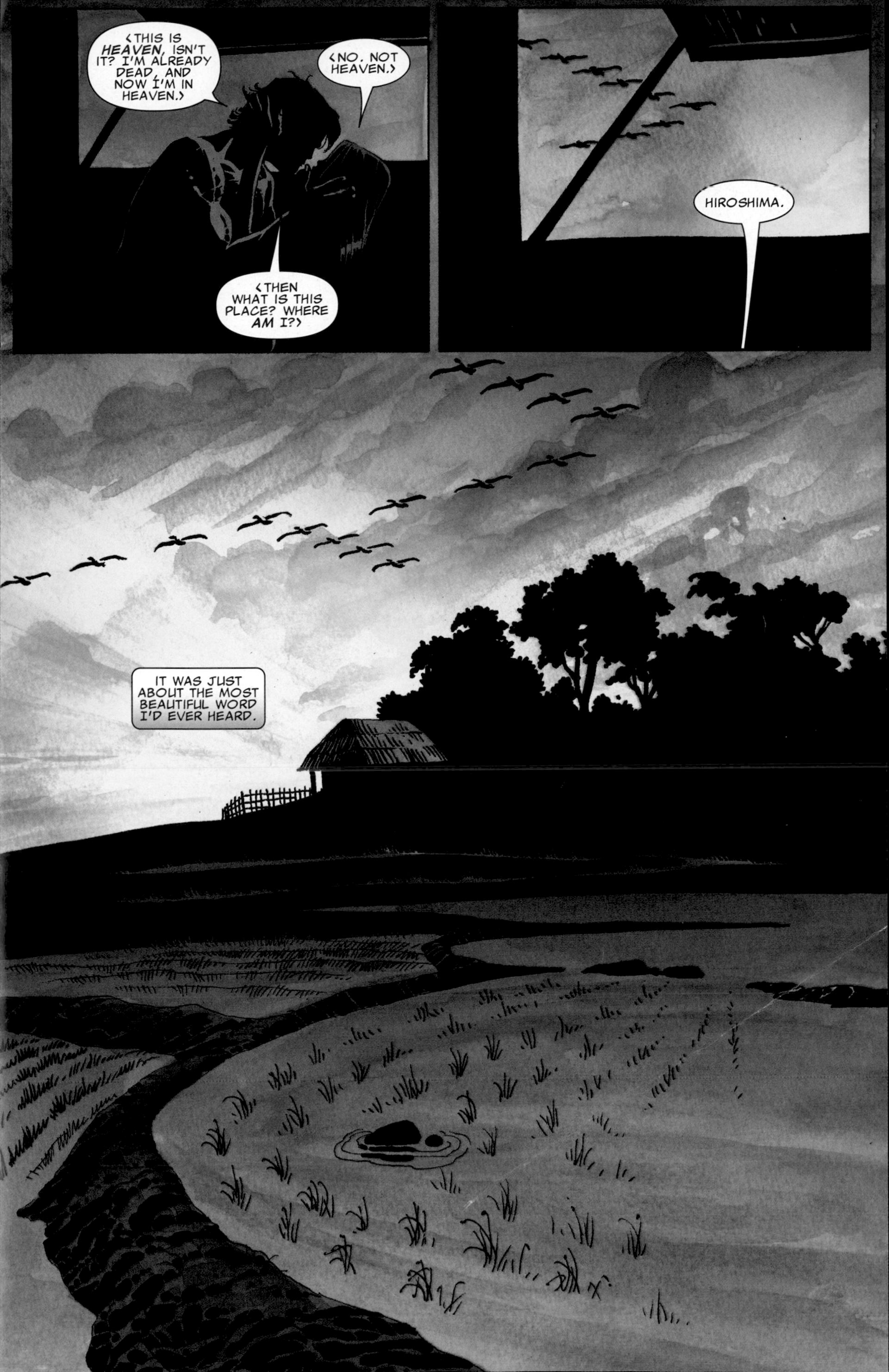
‹THIS IS HEAVEN, ISN'T IT? I'M ALREADY DEAD, AND NOW I'M IN HEAVEN.›
‹NO. NOT HEAVEN.›
‹THEN WHAT IS THIS PLACE? WHERE AM I?›
HIROSHIMA.
IT WAS JUST ABOUT THE MOST BEAUTIFUL WORD I'D EVER HEARD.

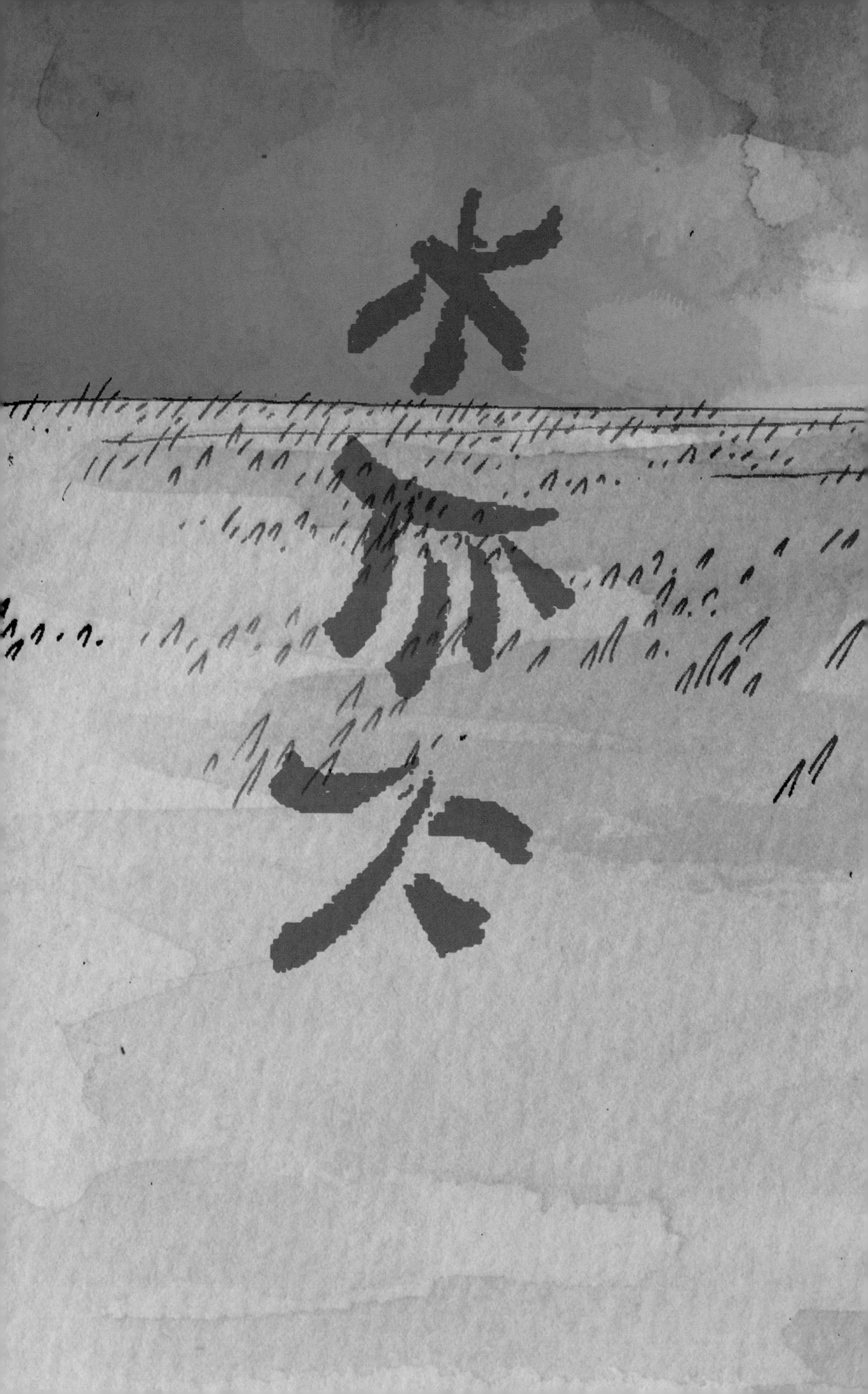

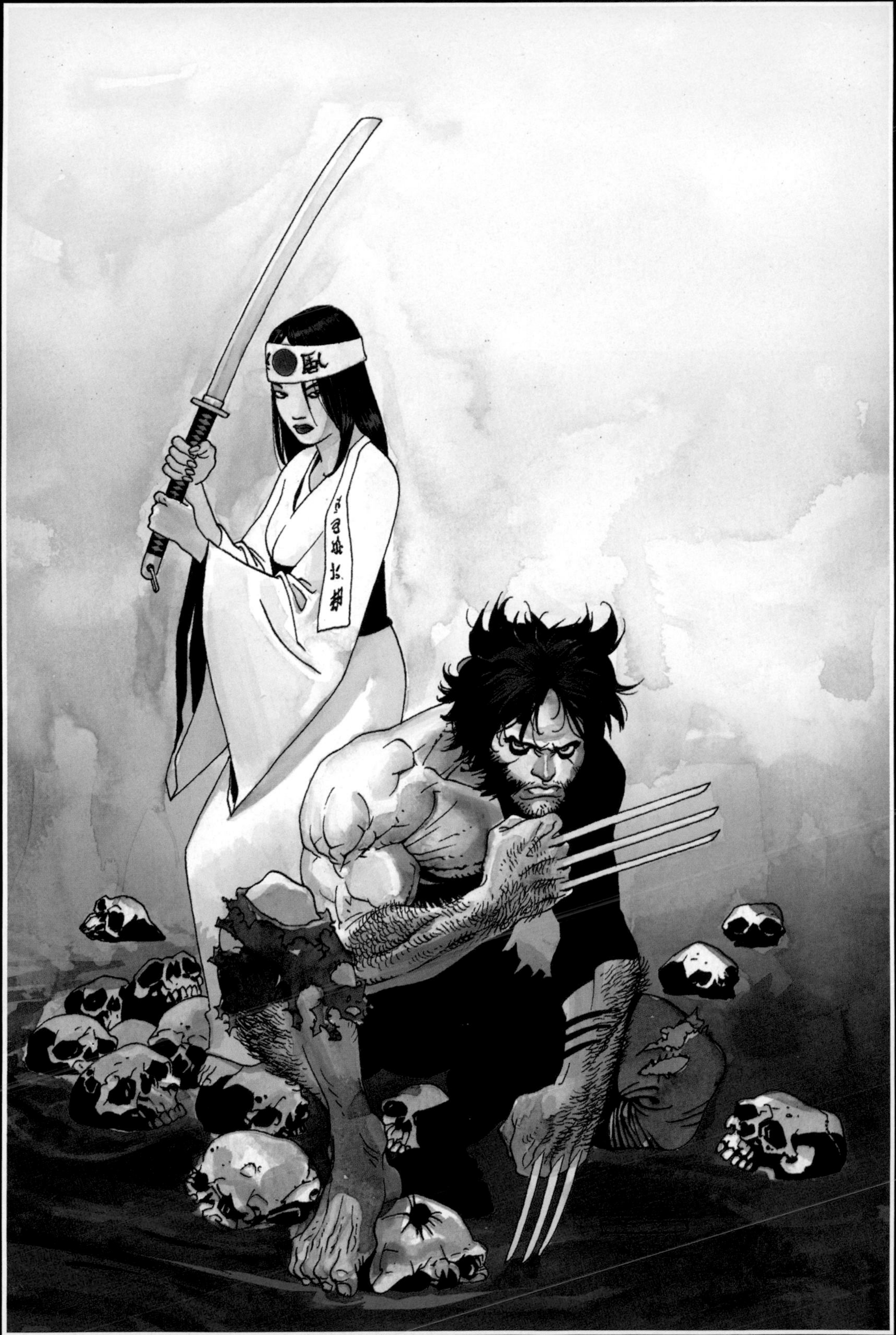

issue number two

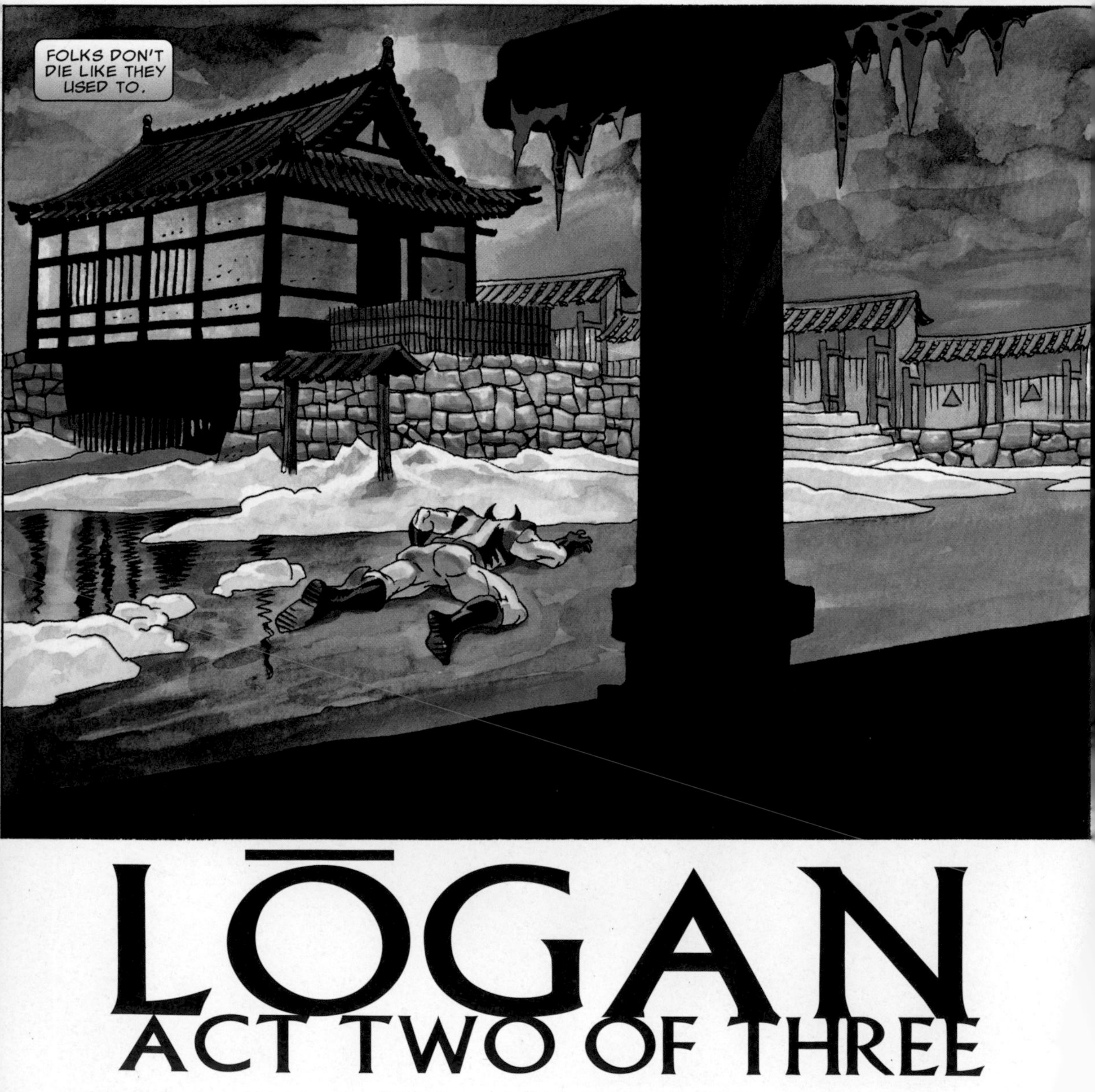
FOLKS DON'T DIE LIKE THEY USED TO.

LŌGAN
ACT TWO OF THREE

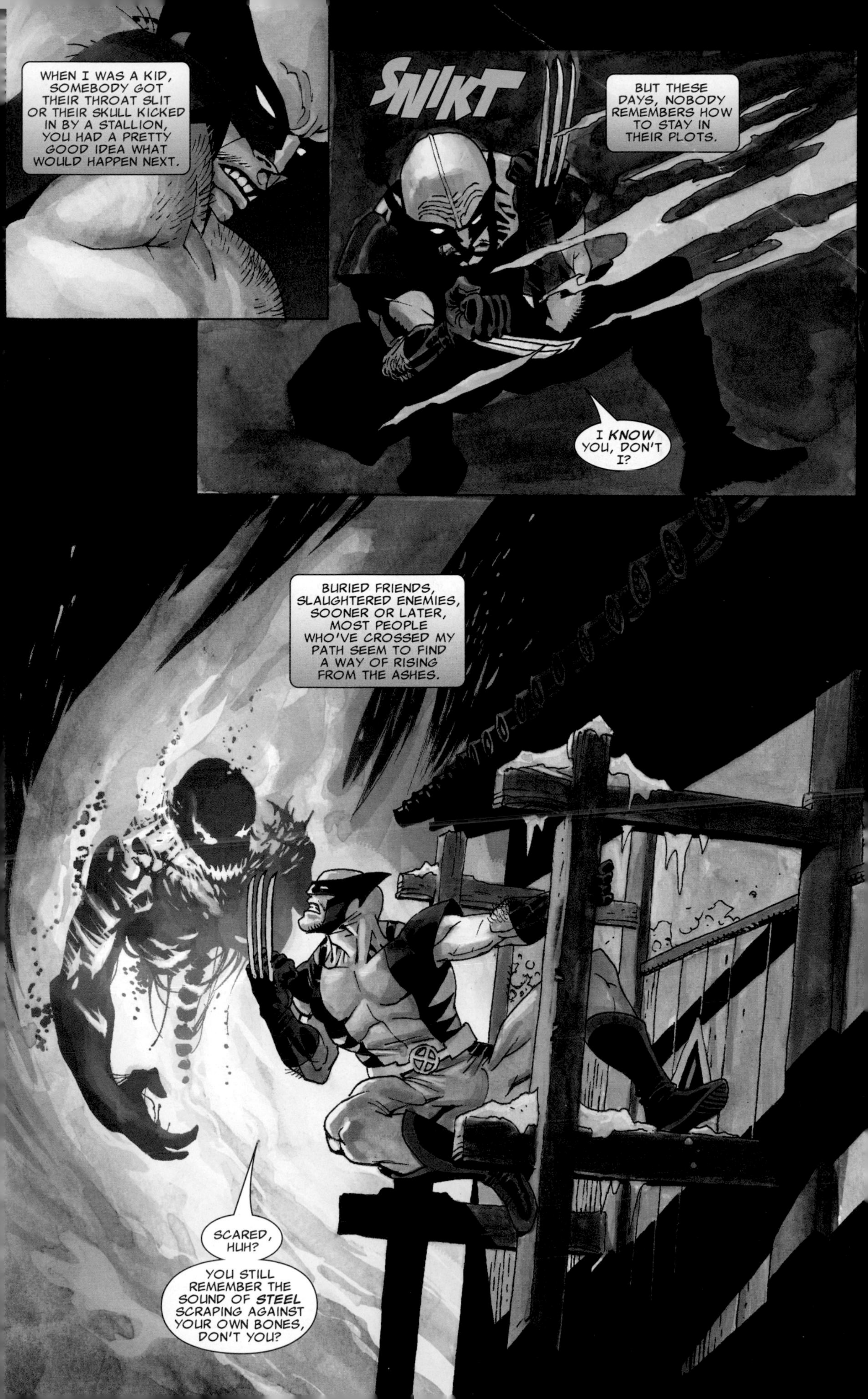

WHEN I WAS A KID, SOMEBODY GOT THEIR THROAT SLIT OR THEIR SKULL KICKED IN BY A STALLION, YOU HAD A PRETTY GOOD IDEA WHAT WOULD HAPPEN NEXT.
SNIKT
BUT THESE DAYS, NOBODY REMEMBERS HOW TO STAY IN THEIR PLOTS.
I KNOW YOU, DON'T I?
BURIED FRIENDS, SLAUGHTERED ENEMIES, SOONER OR LATER, MOST PEOPLE WHO'VE CROSSED MY PATH SEEM TO FIND A WAY OF RISING FROM THE ASHES.
SCARED, HUH?
YOU STILL REMEMBER THE SOUND OF STEEL SCRAPING AGAINST YOUR OWN BONES, DON'T YOU?

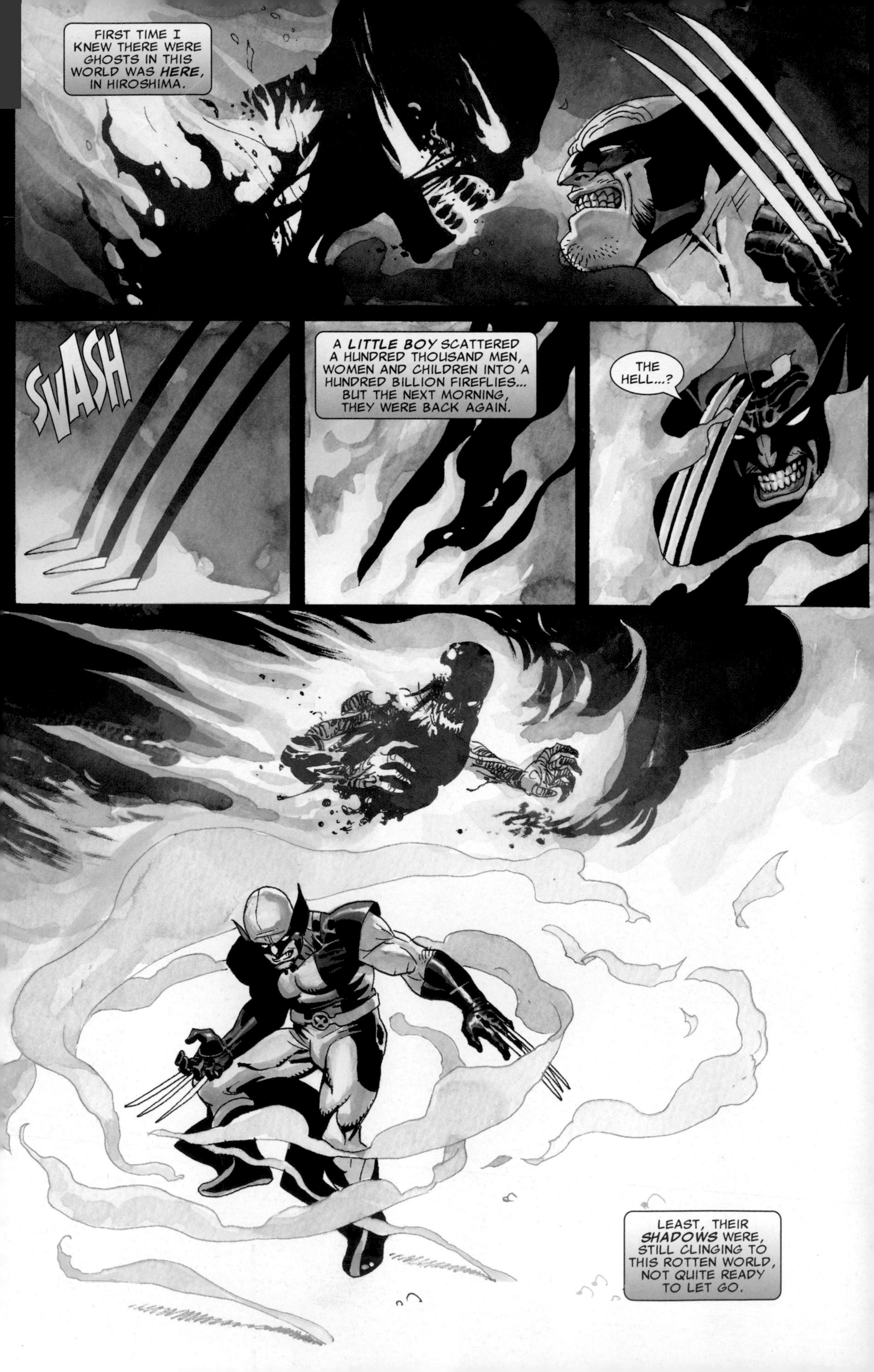
FIRST TIME I KNEW THERE WERE GHOSTS IN THIS WORLD WAS HERE, IN HIROSHIMA.
SVASH
A LITTLE BOY SCATTERED A HUNDRED THOUSAND MEN, WOMEN AND CHILDREN INTO A HUNDRED BILLION FIREFLIES... BUT THE NEXT MORNING, THEY WERE BACK AGAIN.
THE HELL...?
LEAST, THEIR SHADOWS WERE, STILL CLINGING TO THIS ROTTEN WORLD, NOT QUITE READY TO LET GO.

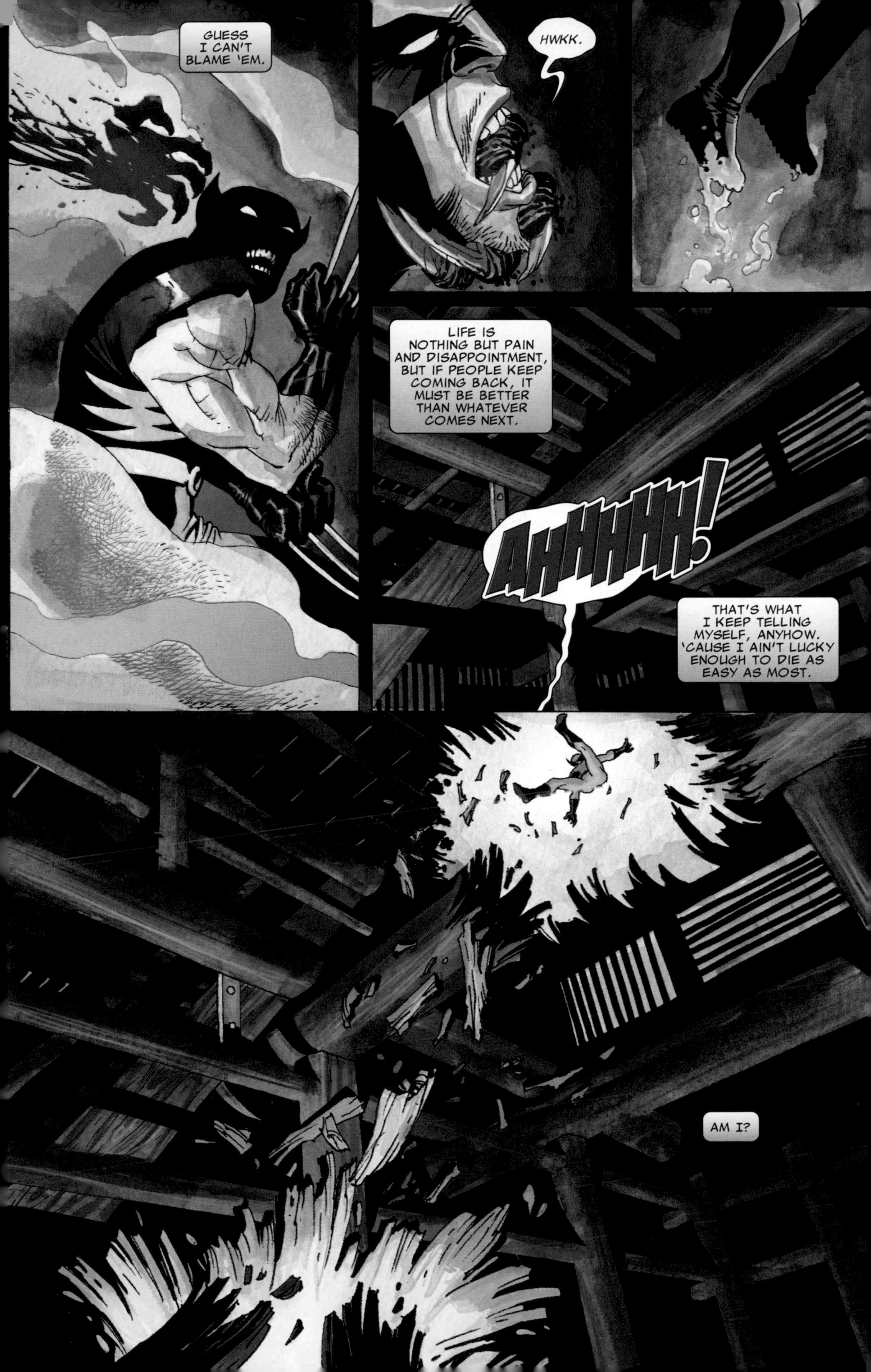
GUESS I CAN'T BLAME 'EM.
HWKK.
LIFE IS NOTHING BUT PAIN AND DISAPPOINTMENT, BUT IF PEOPLE KEEP COMING BACK, IT MUST BE BETTER THAN WHATEVER COMES NEXT.
AHHHHH!
THAT'S WHAT I KEEP TELLING MYSELF, ANYHOW. 'CAUSE I AIN'T LUCKY ENOUGH TO DIE AS EASY AS MOST.
AM I?

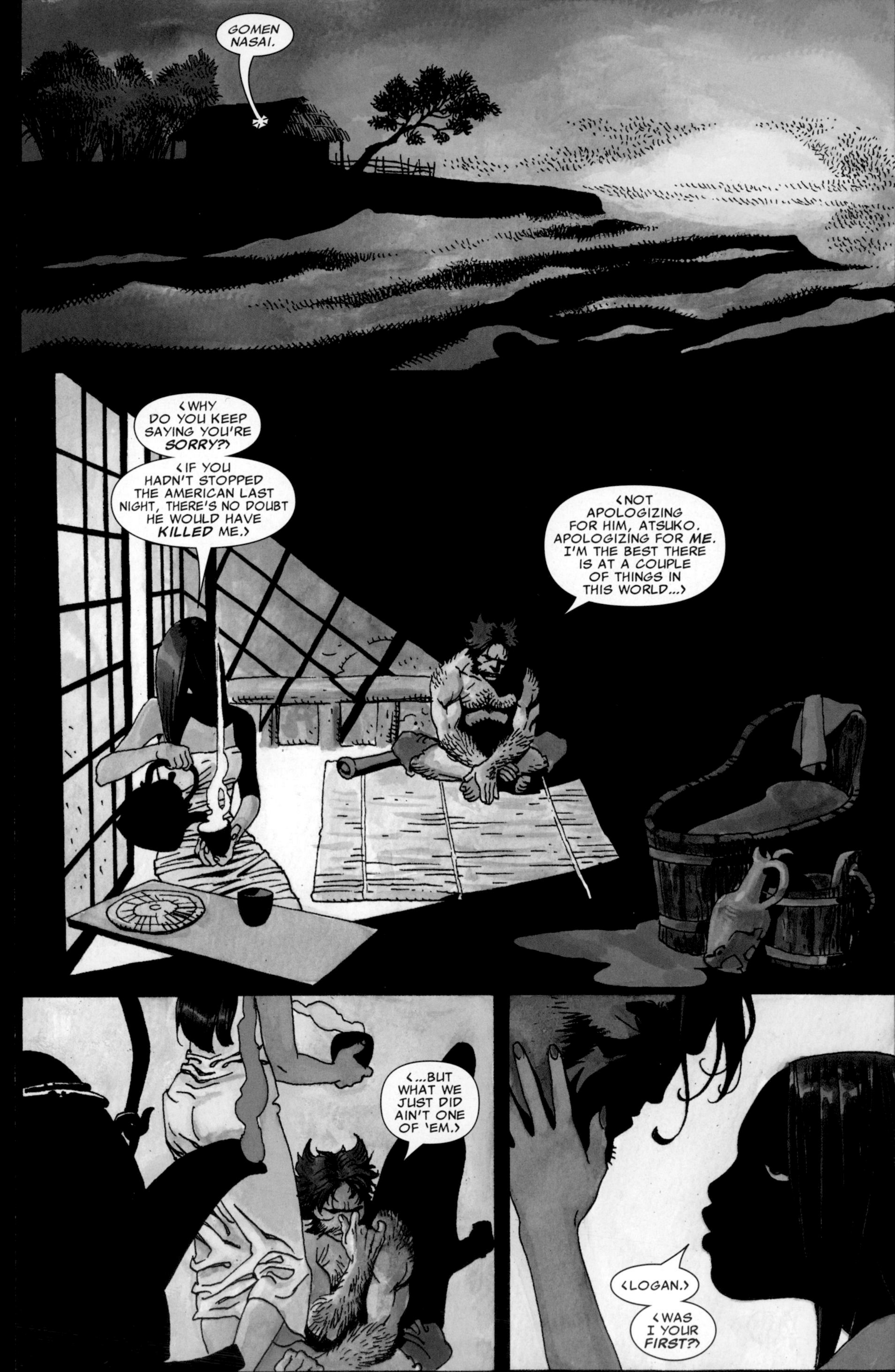
GOMEN NASAI.
‹WHY DO YOU KEEP SAYING YOU'RE SORRY?›
‹IF YOU HADN'T STOPPED THE AMERICAN LAST NIGHT, THERE'S NO DOUBT HE WOULD HAVE KILLED ME.›
‹NOT APOLOGIZING FOR HIM, ATSUKO. APOLOGIZING FOR ME. I'M THE BEST THERE IS AT A COUPLE OF THINGS IN THIS WORLD...›
‹...BUT WHAT WE JUST DID AIN'T ONE OF 'EM.›
‹LOGAN.›
‹WAS I YOUR FIRST?›

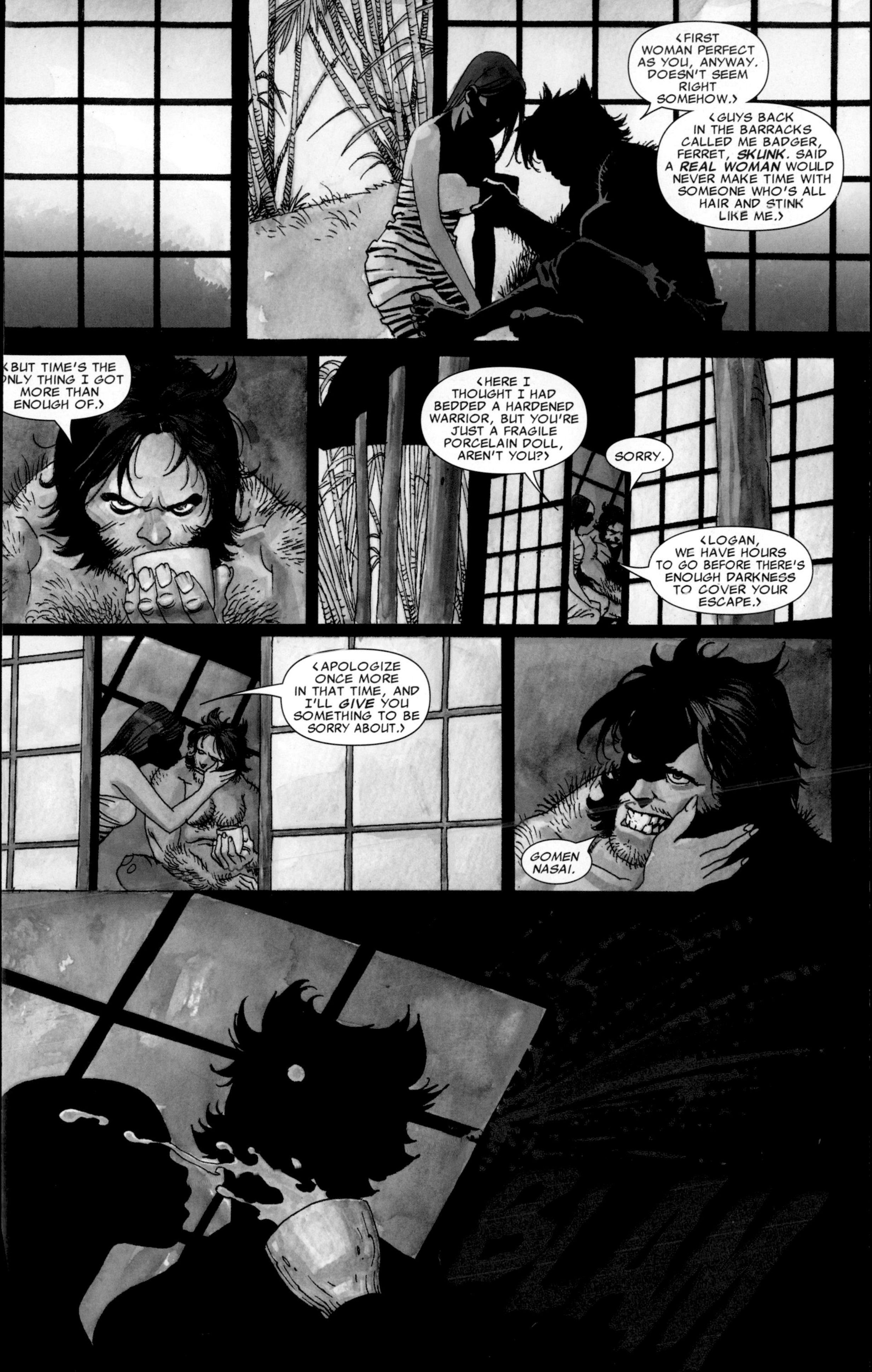
‹FIRST WOMAN PERFECT AS YOU, ANYWAY. DOESN'T SEEM RIGHT SOMEHOW.›
‹GUYS BACK IN THE BARRACKS CALLED ME BADGER, FERRET, SKUNK. SAID A REAL WOMAN WOULD NEVER MAKE TIME WITH SOMEONE WHO'S ALL HAIR AND STINK LIKE ME.›
‹BUT TIME'S THE ONLY THING I GOT MORE THAN ENOUGH OF.›
‹HERE I THOUGHT I HAD BEDDED A HARDENED WARRIOR, BUT YOU'RE JUST A FRAGILE PORCELAIN DOLL, AREN'T YOU?›
SORRY.
‹LOGAN, WE HAVE HOURS TO GO BEFORE THERE'S ENOUGH DARKNESS TO COVER YOUR ESCAPE.›
‹APOLOGIZE ONCE MORE IN THAT TIME, AND I'LL GIVE YOU SOMETHING TO BE SORRY ABOUT.›
GOMEN NASAI.

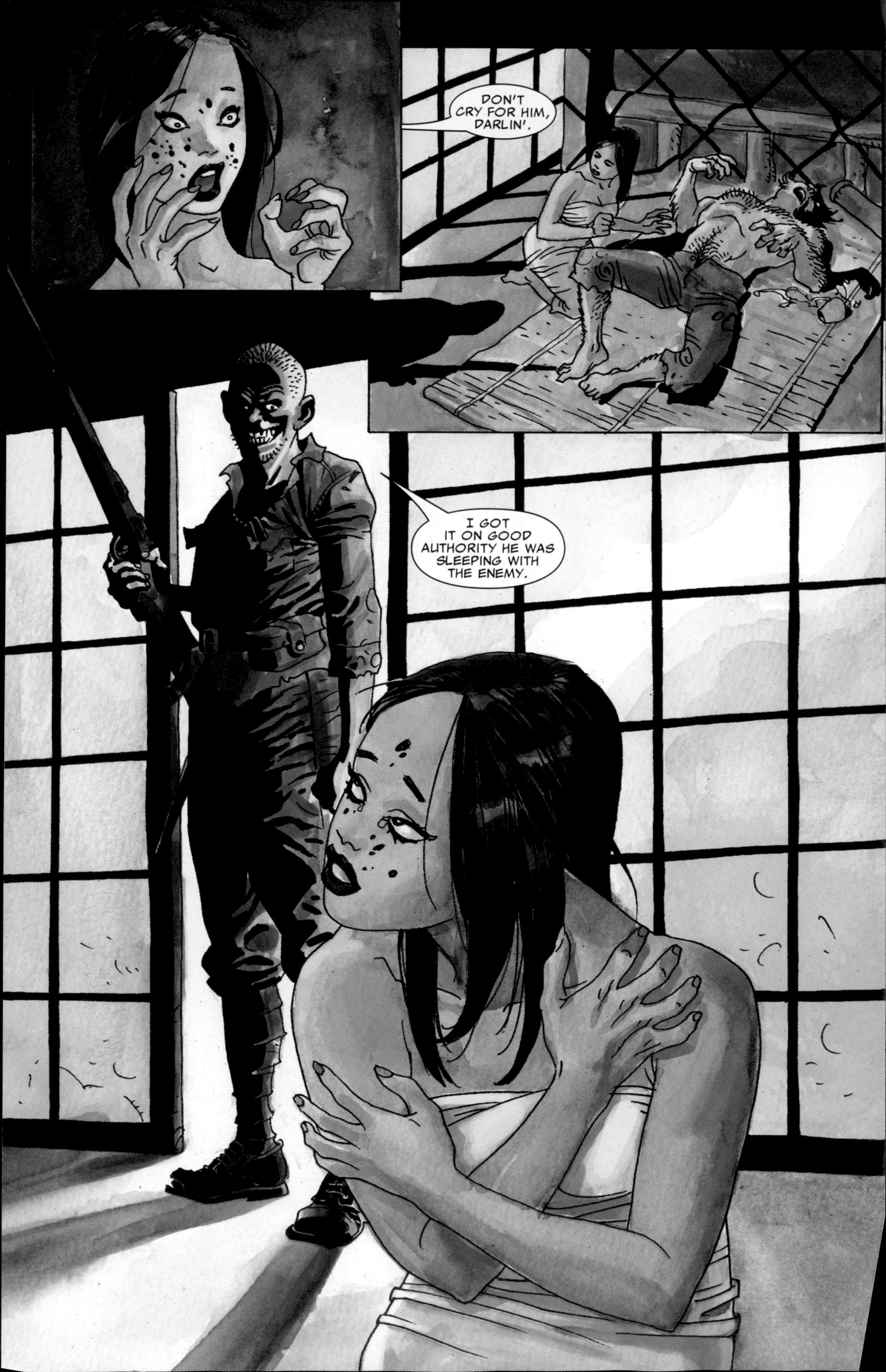
DON'T CRY FOR HIM, DARLIN'.
I GOT IT ON GOOD AUTHORITY HE WAS SLEEPING WITH THE ENEMY.

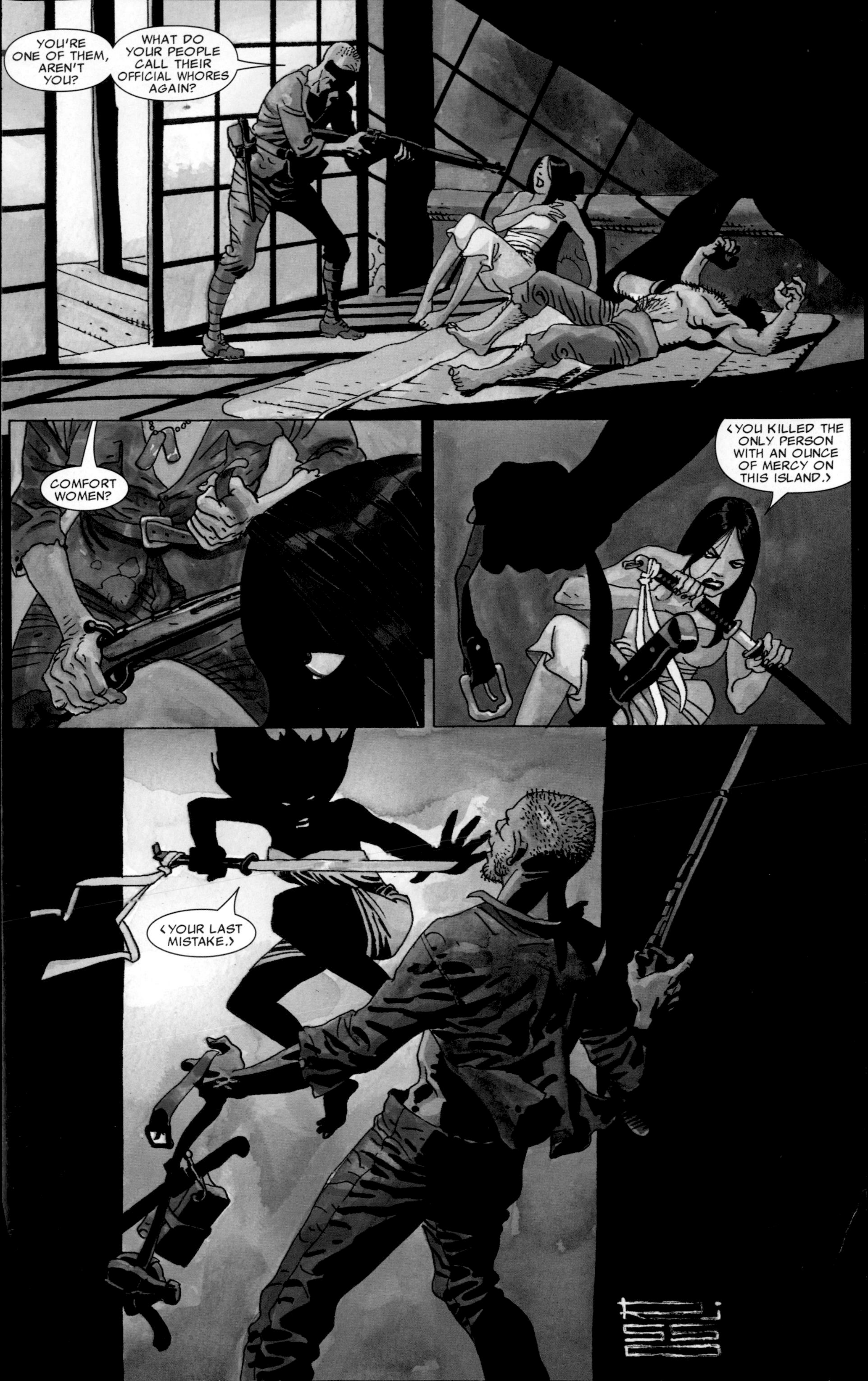
YOU'RE ONE OF THEM, AREN'T YOU?
WHAT DO YOUR PEOPLE CALL THEIR OFFICIAL WHORES AGAIN?
COMFORT WOMEN?
‹YOU KILLED THE ONLY PERSON WITH AN OUNCE OF MERCY ON THIS ISLAND.›
‹YOUR LAST MISTAKE.›

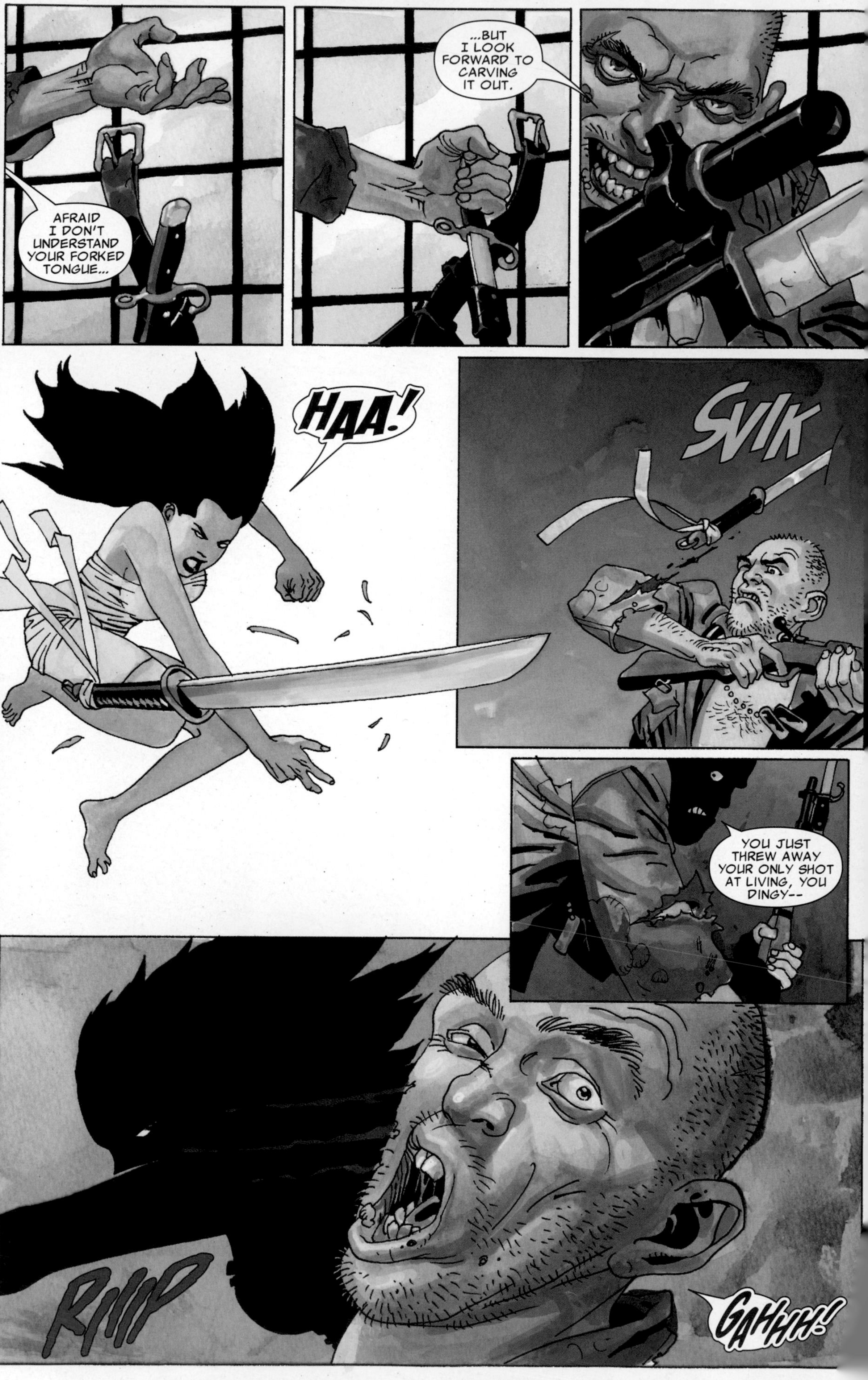
AFRAID I DON'T UNDERSTAND YOUR FORKED TONGUE...
...BUT I LOOK FORWARD TO CARVING IT OUT.
HAA!
SVIK
YOU JUST THREW AWAY YOUR ONLY SHOT AT LIVING, YOU DINGY--
RIIIP
GAHHHH!

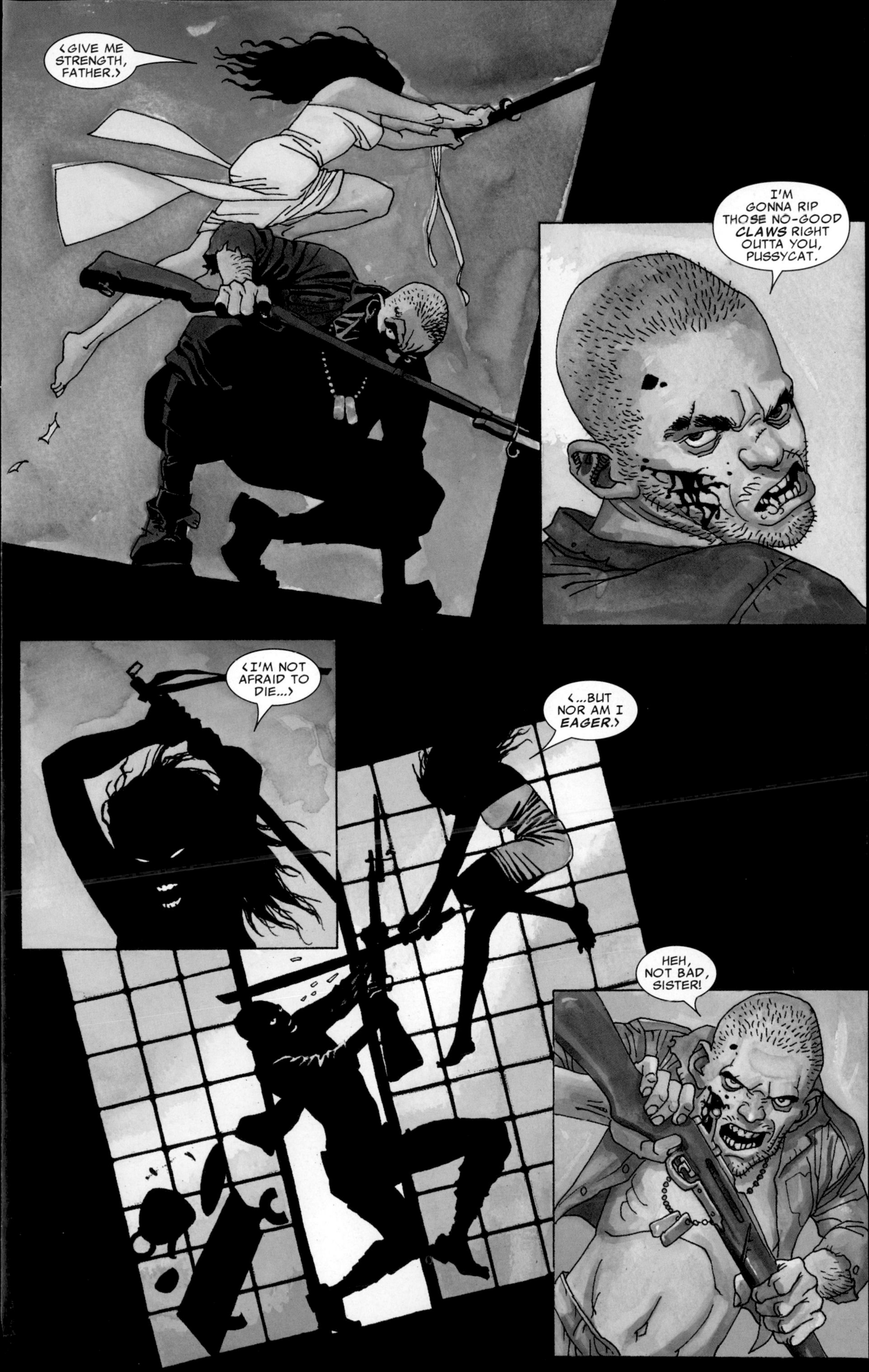
‹GIVE ME STRENGTH, FATHER.›
I'M GONNA RIP THOSE NO-GOOD CLAWS RIGHT OUTTA YOU, PUSSYCAT.
‹I'M NOT AFRAID TO DIE...›
‹...BUT NOR AM I EAGER.›
HEH, NOT BAD, SISTER!

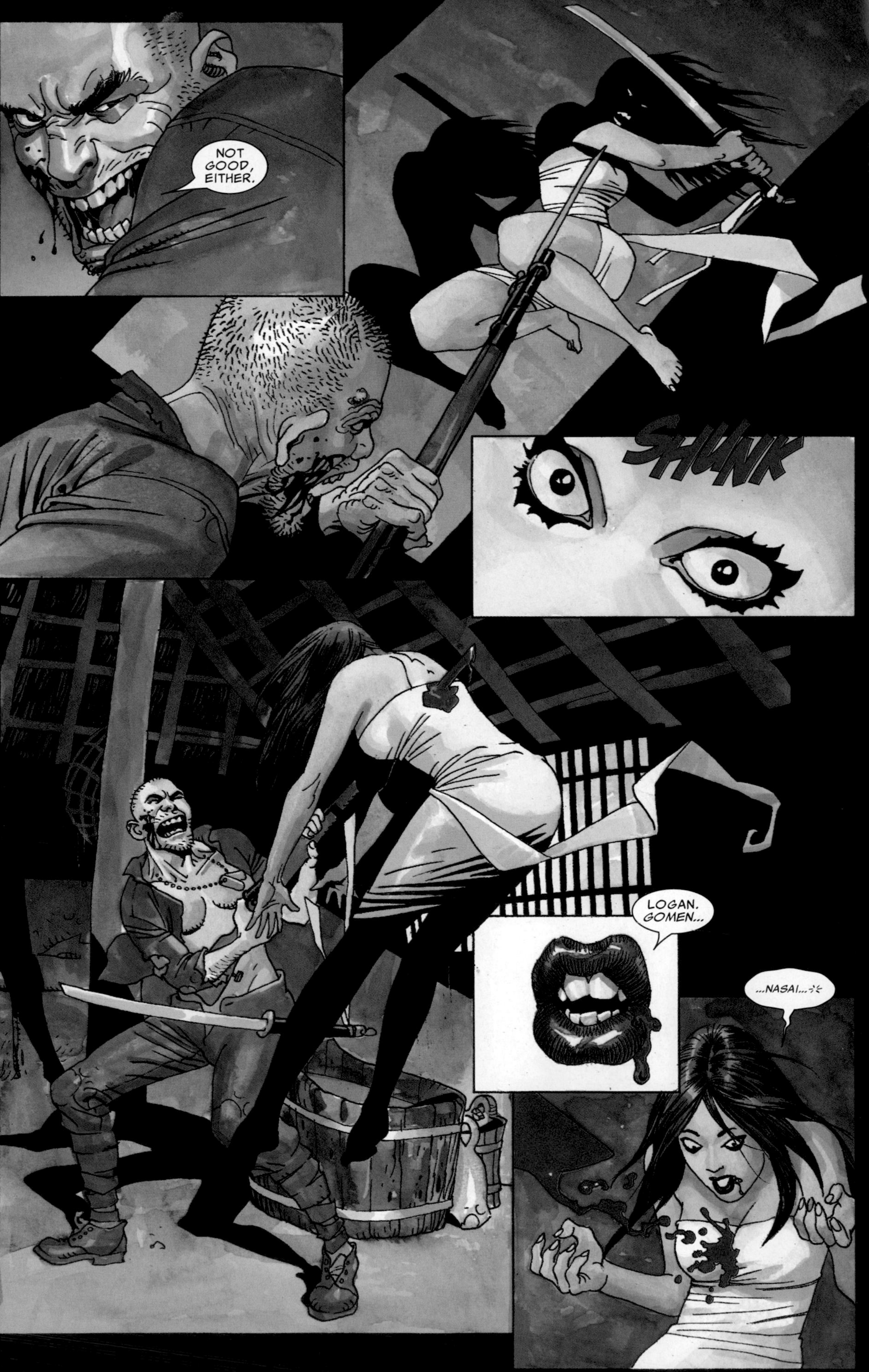
NOT GOOD, EITHER.
SHUNK
LOGAN. GOMEN...
...NASAI...

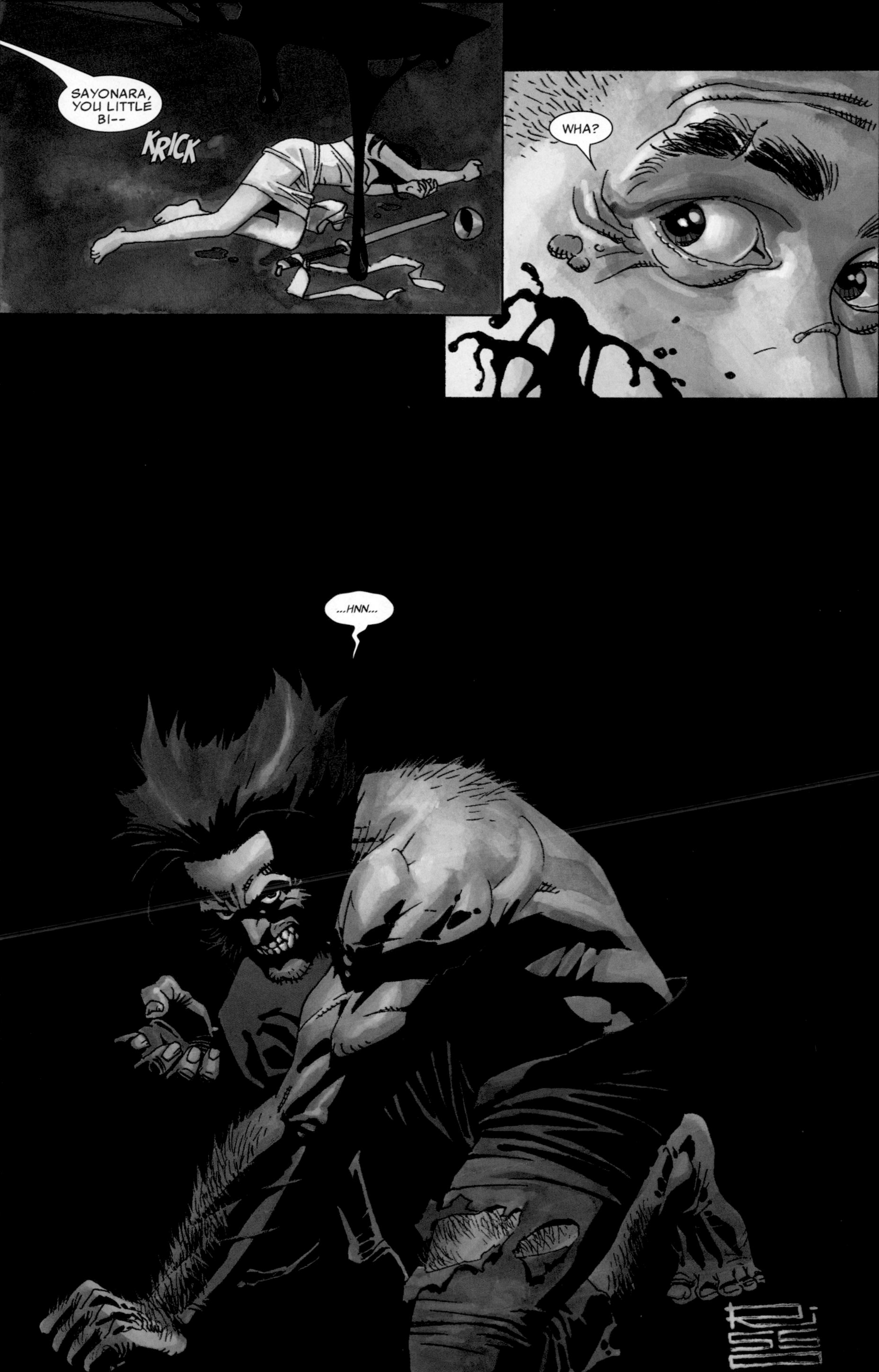
SAYONARA, YOU LITTLE BI--
KRICK
WHA?
...HNN...

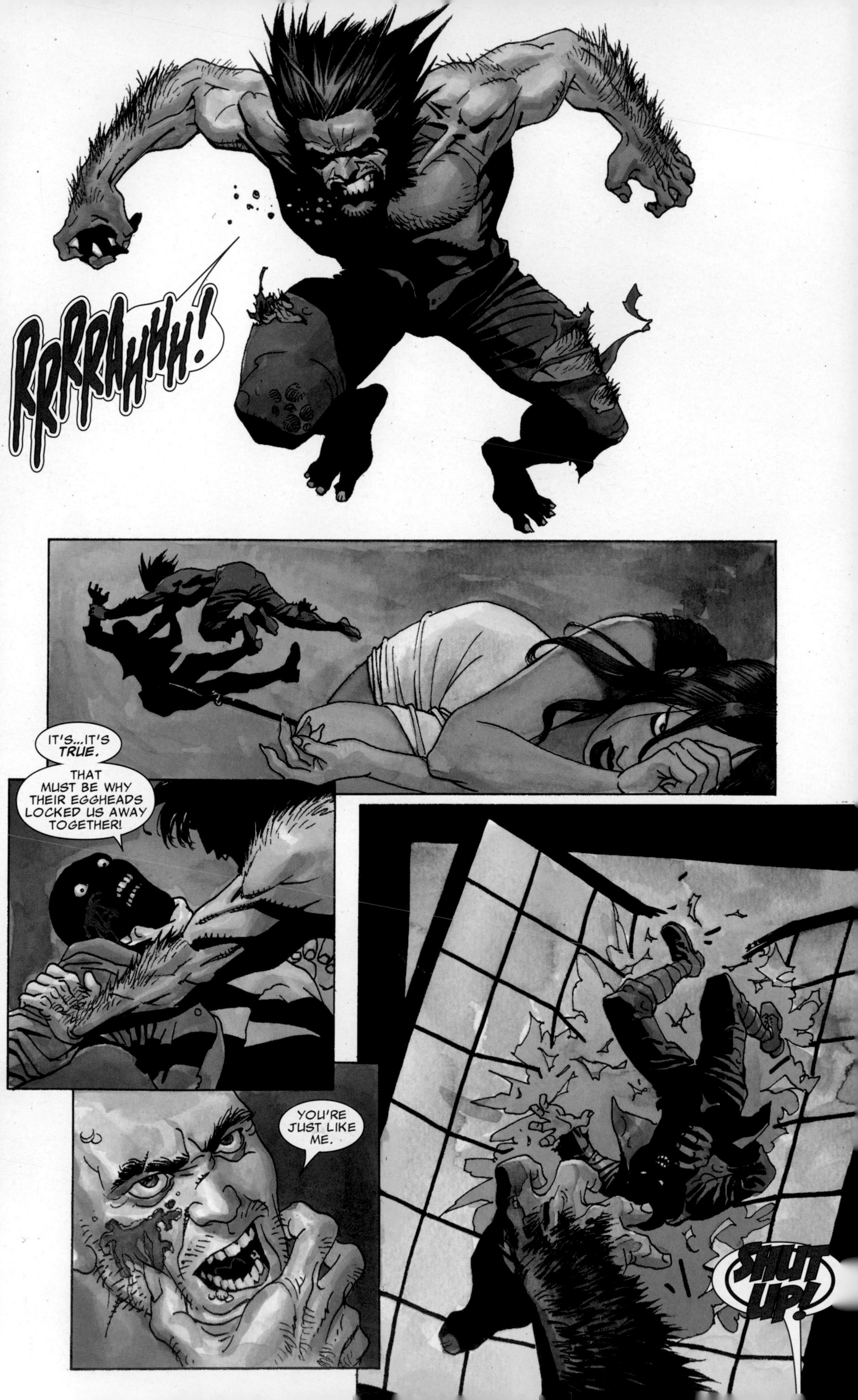
RRRRAHHH!
IT'S...IT'S TRUE.
THAT MUST BE WHY THEIR EGGHEADS LOCKED US AWAY TOGETHER!
YOU'RE JUST LIKE ME.
SHUT UP!

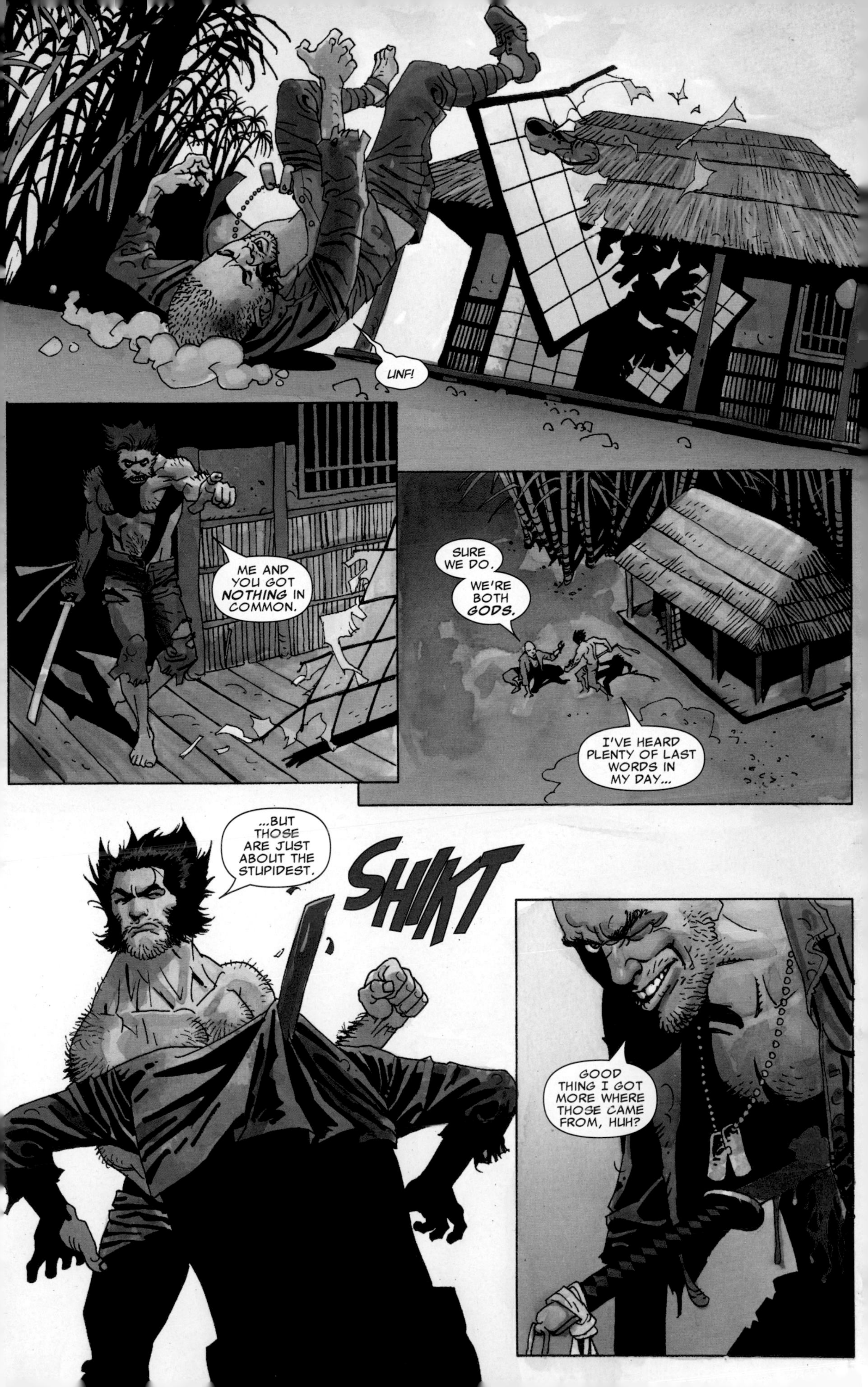
UNF!
ME AND YOU GOT NOTHING IN COMMON.
SURE WE DO.
WE'RE BOTH GODS.
I'VE HEARD PLENTY OF LAST WORDS IN MY DAY...
...BUT THOSE ARE JUST ABOUT THE STUPIDEST.
SHIKT
GOOD THING I GOT MORE WHERE THOSE CAME FROM, HUH?

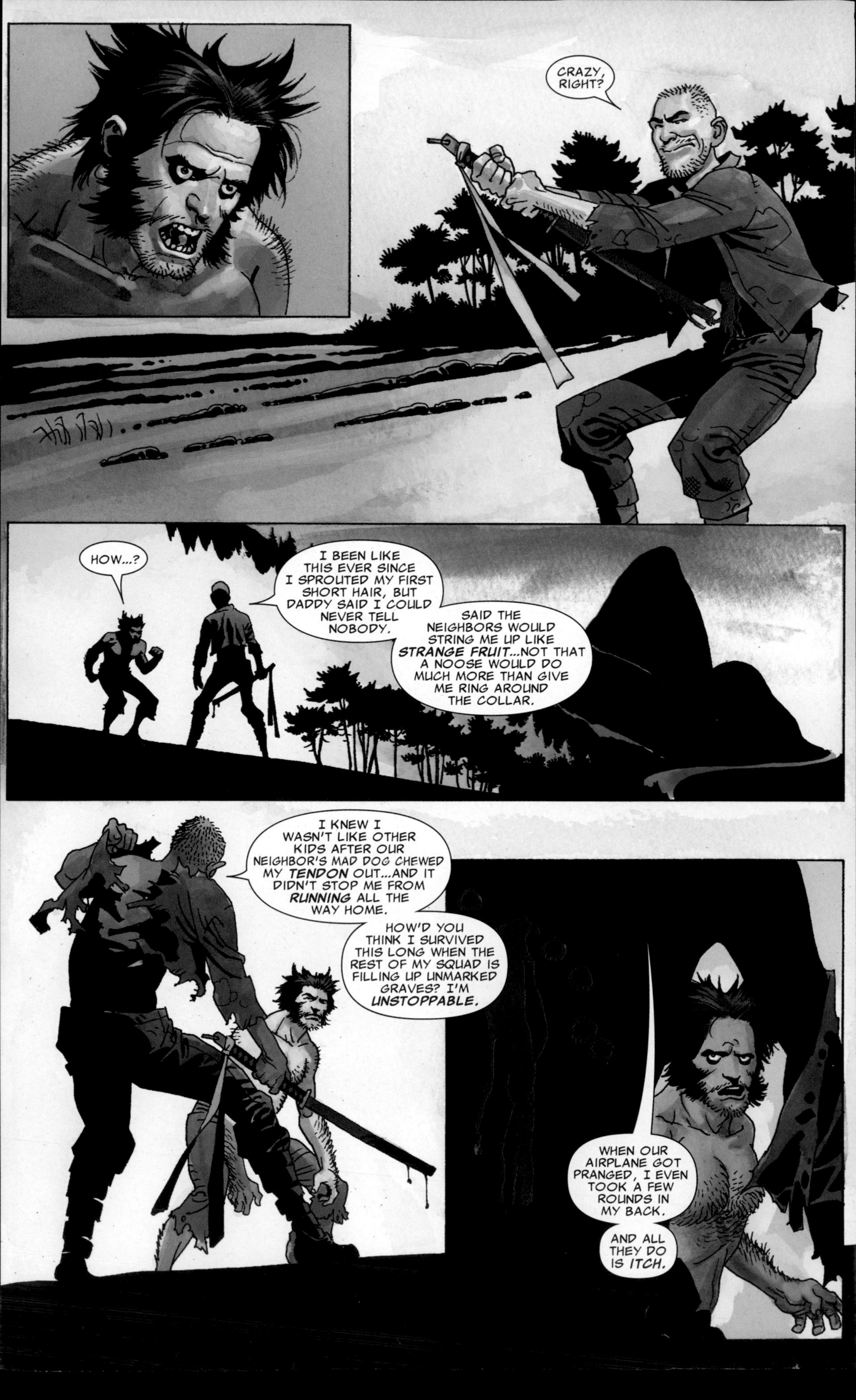
CRAZY, RIGHT?
HOW...?
I BEEN LIKE THIS EVER SINCE I SPROUTED MY FIRST SHORT HAIR, BUT DADDY SAID I COULD NEVER TELL NOBODY.
SAID THE NEIGHBORS WOULD STRING ME UP LIKE STRANGE FRUIT...NOT THAT A NOOSE WOULD DO MUCH MORE THAN GIVE ME RING AROUND THE COLLAR.
I KNEW I WASN'T LIKE OTHER KIDS AFTER OUR NEIGHBOR'S MAD DOG CHEWED MY TENDON OUT...AND IT DIDN'T STOP ME FROM RUNNING ALL THE WAY HOME.
HOW'D YOU THINK I SURVIVED THIS LONG WHEN THE REST OF MY SQUAD IS FILLING UP UNMARKED GRAVES? I'M UNSTOPPABLE.
WHEN OUR AIRPLANE GOT PRANGED, I EVEN TOOK A FEW ROUNDS IN MY BACK.
AND ALL THEY DO IS ITCH.

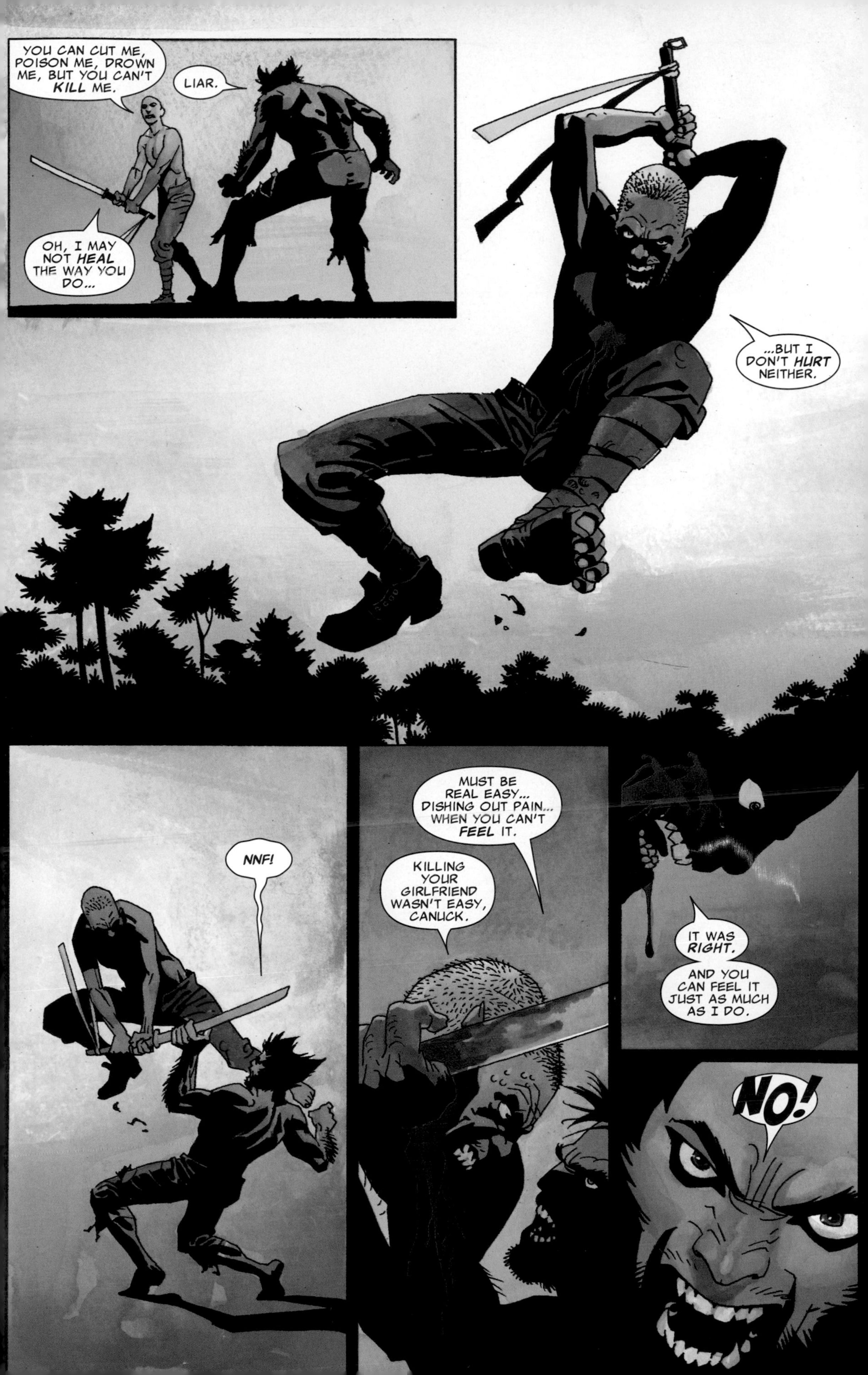

YOU CAN CUT ME, POISON ME, DROWN ME, BUT YOU CAN'T **KILL** ME.
LIAR.
OH, I MAY NOT **HEAL** THE WAY YOU DO...
...BUT I DON'T **HURT** NEITHER.
NNF!
MUST BE REAL EASY... DISHING OUT PAIN... WHEN YOU CAN'T **FEEL** IT.
KILLING YOUR GIRLFRIEND WASN'T EASY, CANUCK.
IT WAS **RIGHT.**
AND YOU CAN FEEL IT JUST AS MUCH AS I DO.
NO!

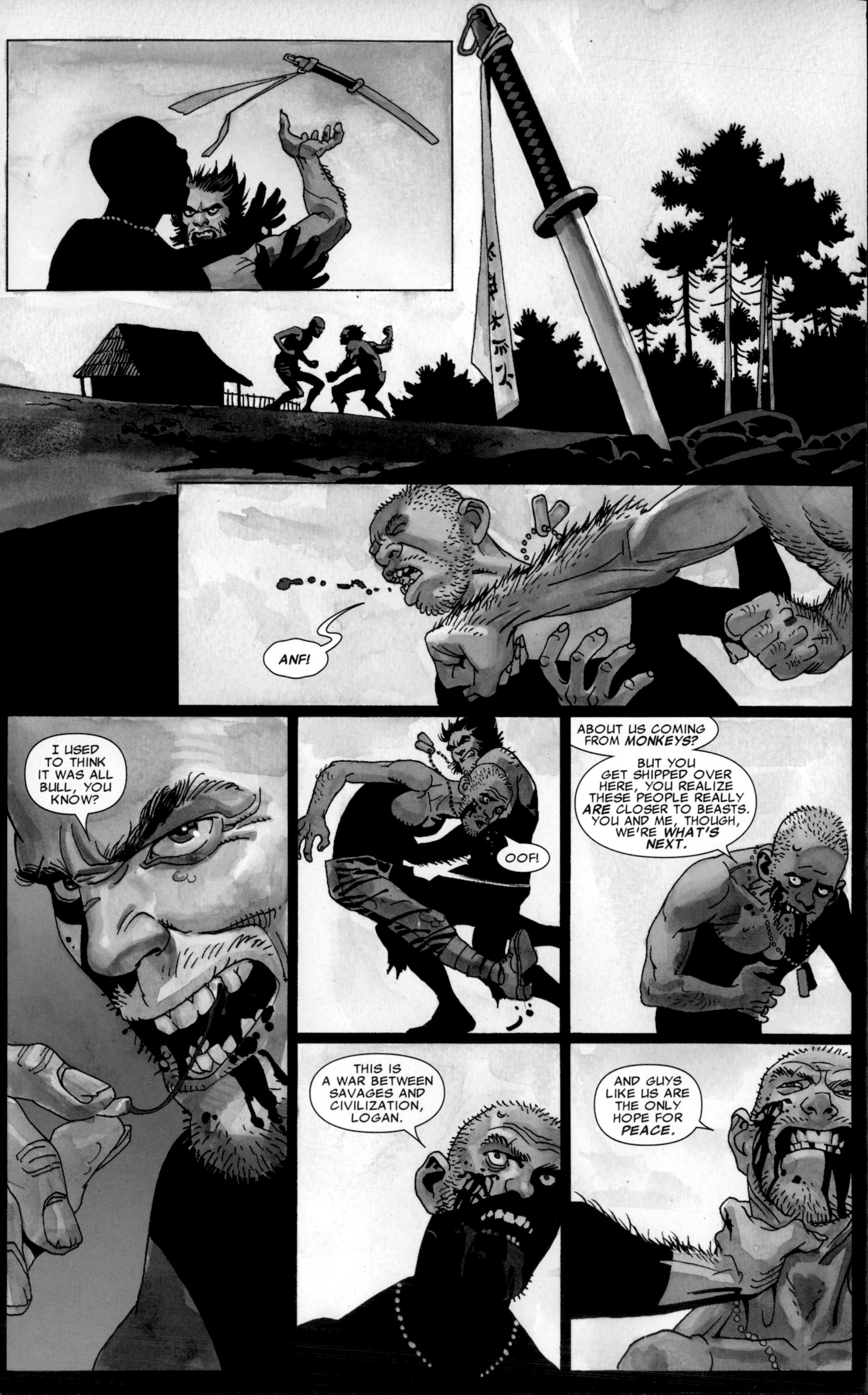
ANF!
I USED TO THINK IT WAS ALL BULL, YOU KNOW?
OOF!
ABOUT US COMING FROM MONKEYS?
BUT YOU GET SHIPPED OVER HERE, YOU REALIZE THESE PEOPLE REALLY ARE CLOSER TO BEASTS. YOU AND ME, THOUGH, WE'RE WHAT'S NEXT.
THIS IS A WAR BETWEEN SAVAGES AND CIVILIZATION, LOGAN.
AND GUYS LIKE US ARE THE ONLY HOPE FOR PEACE.

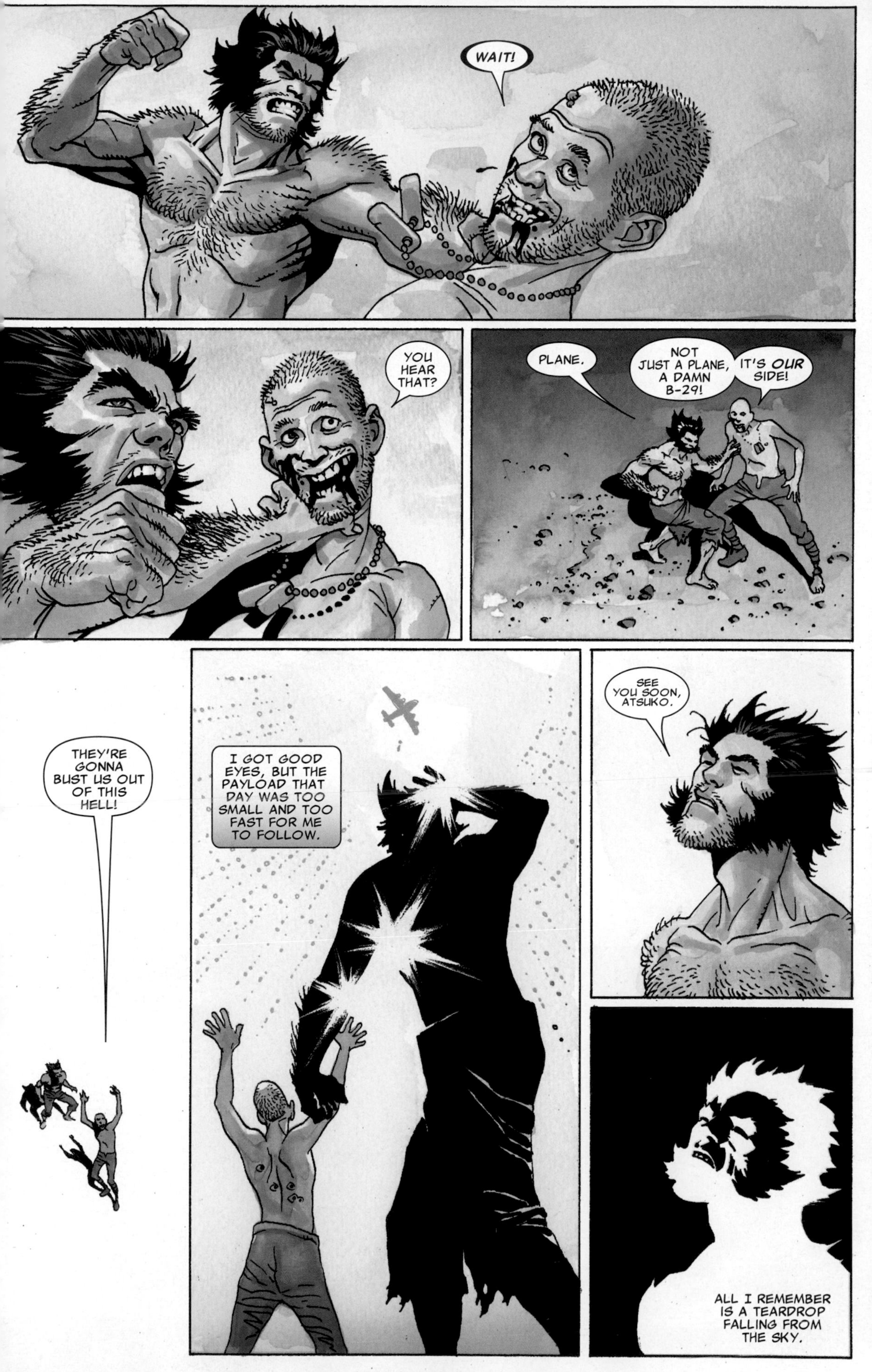
WAIT!
YOU HEAR THAT?
PLANE.
NOT JUST A PLANE, A DAMN B-29!
IT'S OUR SIDE!
THEY'RE GONNA BUST US OUT OF THIS HELL!
I GOT GOOD EYES, BUT THE PAYLOAD THAT DAY WAS TOO SMALL AND TOO FAST FOR ME TO FOLLOW.
SEE YOU SOON, ATSUKO.
ALL I REMEMBER IS A TEARDROP FALLING FROM THE SKY.

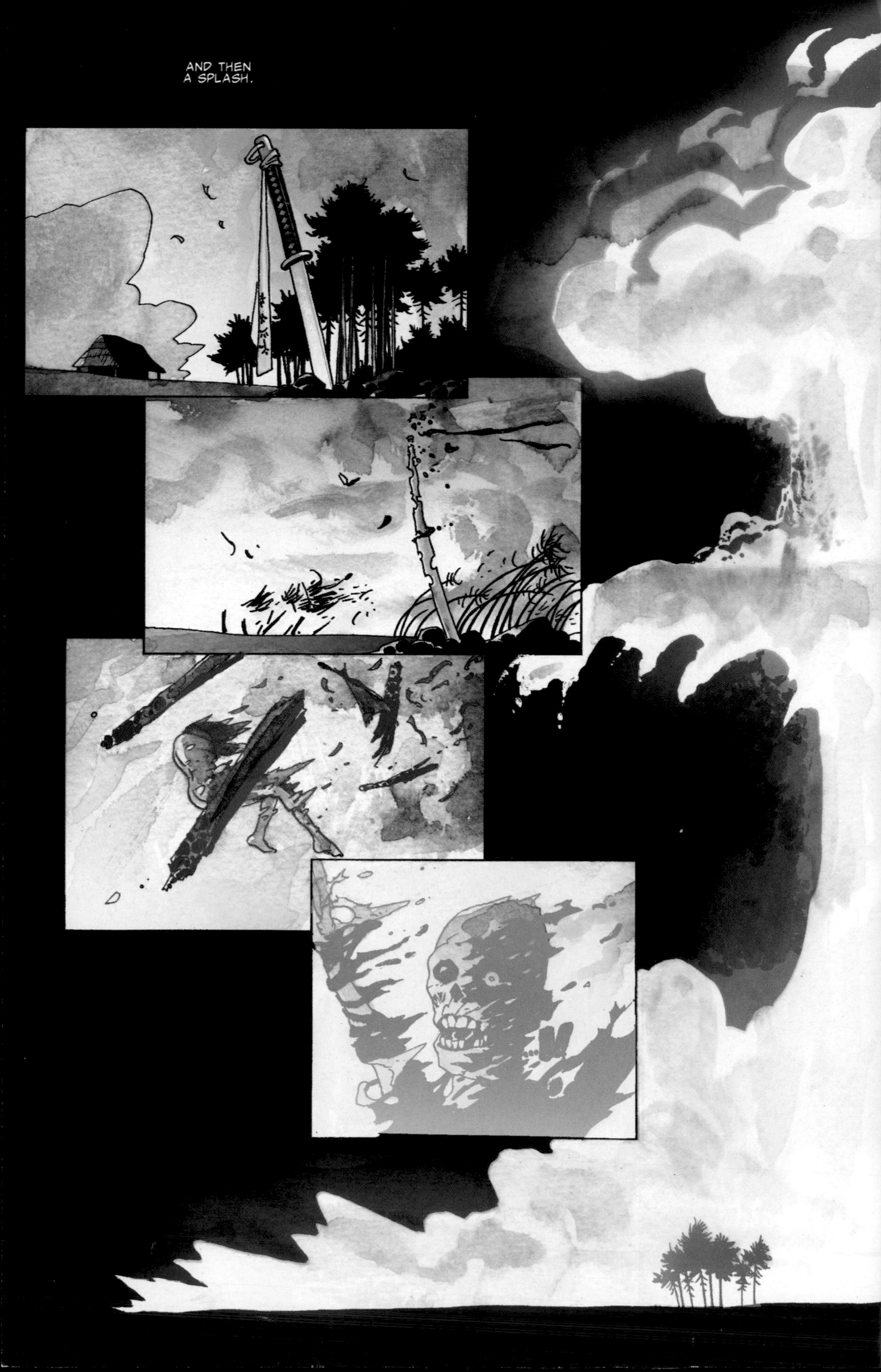
AND THEN
A SPLASH.

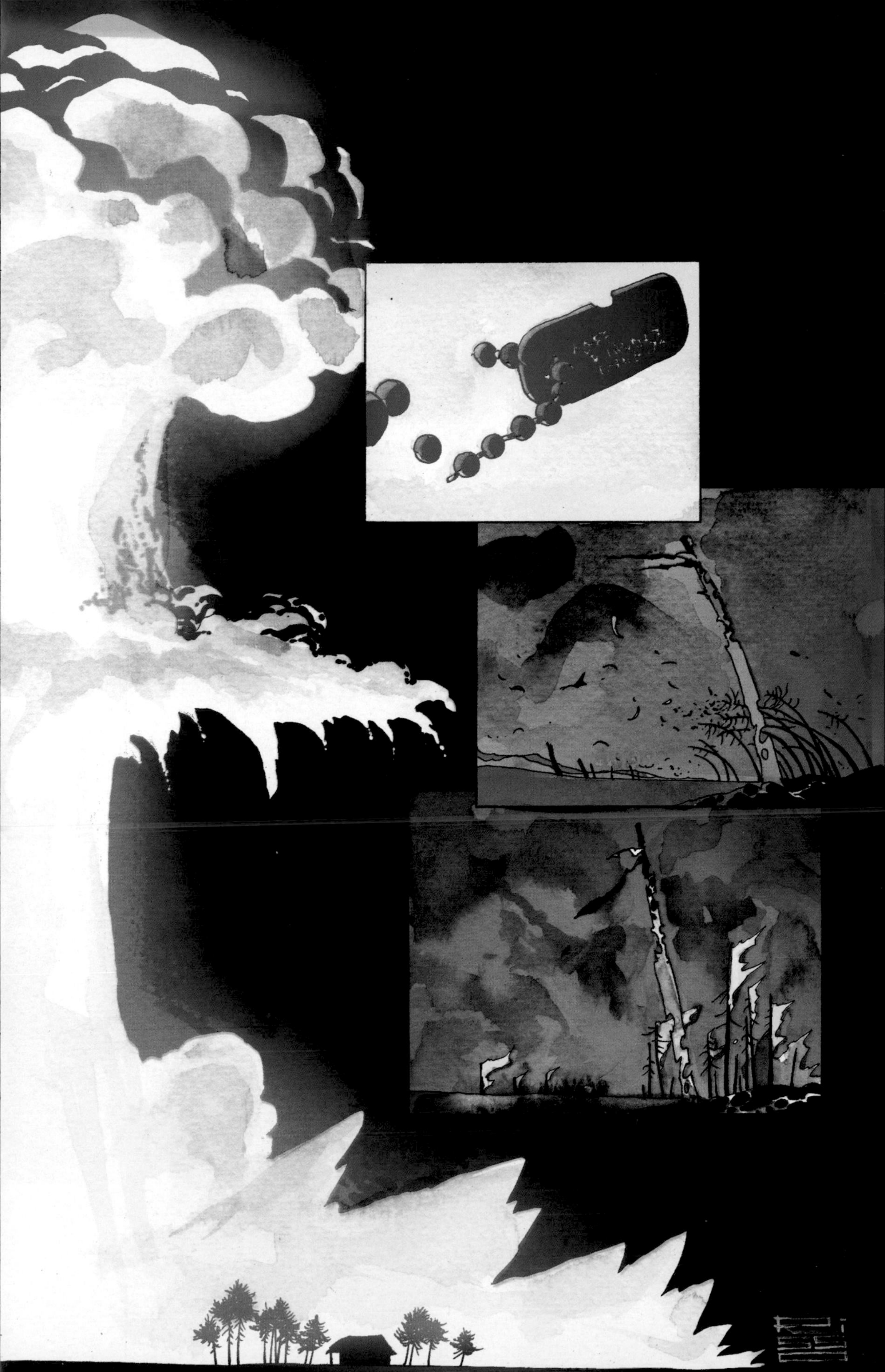

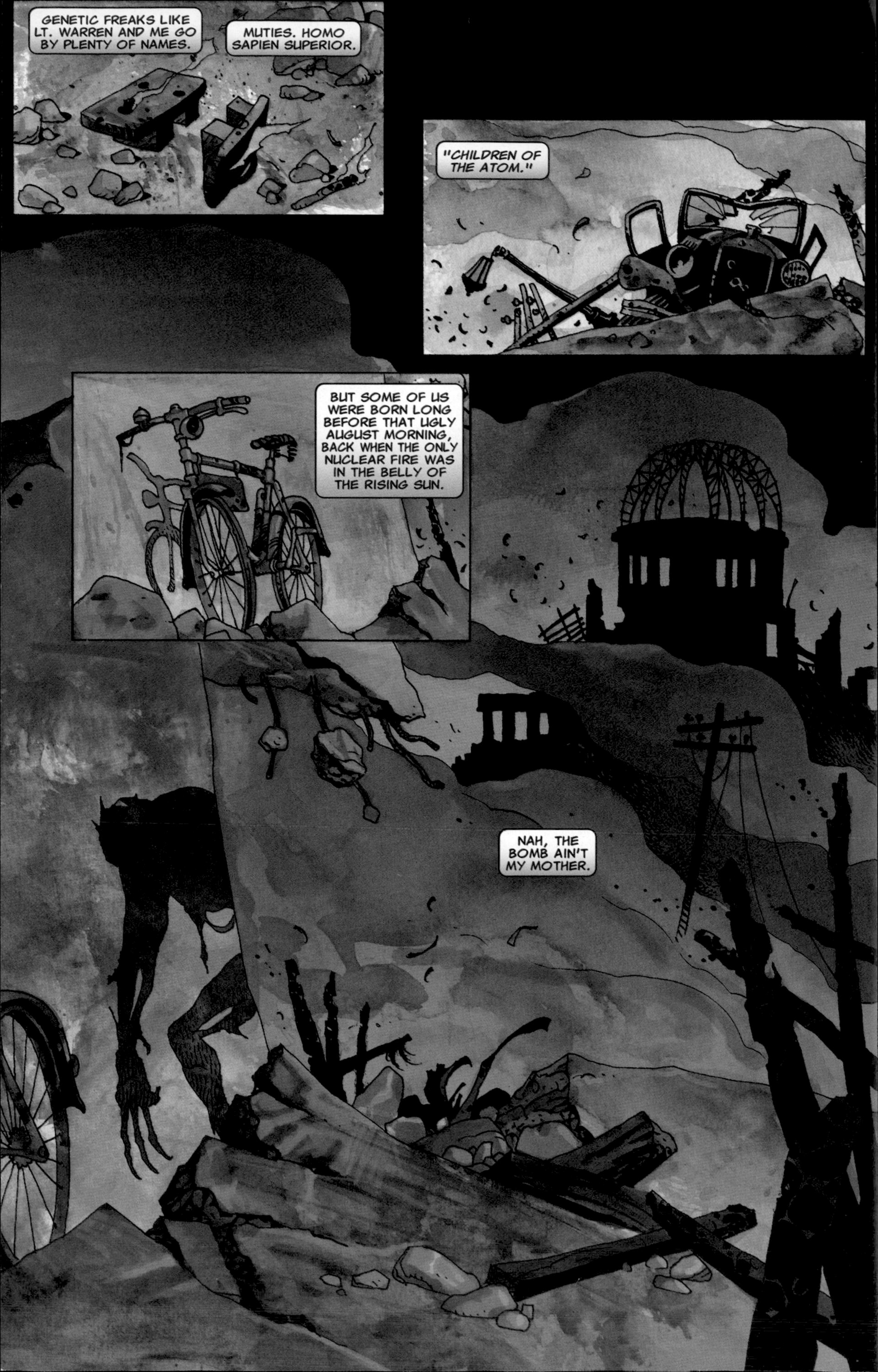
GENETIC FREAKS LIKE LT. WARREN AND ME GO BY PLENTY OF NAMES.
MUTIES. HOMO SAPIEN SUPERIOR.
"CHILDREN OF THE ATOM."
BUT SOME OF US WERE BORN LONG BEFORE THAT UGLY AUGUST MORNING, BACK WHEN THE ONLY NUCLEAR FIRE WAS IN THE BELLY OF THE RISING SUN.
NAH, THE BOMB AIN'T MY MOTHER.

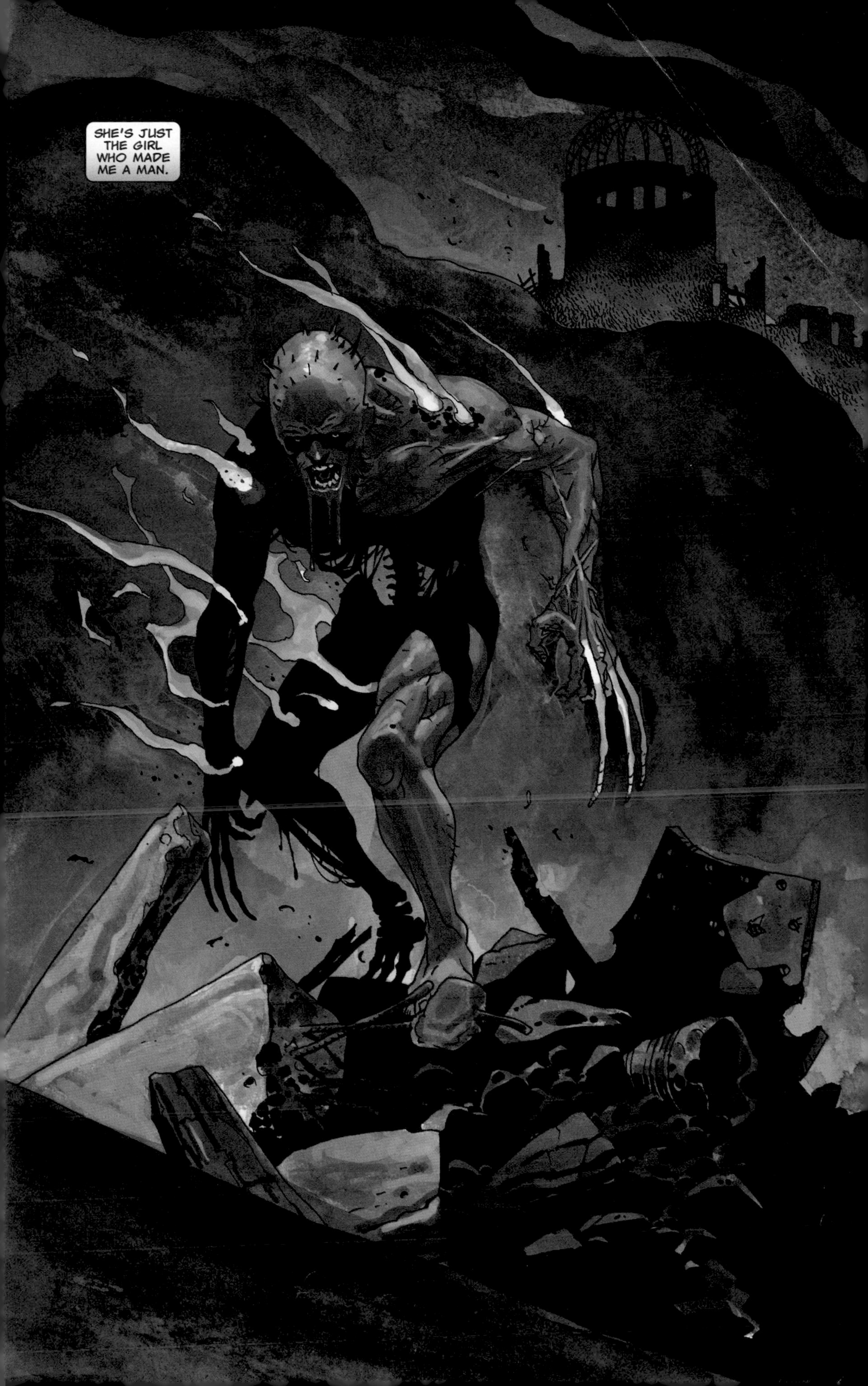
SHE'S JUST THE GIRL WHO MADE ME A MAN.

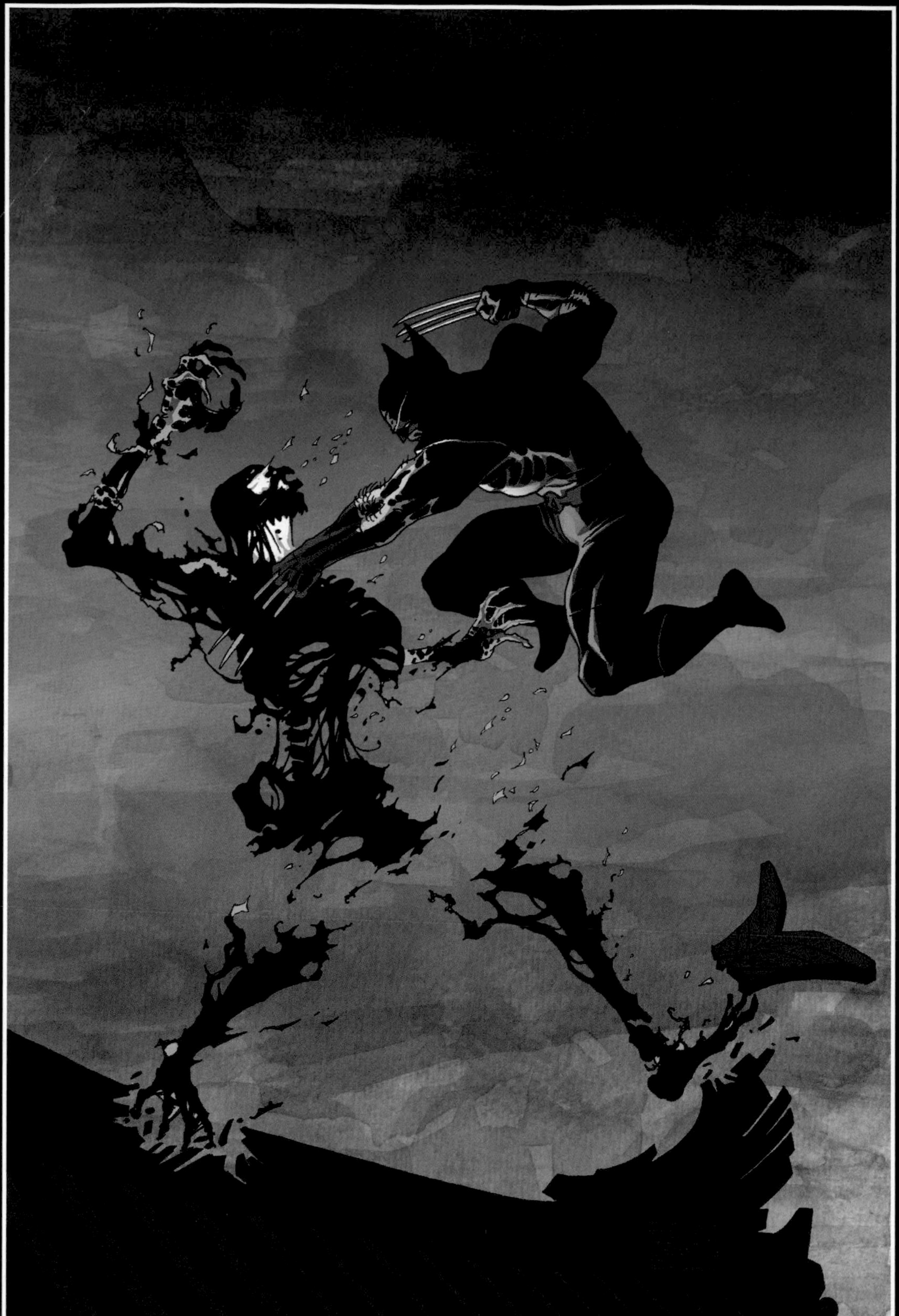

issue number three

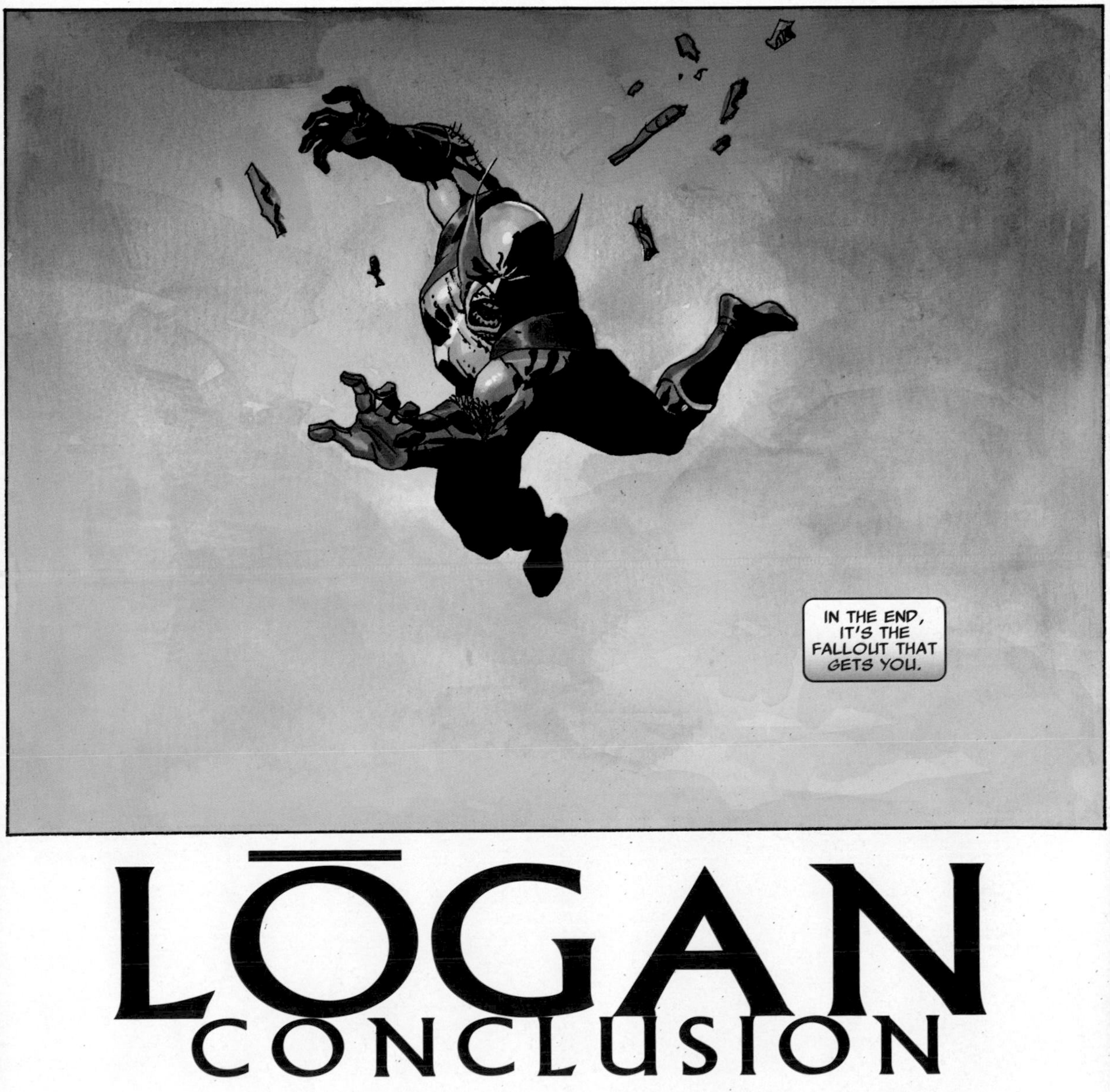
IN THE END, IT'S THE FALLOUT THAT GETS YOU.

LŌGAN
CONCLUSION

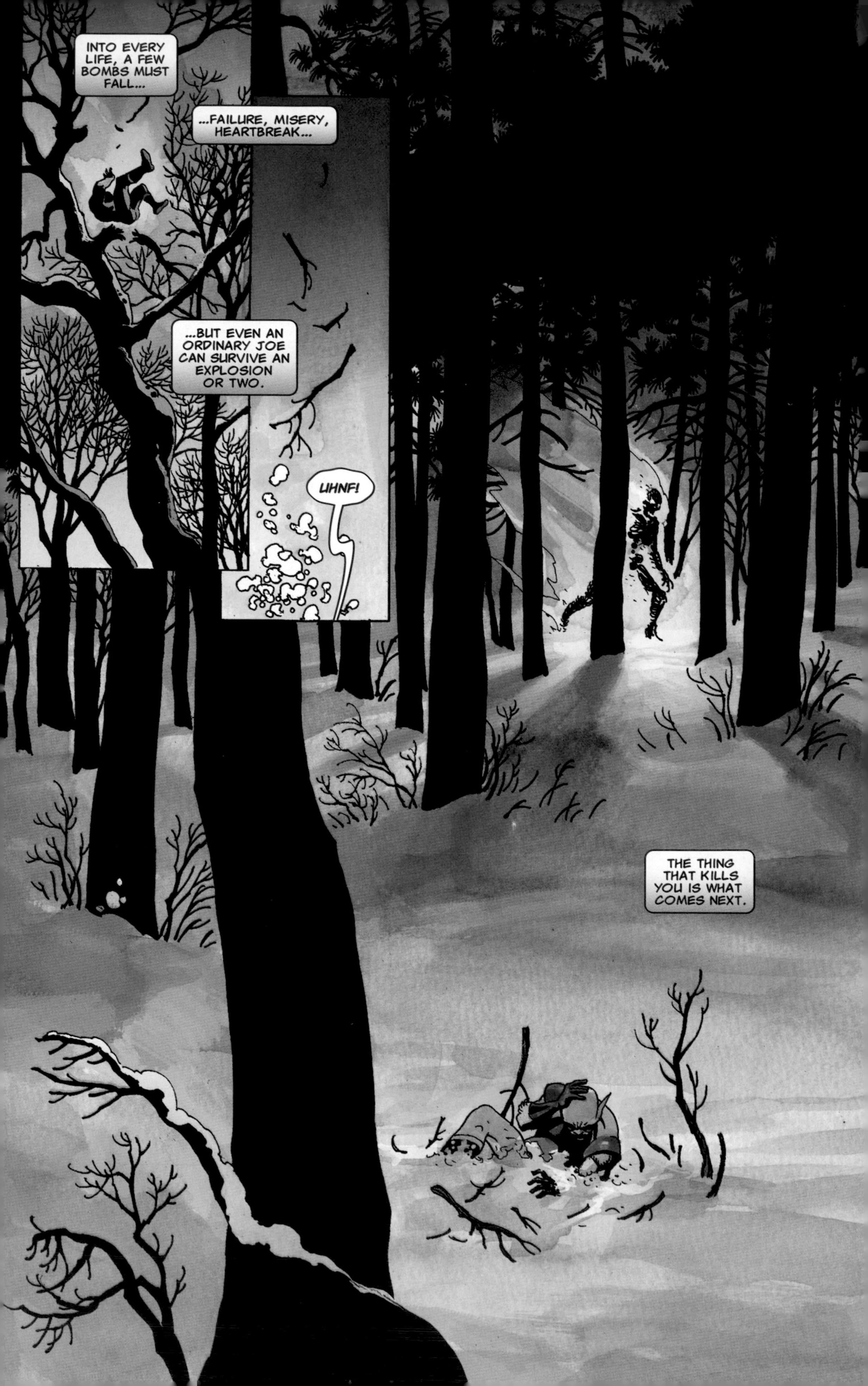
INTO EVERY LIFE, A FEW BOMBS MUST FALL...
...FAILURE, MISERY, HEARTBREAK...
...BUT EVEN AN ORDINARY JOE CAN SURVIVE AN EXPLOSION OR TWO.
UHNF!
THE THING THAT KILLS YOU IS WHAT COMES NEXT.

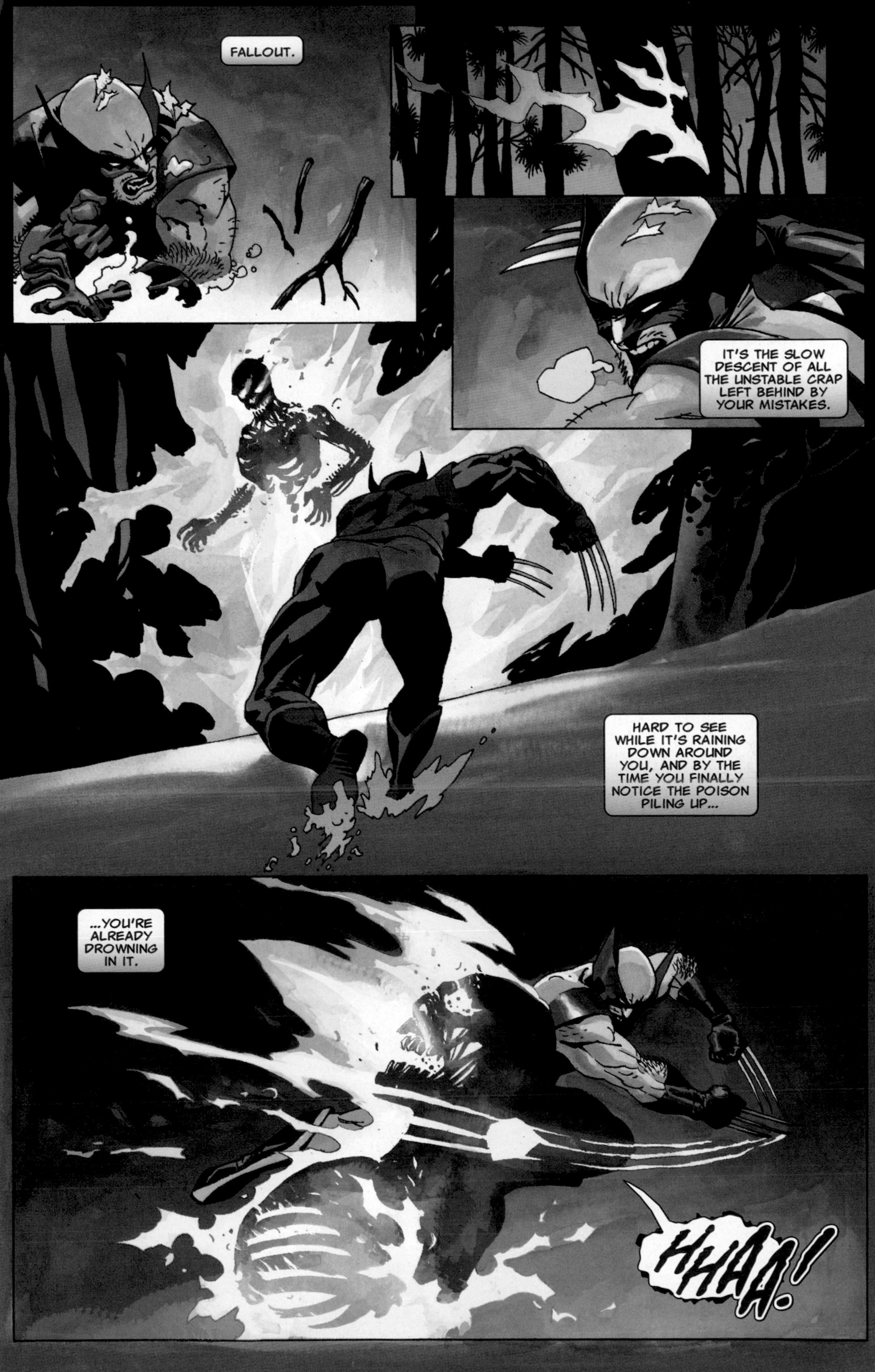
FALLOUT.
IT'S THE SLOW DESCENT OF ALL THE UNSTABLE CRAP LEFT BEHIND BY YOUR MISTAKES.
HARD TO SEE WHILE IT'S RAINING DOWN AROUND YOU, AND BY THE TIME YOU FINALLY NOTICE THE POISON PILING UP...
...YOU'RE ALREADY DROWNING IN IT.
HHAA!

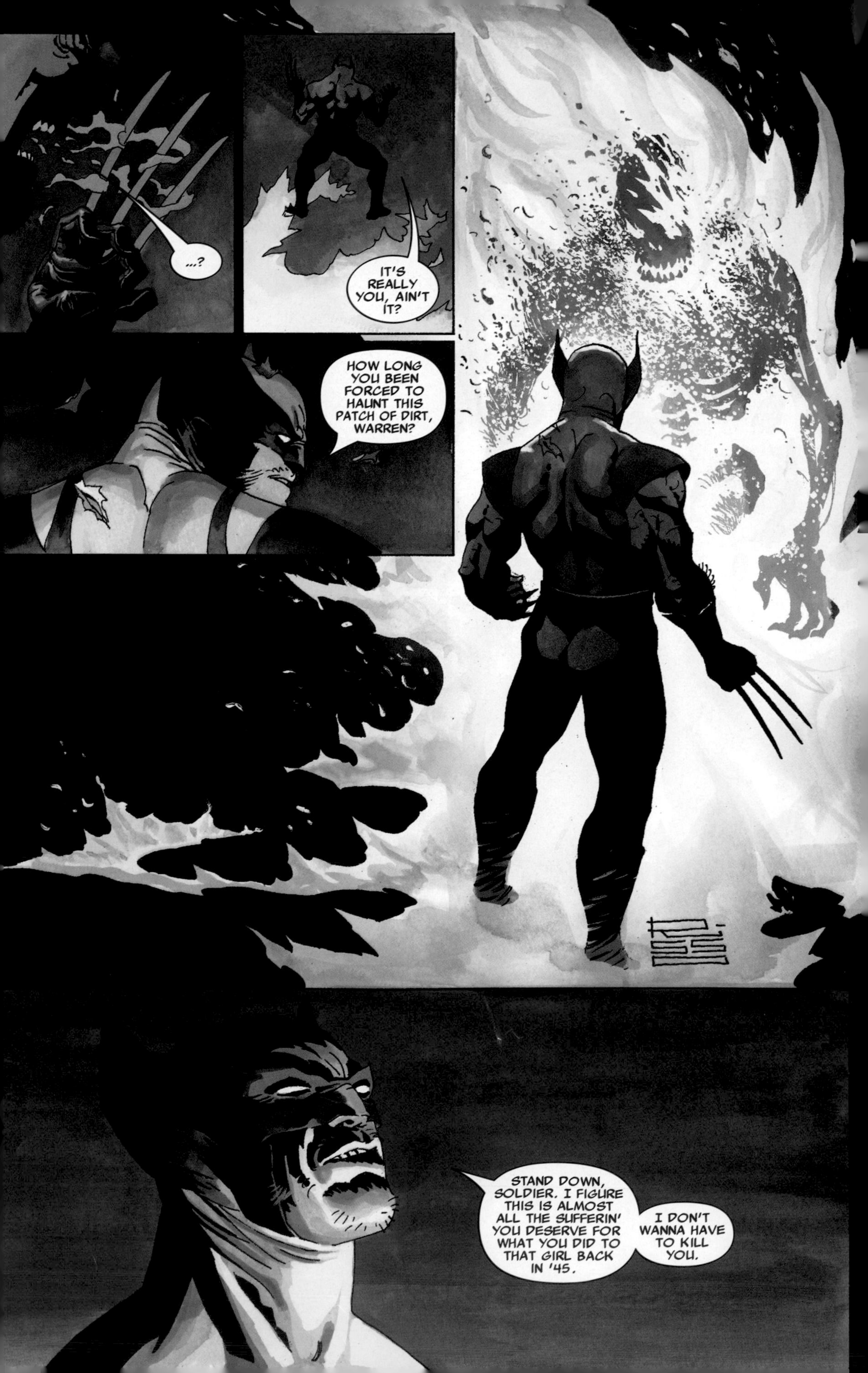
...?
IT'S REALLY YOU, AIN'T IT?
HOW LONG YOU BEEN FORCED TO HAUNT THIS PATCH OF DIRT, WARREN?
STAND DOWN, SOLDIER. I FIGURE THIS IS ALMOST ALL THE SUFFERIN' YOU DESERVE FOR WHAT YOU DID TO THAT GIRL BACK IN '45.
I DON'T WANNA HAVE TO KILL YOU.

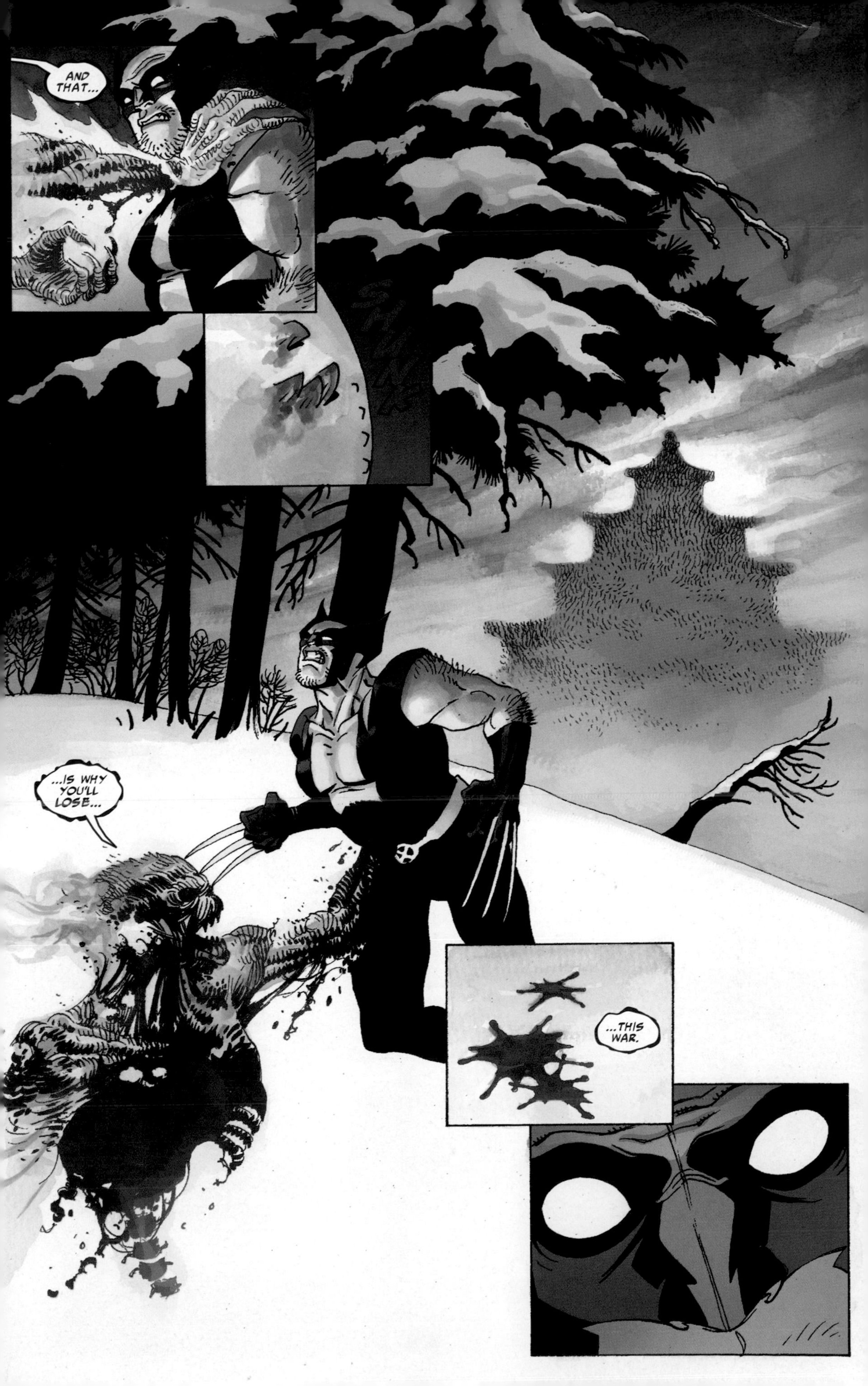
AND THAT...
...IS WHY YOU'LL LOSE...
...THIS WAR.

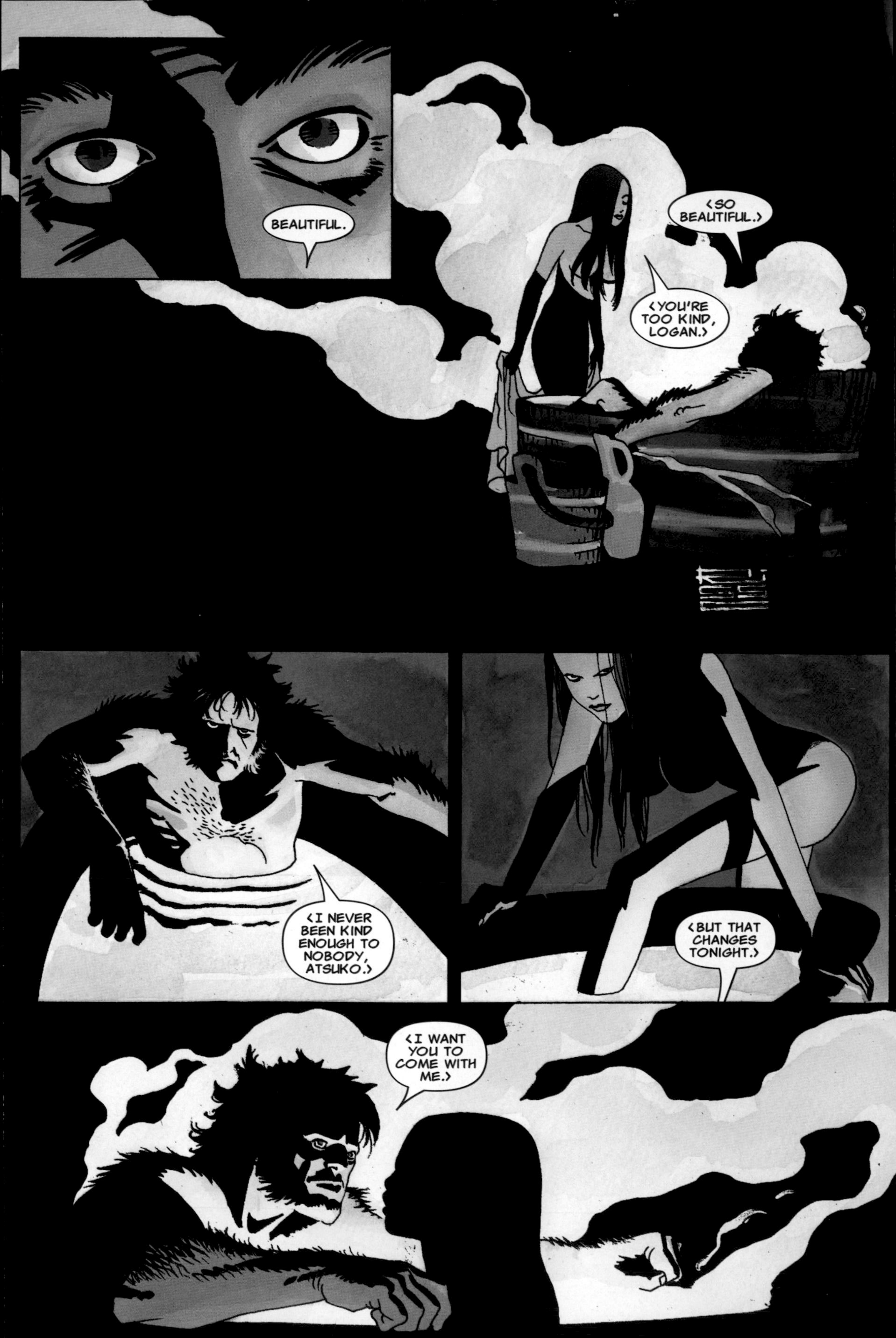
BEAUTIFUL.
‹SO BEAUTIFUL.›
‹YOU'RE TOO KIND, LOGAN.›
‹I NEVER BEEN KIND ENOUGH TO NOBODY, ATSUKO.›
‹BUT THAT CHANGES TONIGHT.›
‹I WANT YOU TO COME WITH ME.›

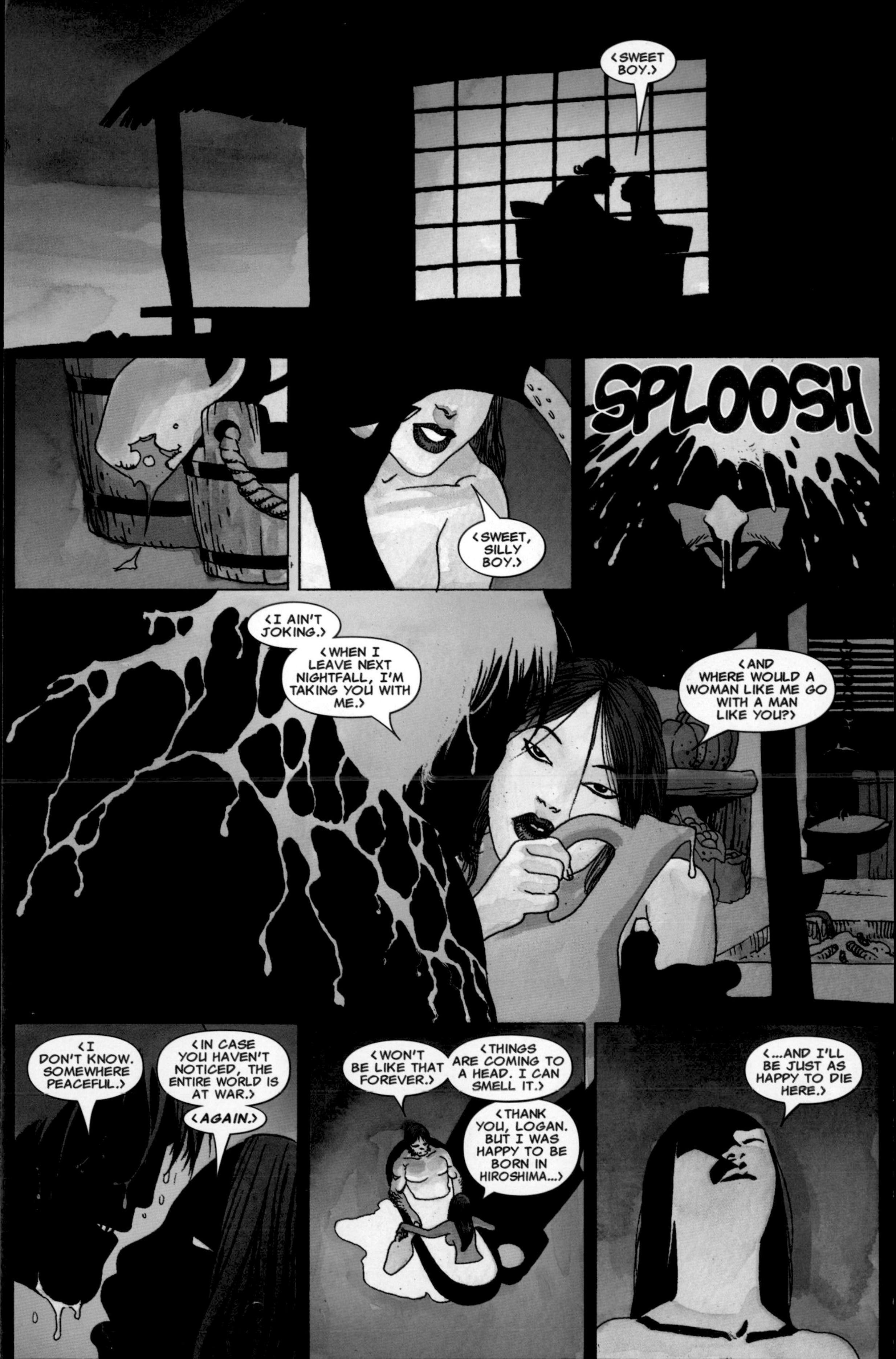
‹SWEET BOY.›
‹SWEET, SILLY BOY.›
SPLOOSH
‹I AIN'T JOKING.›
‹WHEN I LEAVE NEXT NIGHTFALL, I'M TAKING YOU WITH ME.›
‹AND WHERE WOULD A WOMAN LIKE ME GO WITH A MAN LIKE YOU?›
‹I DON'T KNOW. SOMEWHERE PEACEFUL.›
‹IN CASE YOU HAVEN'T NOTICED, THE ENTIRE WORLD IS AT WAR.›
‹AGAIN.›
‹WON'T BE LIKE THAT FOREVER.›
‹THINGS ARE COMING TO A HEAD. I CAN SMELL IT.›
‹THANK YOU, LOGAN. BUT I WAS HAPPY TO BE BORN IN HIROSHIMA...›
‹...AND I'LL BE JUST AS HAPPY TO DIE HERE.›

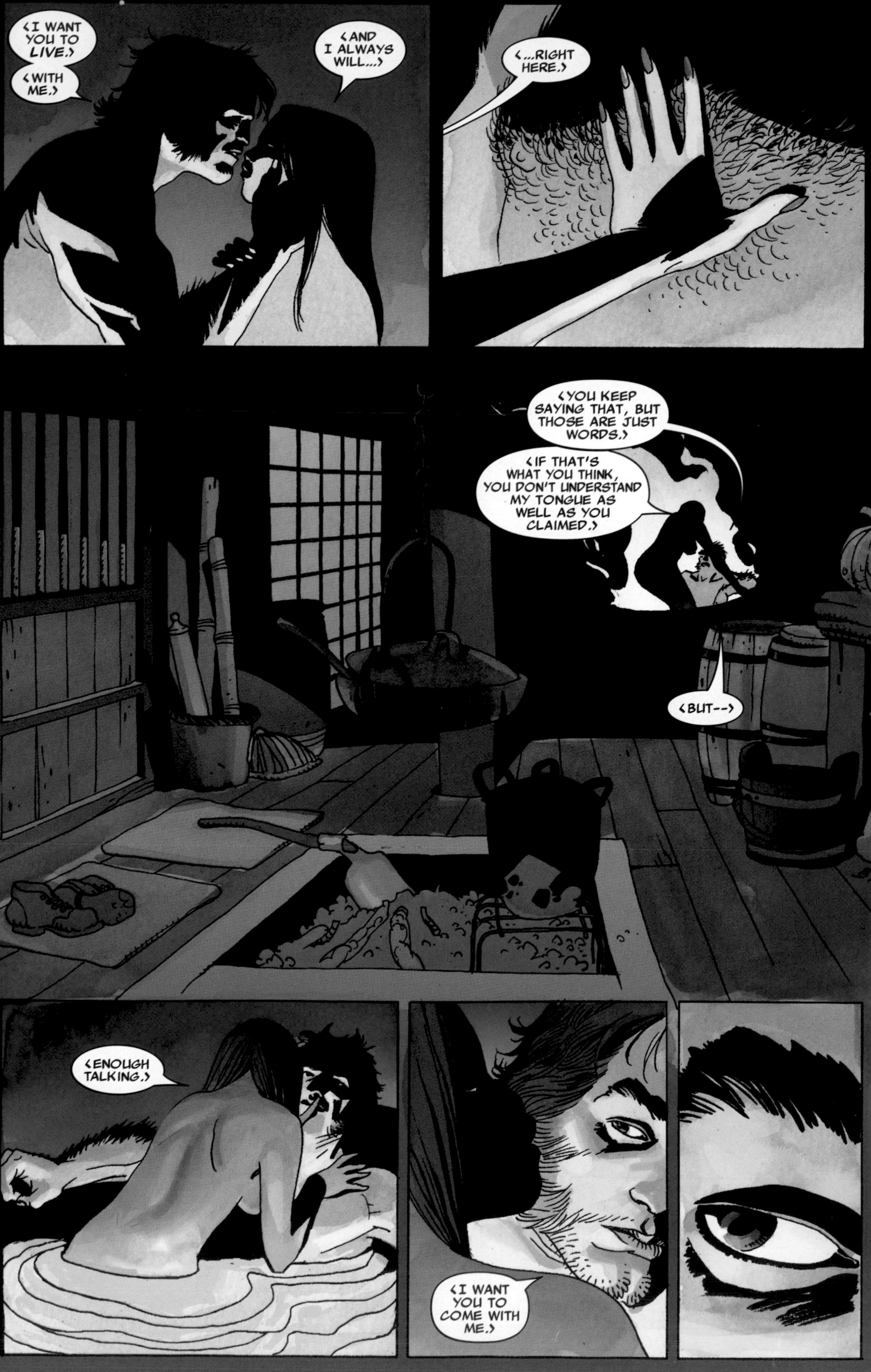
‹I WANT YOU TO LIVE.›
‹WITH ME.›
‹AND I ALWAYS WILL...›
‹...RIGHT HERE.›
‹YOU KEEP SAYING THAT, BUT THOSE ARE JUST WORDS.›
‹IF THAT'S WHAT YOU THINK, YOU DON'T UNDERSTAND MY TONGUE AS WELL AS YOU CLAIMED.›
‹BUT--›
‹ENOUGH TALKING.›
‹I WANT YOU TO COME WITH ME.›

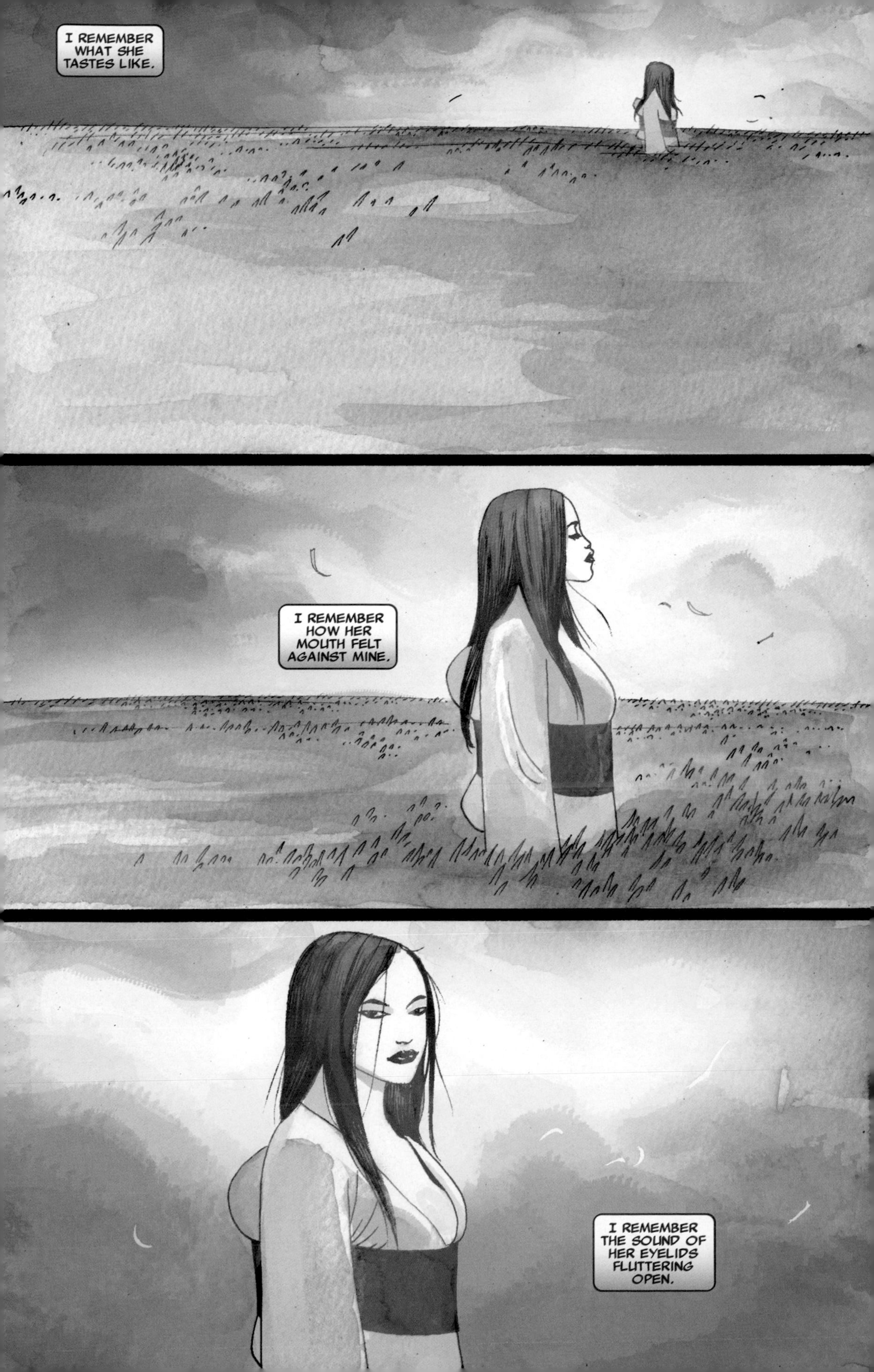
I REMEMBER WHAT SHE TASTES LIKE.
I REMEMBER HOW HER MOUTH FELT AGAINST MINE.
I REMEMBER THE SOUND OF HER EYELIDS FLUTTERING OPEN.

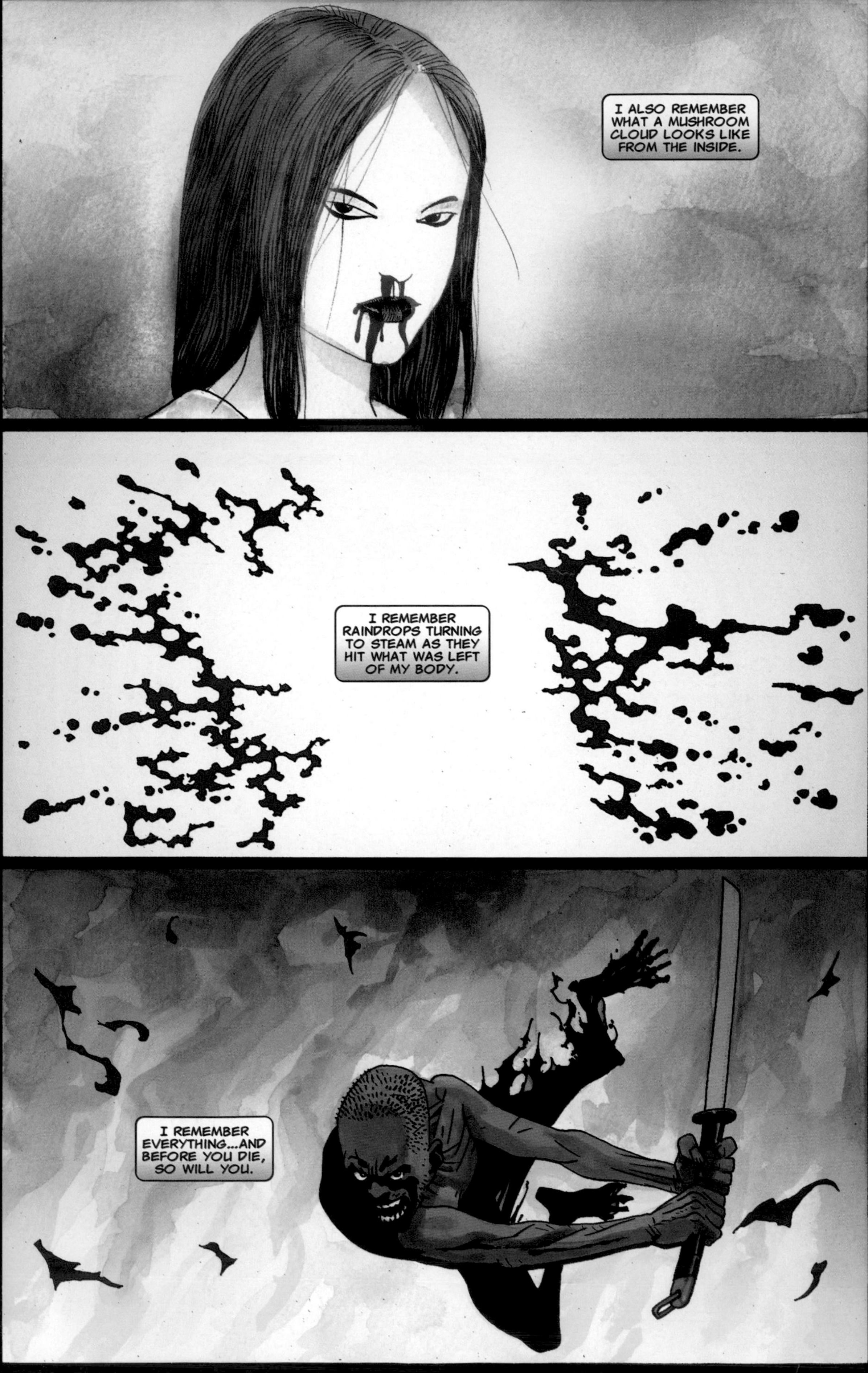
I ALSO REMEMBER WHAT A MUSHROOM CLOUD LOOKS LIKE FROM THE INSIDE.
I REMEMBER RAINDROPS TURNING TO STEAM AS THEY HIT WHAT WAS LEFT OF MY BODY.
I REMEMBER EVERYTHING...AND BEFORE YOU DIE, SO WILL YOU.

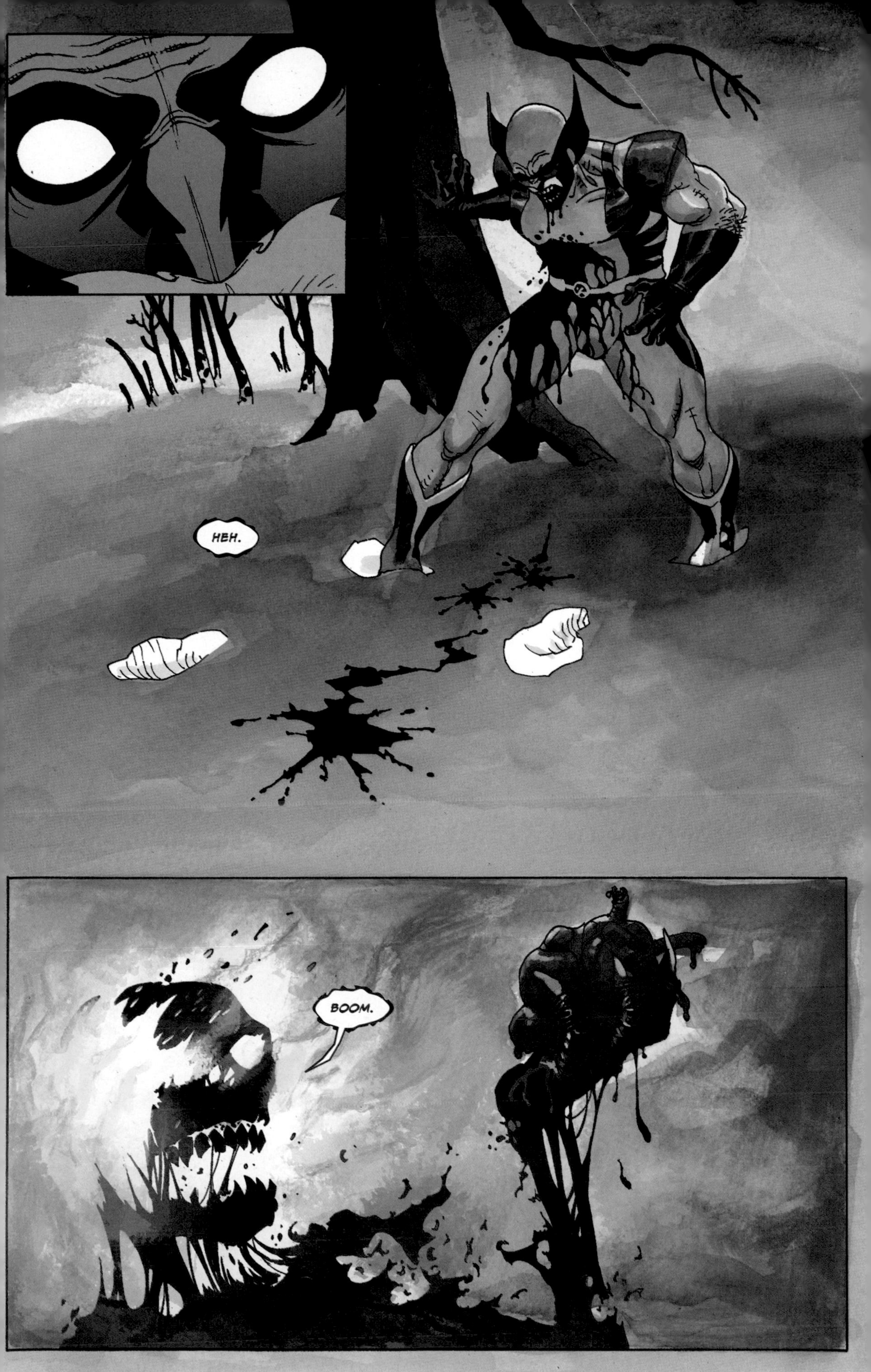
HEH.
BOOM.

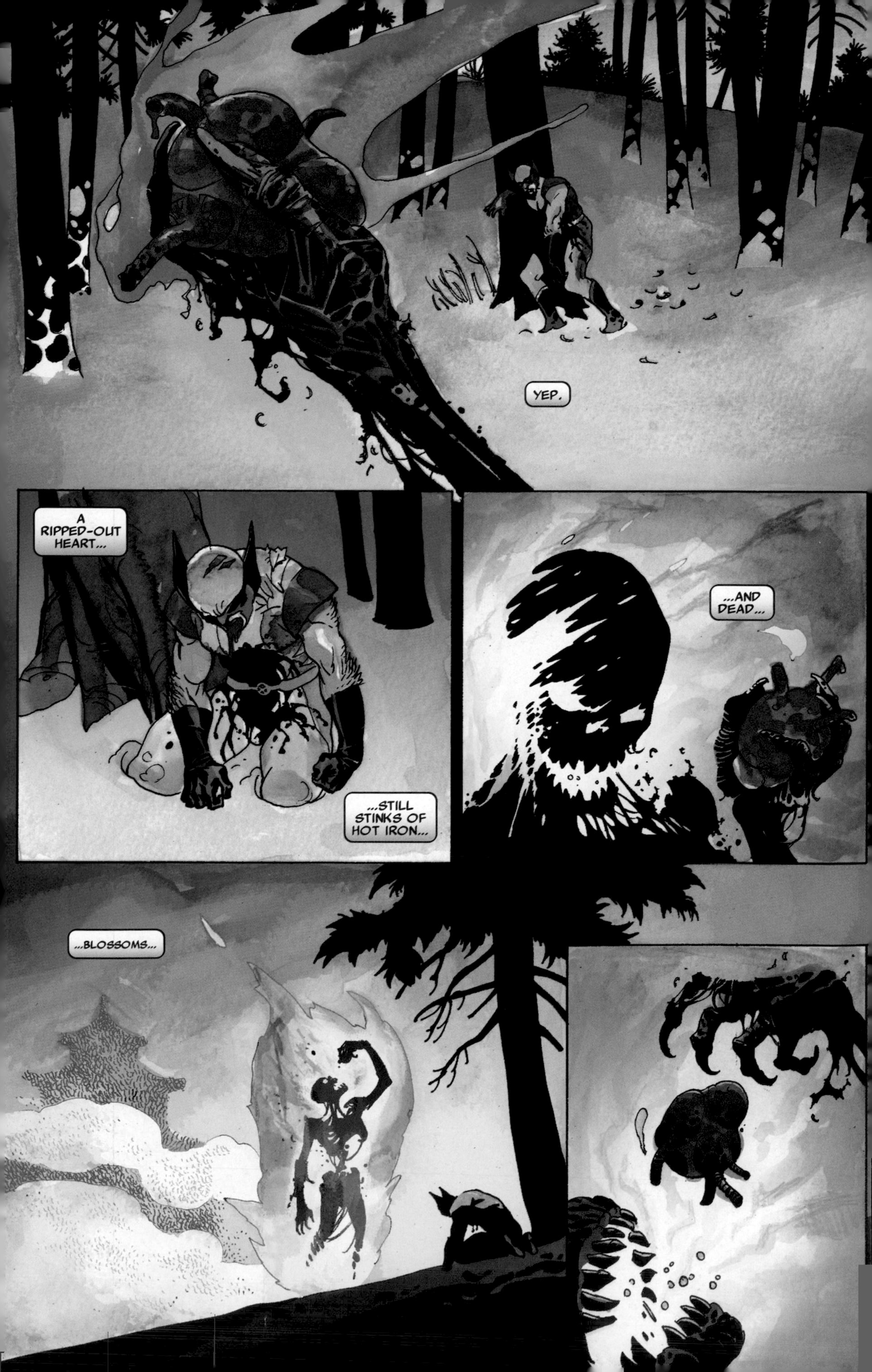
YEP.
A RIPPED-OUT HEART...
...STILL STINKS OF HOT IRON...
...AND DEAD...
...BLOSSOMS...

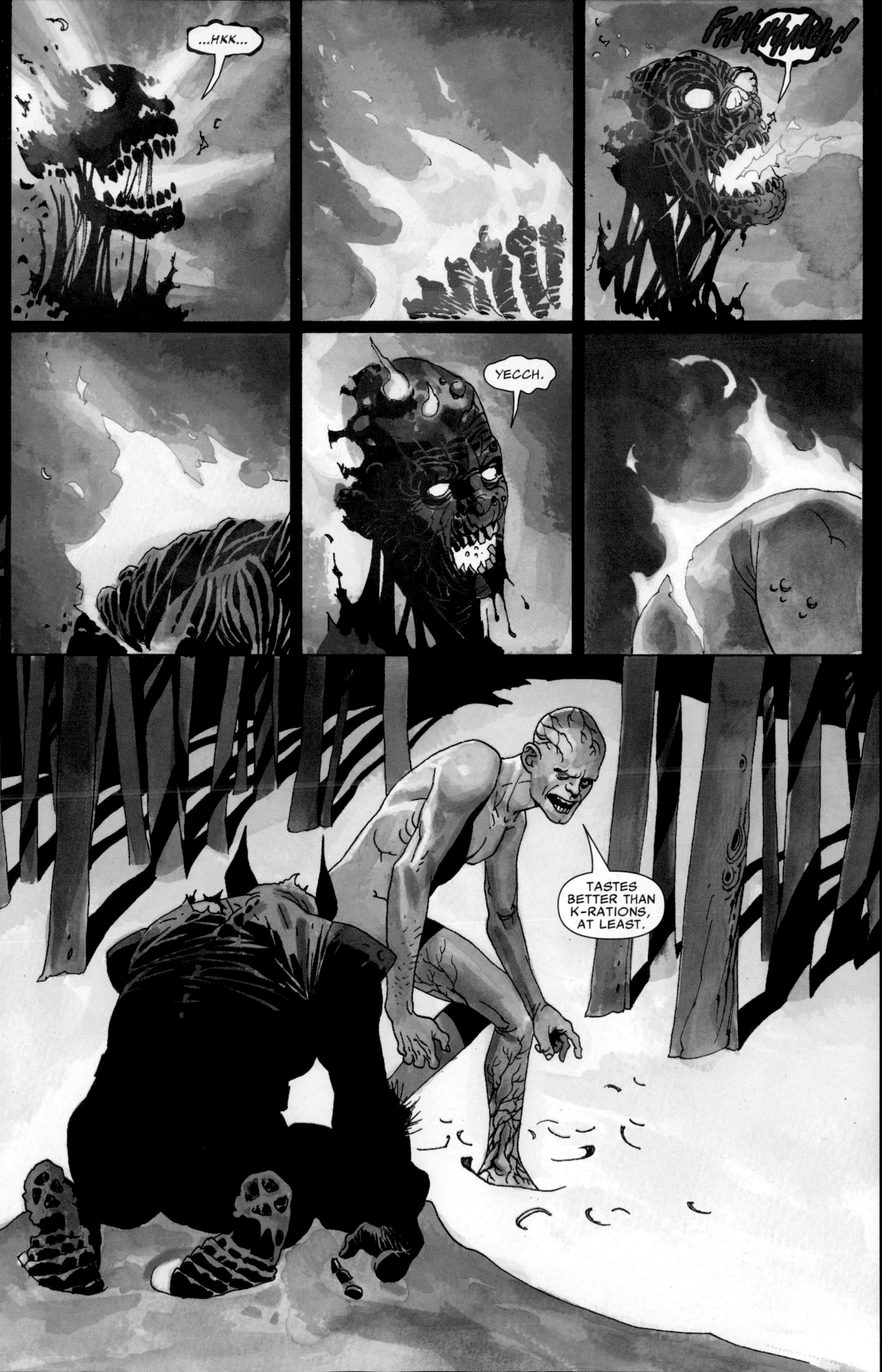
...HKK...
FWHHHHHMUH!
YECCH.
TASTES BETTER THAN K-RATIONS, AT LEAST.

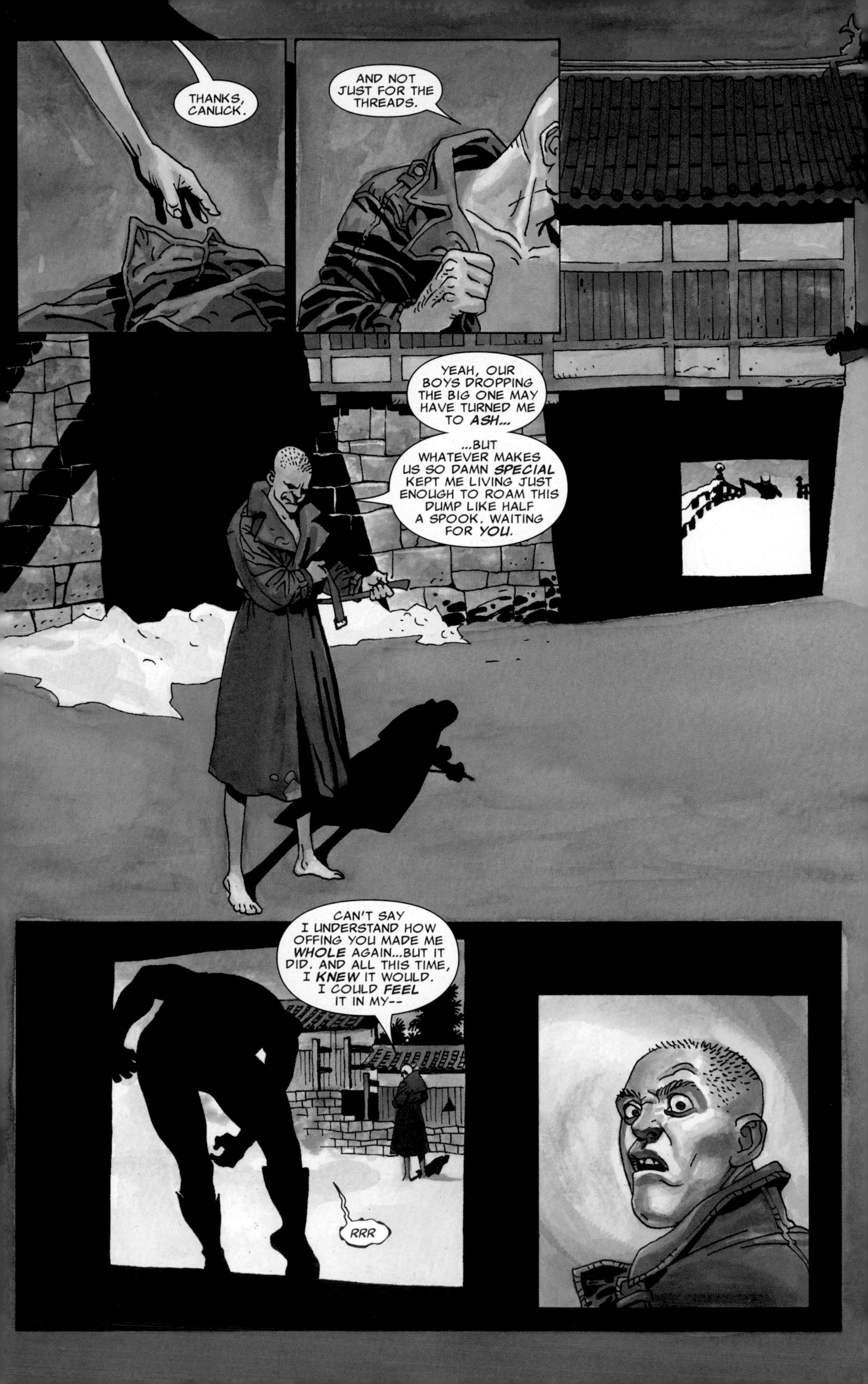
THANKS, CANUCK.
AND NOT JUST FOR THE THREADS.
YEAH, OUR BOYS DROPPING THE BIG ONE MAY HAVE TURNED ME TO ASH...
...BUT WHATEVER MAKES US SO DAMN SPECIAL KEPT ME LIVING JUST ENOUGH TO ROAM THIS DUMP LIKE HALF A SPOOK. WAITING FOR YOU.
CAN'T SAY I UNDERSTAND HOW OFFING YOU MADE ME WHOLE AGAIN...BUT IT DID. AND ALL THIS TIME, I KNEW IT WOULD. I COULD FEEL IT IN MY--
RRR

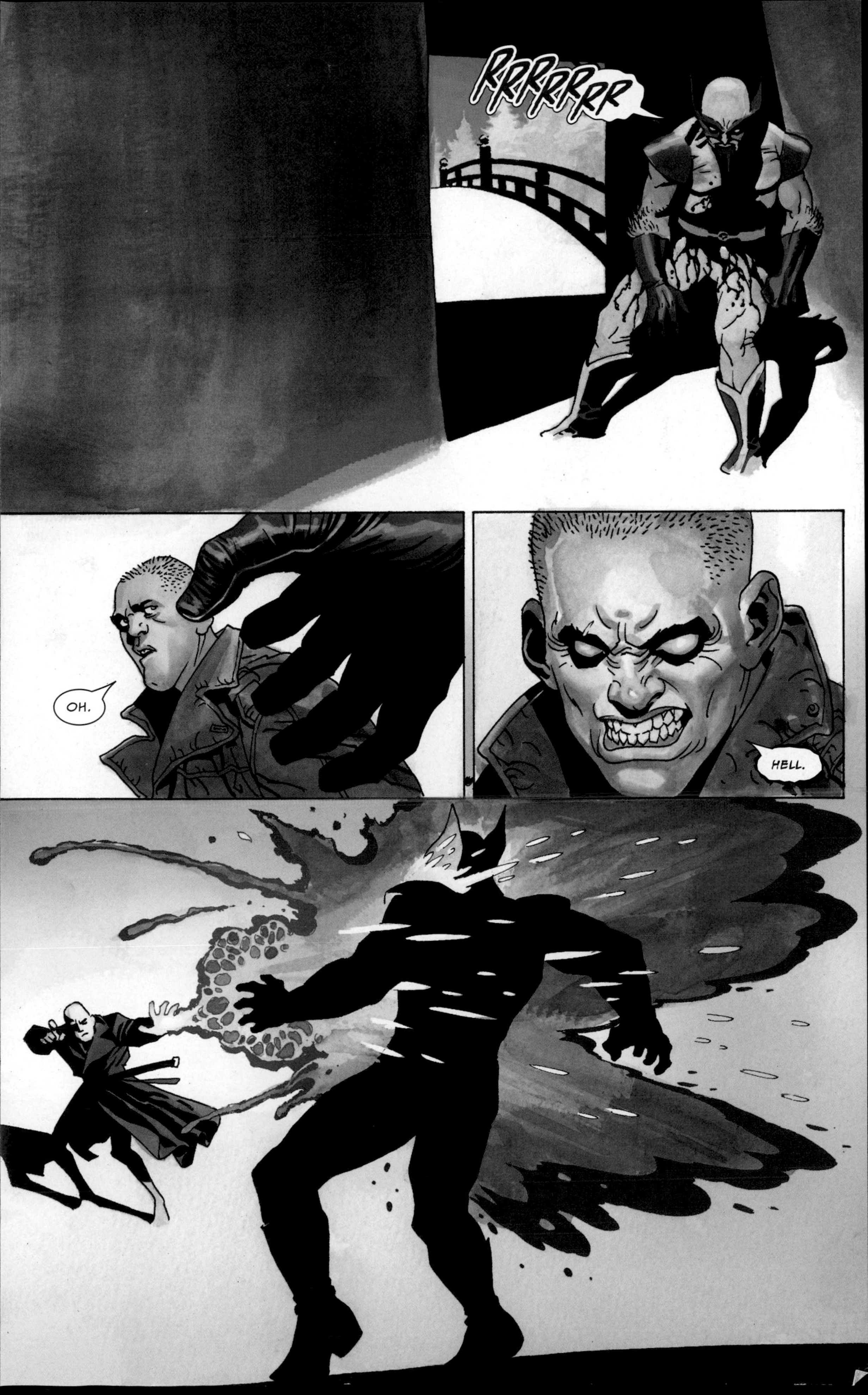
RRRRRRRR
OH.
HELL.

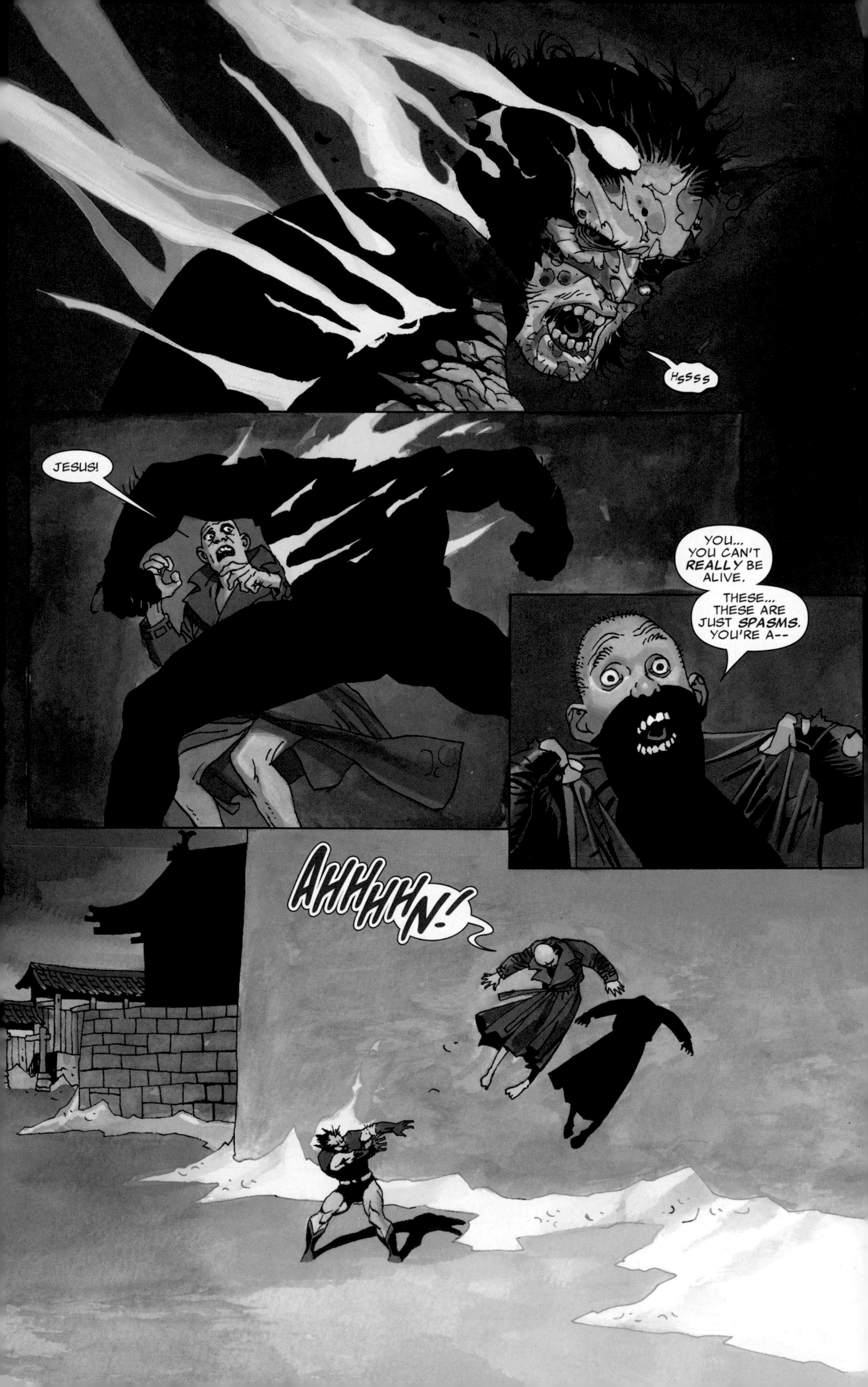
HSSSS
JESUS!
YOU... YOU CAN'T **REALLY** BE ALIVE.
THESE... THESE ARE JUST **SPASMS**. YOU'RE A--
AHHHHN!

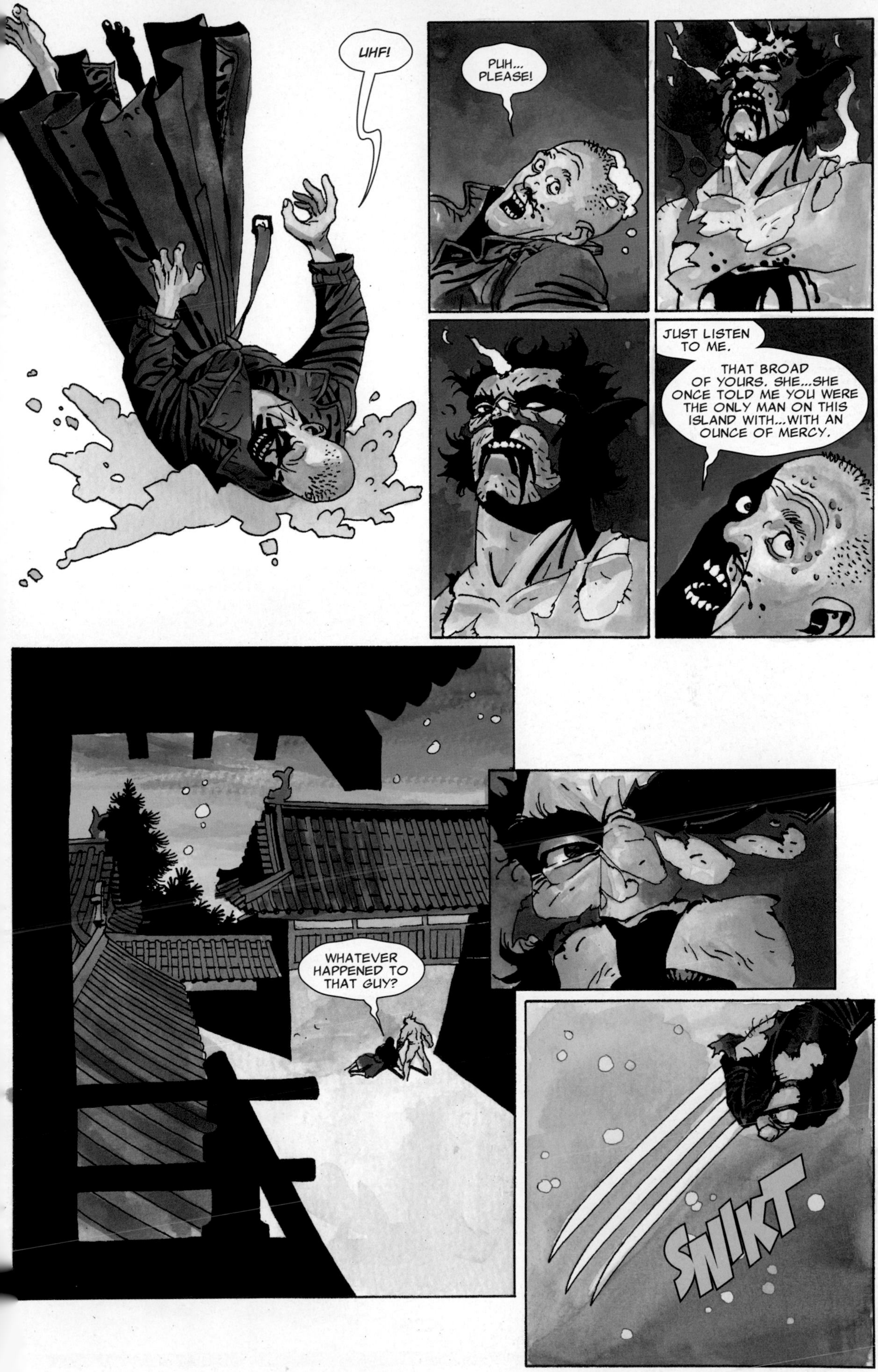
UHF!
PUH... PLEASE!
JUST LISTEN TO ME.
THAT BROAD OF YOURS. SHE...SHE ONCE TOLD ME YOU WERE THE ONLY MAN ON THIS ISLAND WITH...WITH AN OUNCE OF MERCY.
WHATEVER HAPPENED TO THAT GUY?
SNIKT

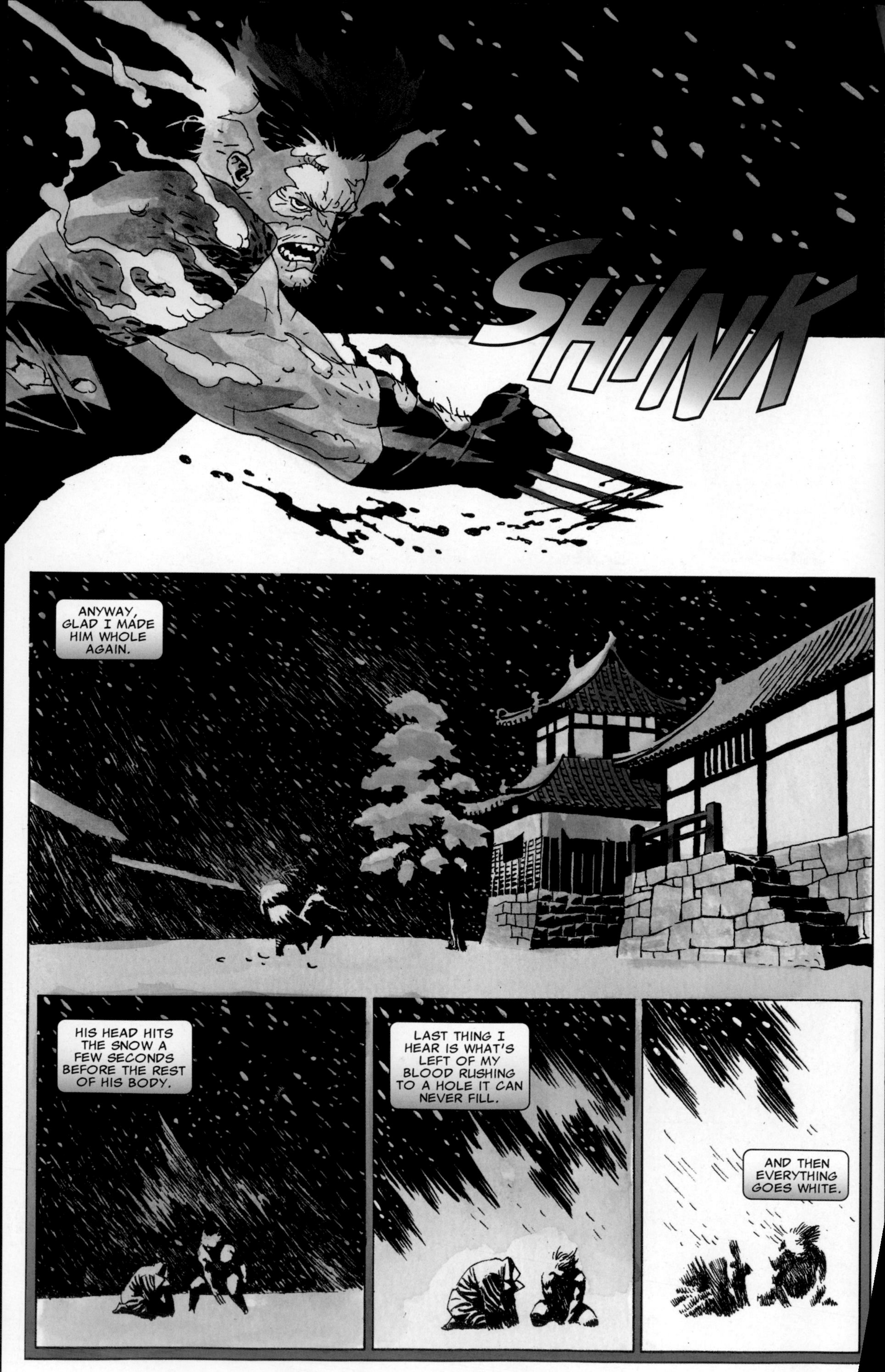
SHINK
ANYWAY, GLAD I MADE HIM WHOLE AGAIN.
HIS HEAD HITS THE SNOW A FEW SECONDS BEFORE THE REST OF HIS BODY.
LAST THING I HEAR IS WHAT'S LEFT OF MY BLOOD RUSHING TO A HOLE IT CAN NEVER FILL.
AND THEN EVERYTHING GOES WHITE.

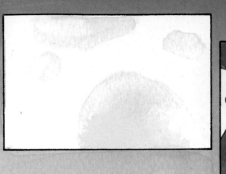

HELLO, LOGAN.

ATSUKO. AM I...?

DEAD? NO. AS EVER, WHAT WAS TAKEN FROM YOU NOW GROWS ANEW.

BUT, I JUST WANT THIS TO BE OVER.

I WANT TO BE WITH...

...YOU.

I'M AFRAID THAT'S NOT YET POSSIBLE.

STILL, YOU AVENGED MY SPIRIT. THE LEAST I OWE YOU IS SOME SMALL TASTE OF TRANQUILITY.

I DON'T FOLLOW...

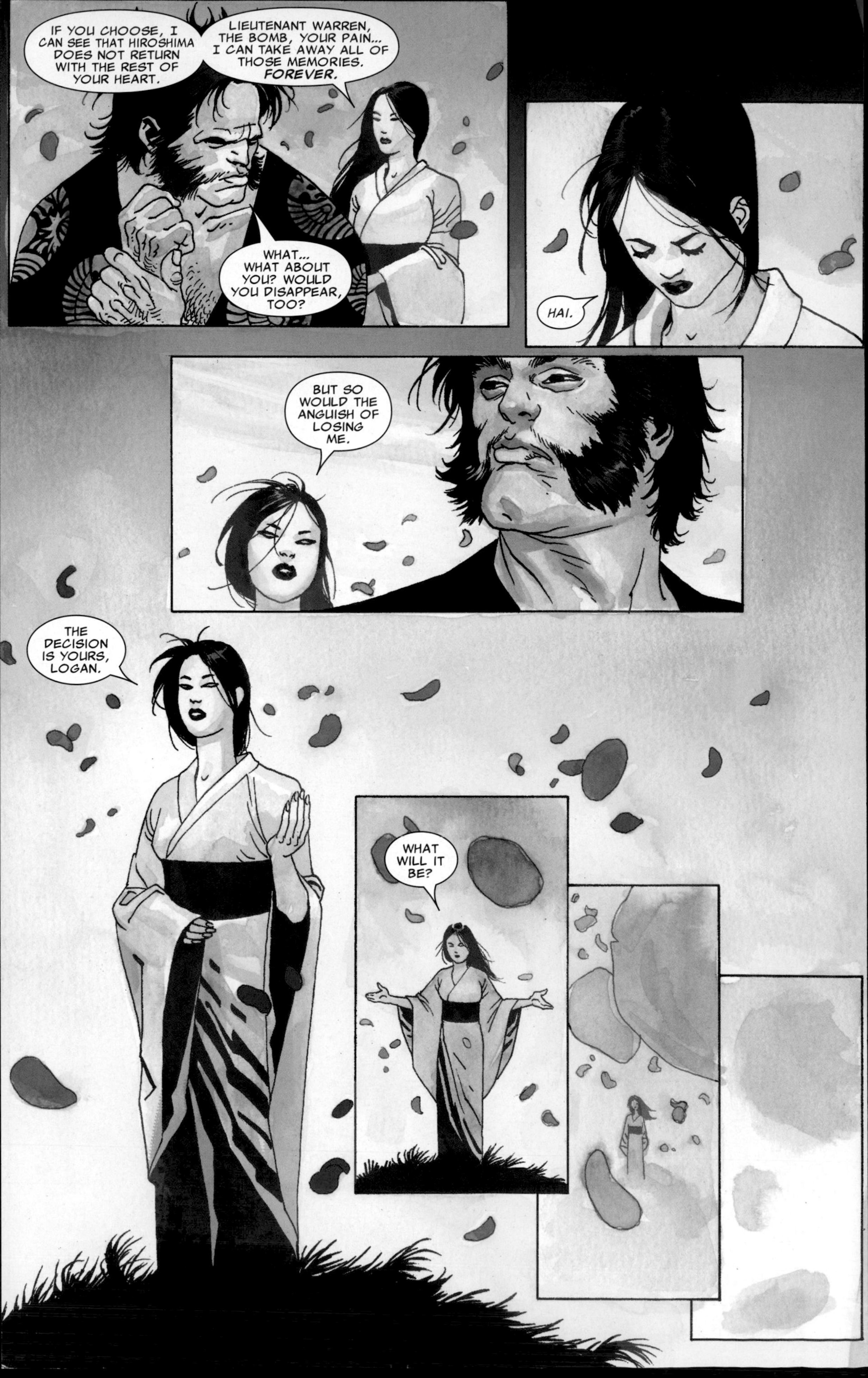
IF YOU CHOOSE, I CAN SEE THAT HIROSHIMA DOES NOT RETURN WITH THE REST OF YOUR HEART.
LIEUTENANT WARREN, THE BOMB, YOUR PAIN... I CAN TAKE AWAY ALL OF THOSE MEMORIES. FOREVER.
WHAT... WHAT ABOUT YOU? WOULD YOU DISAPPEAR, TOO?
HAI.
BUT SO WOULD THE ANGUISH OF LOSING ME.
THE DECISION IS YOURS, LOGAN.
WHAT WILL IT BE?

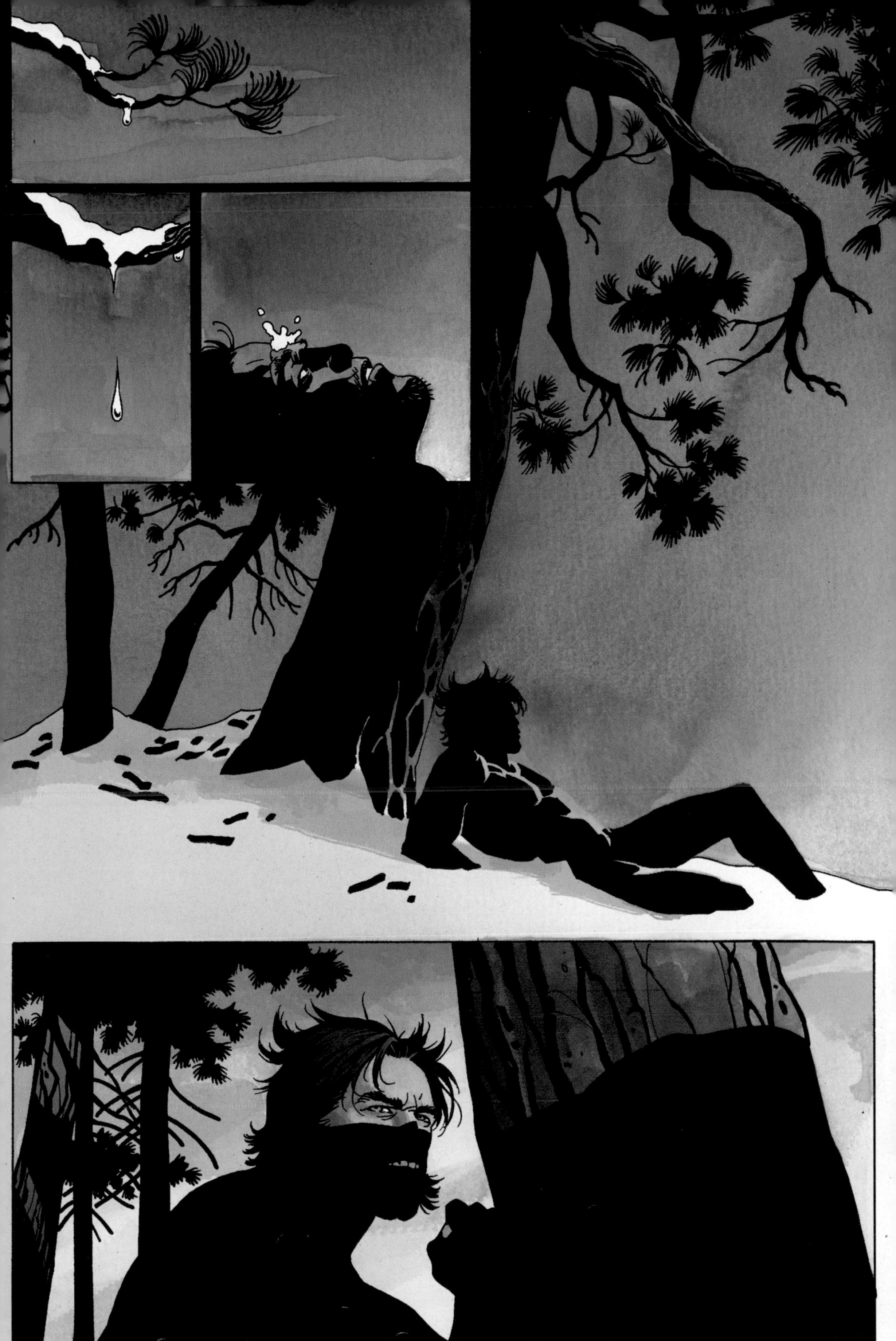

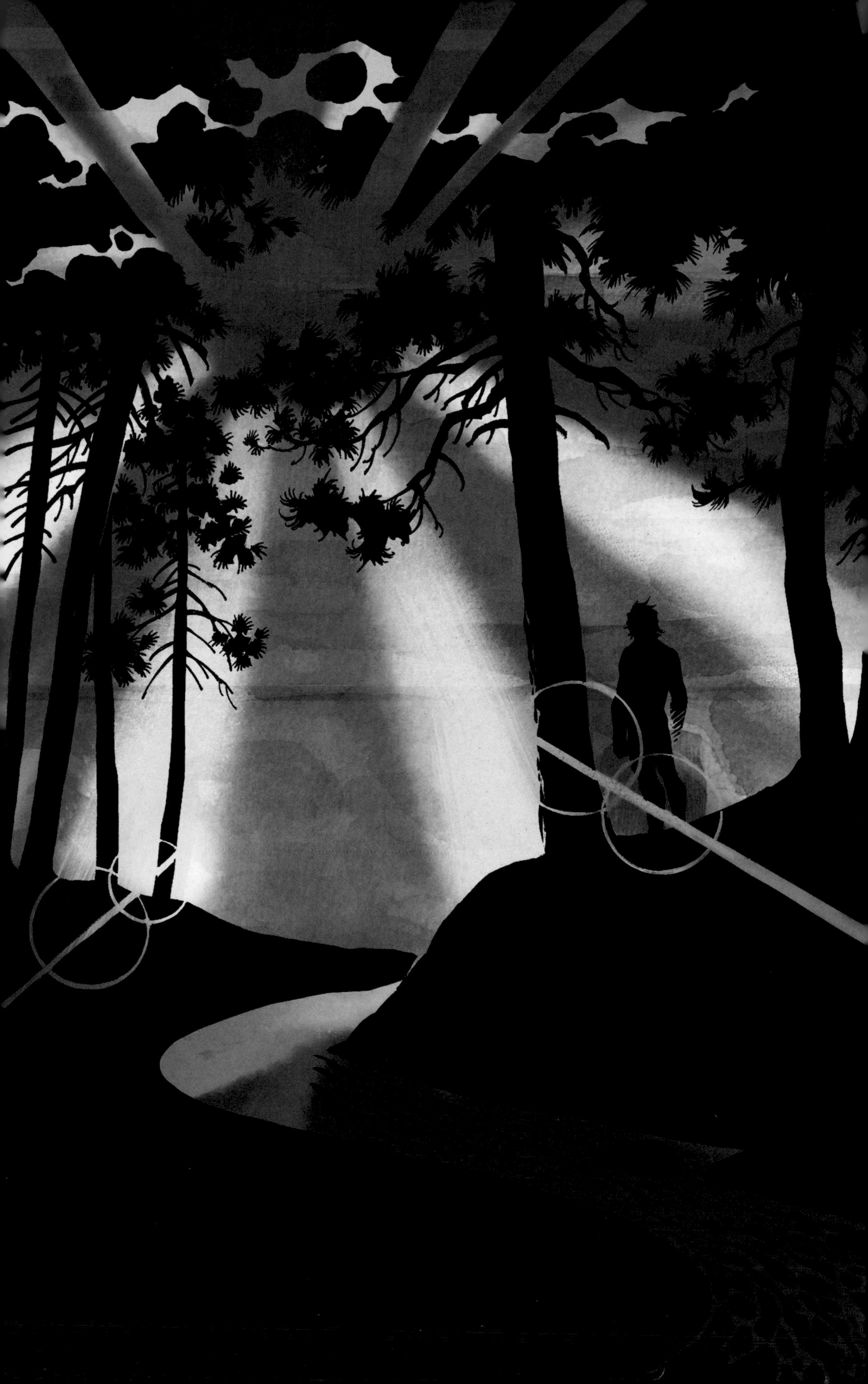

BRIAN K. VAUGHAN
EDUARDO RISSO

—

LOGAN

ORIGIN introduced us to the boy.

X-MEN showed us the hero.

LOGAN finally reveals the day the <u>man</u> was born.

The fates of a young soldier, a beautiful woman, and a vicious monster are forever linked amidst the burning shadows of Nagasaki in this three-part epic, spanning sixty years of the nuclear age.

THE MISSION

There are three things I'd like to accomplish with our three-issue miniseries:

1) Create a story that will showcase the considerable talents of Eduardo Risso, who I've been a huge fan of ever since *Johnny Double*. There are countless Marvel readers who have yet to be exposed to Risso's artwork, and I hope *Logan* will give fans a chance to see what he does best (sophisticated storytelling, visceral action and beautiful women), while also giving Eduardo an opportunity to stretch his muscles and show a whole new side of his work (costumed heroes, misshapen mutants and period drama).

2) Tell a timeless Wolverine story that can stand alongside Miller and Claremont's original miniseries. *Logan* will be a classic, "evergreen" adventure that will appeal to both hardcore fans of the X-Men, and the much larger readership of those only familiar with the character through the movies.

3) Japan and World War II have always been integral parts of Wolverine's shadowy past, but they've usually been shown in a more cartoonish light (with Logan fighting against ninjas or alongside Captain America). With *Logan*, I want to set our hero in a more realistic, relevant version of this time and place. After all, fictional mutants like Wolverine were born in the all-too-real age of atomic paranoia, an era that began in earnest the morning of August 6, 1945.

THE STORY

We'll open in the present, with our modern-day WOLVERINE traveling to Japan after being haunted by nightmares of a beautiful woman from his long-forgotten past.

Flashing back to 1945, we meet up with a young CORPORAL LOGAN of the First Canadian Parachute Battalion, who's being held as a prisoner of war in the terrifying Koyagi Island POW camp in Nagasaki, Japan. Along with a fellow POW, a seemingly indestructible American infantryman (and veteran of several tours of duty) named PRIVATE WARREN, Logan kills his captors before escaping into the night.

On the run, the two fugitives soon encounter a beautiful young Japanese woman named ATSUKO. Eager to punish any member of the race he holds responsible for his brutal treatment in the camps, Private Warren tries to murder this farm girl, only to be beaten down by Logan, who leaves the shamed American to fend for himself.

A grateful Atsuko (orphaned by the war) takes Logan back to her modest farm, where the two wordlessly bond over her family's samurai heirlooms. Fearing that this global war will soon claim them both, Atsuko eventually convinces Logan to join her in one last night of passion.

The next morning, a horrified Logan awakens to find Atsuko's lifeless body lying next to his. A smiling Private Warren is standing over the woman's corpse, chastising a "traitorous" Logan for sleeping with the enemy.

A spectacular clash ensues as Logan uses the ancient samurai weapons to battle his former ally. Ultimately knocking Logan to the ground, Warren prepares to deliver the deathblow… but it's out of the frying pan and into the hellfire, as both men are soon engulfed in the nuclear explosion of an American A-bomb. A nearly skeletonized Logan crawls out of the blast, barely alive and presuming his enemy to be dead.

The rest of our story will take place in the present, as a costumed Wolverine is confronted by a hideous monster (really what's left of Private Warren), who rose from the ashes of Nagasaki after the radiation severely mutated his body. This unstoppable creature is looking to finish a decades-old fight that Wolverine doesn't even remember starting.

But if Logan kills this "son of the atom," he risks destroying his last link to the beautiful young woman who exists only in his dreams.

He's already lived through the war, but now Wolverine will have to survive the fallout.

***

Axel, these are just the very broad strokes of our story, which I'll flesh out in more detail if you and Eduardo feel comfortable with this basic outline. Looking forward to hearing your thoughts!

***

These are some very quick thoughts I had for possible covers, if you want to pass them along to Eduardo. These are all just suggestions, nothing I'm married to at all, and I fully encourage you guys to go in a completely different direction.

Either way, I'm picturing each of these covers featuring one of our three main characters: the man (Wolverine), the woman (a Japanese farm girl named Atsuko), and our monster (Logan's American friend, who will be transformed into a hideous creature):

ISSUE #1: The inspiration for our title (down to the line over the "O" in "Logan") is the novel/movie called SHOGUN.

Like the posters and book covers for that work of fiction, I think our first cover should definitely have clearly Japanese background elements: a temple, a setting red sun, etc. But in the foreground of this shot, because we've seen Wolverine dressed as a samurai/ninja plenty of times before, I think it might be more interesting to see a young Logan dressed in his World War II Canadian soldier outfit (minus the helmet).

Maybe the gun-toting grunt's clothes are torn and dirty, and his silver dog tags are hanging out of his shirt. I think seeing a young Logan in this attire would suggest that this is a story about WAR as much as it is about Japan, and also shows that it's going to reveal an important missing chapter from the character's past.

ISSUE #2: While Logan should definitely be seen somewhere on this cover (maybe we're looking through his metal claws in the foreground?), I think the focus should be Atsuko, Logan's love interest. This beautiful young Japanese woman is a poor farm girl living in Nagasaki during World War II. She was orphaned after her father left her to die for his country as a Kamikaze pilot. On this cover, maybe she's holding his samurai sword (a gift the military sent to pilots' families), and wearing his kamikaze headband.

Families of kamikaze pilots were also given small wooden boxes containing their fingernail clippings (which they cut before their missions, so their families would have a piece of them to bury). That might be a nice touch to incorporate.

Because she's going to die in this issue, maybe Atsuko's wearing a white kimono, and standing in a shallow river (both signs of death/ghosts in Japanese culture).

She should be incredibly sexy (Eduardo's specialty), but also strong.

ISSUE #3: I'm honestly not sure about this cover, and I'd welcome any suggestions from Eduardo. I think this one should feature Wolverine in modern-day Japan (wearing his contemporary costume?), as he battles his nemesis: an American soldier who was mutated by the atomic bomb in Nagasaki.

There are several directions we could go with this villain, and I'm open to any of them. We could make him a shadow creature, to play off the shadows that were burned into the ground by the nuclear explosion in Nagasaki. We could also make him more of a classical demon-type creature. Our third option is to make him a real MONSTER, like Godzilla or the other creatures created by the Japanese in the era of nuclear paranoia. Maybe our villain uses FUSION (like the

A-Bomb) to incorporate aspects of the environment and other living creatures into his massive mutating body, a bit like the Tetsuo character from Akira.

But again, if Eduardo would rather go in a more quiet, grounded direction, I'm fine with that as well. The important thing is that this character represents unchecked American aggression; he possesses all of Wolverine's rage and bloodlust, without being tempered by Logan's sense of mercy.

****

Guys, those are just my really broad initial thoughts. I have the opening of our story pretty well thought out, but the conclusion is still forming in my head. I'm honored to have Eduardo as a collaborator on this project, and I really want him to have a say in our story's direction. I'm open to any and all ideas, so I welcome input from both of you!

More soon,
BKV

The Full Script for

——

LOGAN

Brian K. Vaughan

Prepared for Marvel Comics
August 6, 2005

Eduardo--Once again, it's a tremendous honor to be working with one of my favorite artists. My scripts are somewhat detailed (to help save you time gathering reference, I'll occasionally throw in some annoying web links), but these panel descriptions are only suggestions. *You're the best storyteller working in comics, so if you ever see a better way to layout a page or frame a shot, or think of a way to add or subtract panels, please do so with my blessing! And feel free to email me anytime with questions. Many thanks--BKV*

PAGE ONE

Page One, SPLASH
We're going to open with a dramatic full-page SPLASH of modern-day Japan, specifically, the rebuilt HIROSHIMA CASTLE. It's night out, so this scene can be lit by moonlight. It's winter, and snowing heavily. We're *behind* WOLVERINE in the foreground of this shot, looking at his back as he stares up at this impressive building. He has a black trenchcoat on, which we'll eventually reveal is covering his current X-Men uniform.

    1)   <u>Caption</u>: When you rip a guy's heart out, the blood inside stinks of hot iron and dead blossoms.

    2)   <u>Caption</u>: After all these years, that's still what Japan smells like to me.

PAGE TWO

Page Two, Panel One
We're looking at Wolverine's face here, as he exhales an icy breath. He's not yet wearing his mask.

    1)   Caption: In case you hadn't heard, I'm a mutant. A

son of the atom ((Save phrase for next issue?)).

2)   Caption: I was cursed with a body that just won't break, no matter what the world does to it.

Page Two, Panel Two
Change angles, as Wolverine walks towards the dark woods that surround this building.

3)   Caption: I've lived enough years to fill a few lifetimes, but most of those I've been lucky enough to forget.

4)   Caption: Least I was…until every last memory came flooding back into my rotten gourd.

5)   Caption: Anyway, that's what brings me here.

Page Two, Panel Three
Pull out to the largest panel of the page, as Wolverine walks through the ominous woods. It continues to snow.

6)   Caption: See, in the Great White North, a sickly kid named James Howlett was born.

7)   Caption: In the backroom butcher shops of evil men, a killer named Weapon X was created.

8)   Caption: And in a little school in Westchester, a "hero" named Wolverine was forged.

Page Two, Panel Four
Push in close on our hero, as he suddenly SNIFFS at the air, having smelled a threat nearby.

9)   Caption: I been a lot of things in a lot of places, but this…this is where I became a man.

10)   SFX: snff

PAGE THREE

Page Three, Panel One
Change angles, as Wolverine looks around. There's nothing but shadows.

1) Wolverine: You been waiting sixty years, haven't you?

2) Wolverine: Let's finish this already.

Page Three, Panel Two
Wolverine now PULLS ON his mask, and shrugs off his trenchcoat, revealing his yellow and blue uniform.

3) SFX: aheh heh heh heh

4) Wolverine: You wanna be dramatic, I can do the kabuki thing…

Page Three, Panel Three
This is a cool, iconic shot of Wolverine as he POPS his glistening metal claws.

5) Wolverine: …but I ain't got all night.

6) SFX: SNIKT

7) Caption: I've made a hell of a lot of enemies over the decades, but I don't lose sleep over 'em.

Page Three, Panel Four
Change angles, as Wolverine is suddenly STRUCK in the back of his head by a MASSIVE FIST OF FIRE belonging to a mysterious creature (more on this creature on the next page).

8) Wolverine: UHN!

9) Caption: No, it's the women that keep me up at night, the handful of girls I was dumb enough to fall for over the last century or so.

10) Caption: After all, I can recover from just about anything…

PAGE FOUR

Page Four, SPLASH
We're with a now *unconscious* Wolverine in the foreground of this shot, as he collapses onto the fresh snow. Standing over him is our MONSTER, a creature whose large body seems to be comprised of BURNING SHADOWS. He or she (we shouldn't be able to tell its sex

yet) is a jet-black monstrosity, whose inky flesh is covered in flames. Maybe a sudden whirlwind of snow partially obscures this strange beast, so we can't yet see it in full detail.

(Eduardo, that's just a suggestion, but feel free to use your imagination. Either way, we'll eventually reveal that this villain is what's left of Lieutenant Warren, an American soldier we're about to meet, who was transformed into this creature by an atomic blast. He's been dormant for sixty years, waiting for Wolverine's return.)

1)   Caption: …anything but getting my heart ripped out.

2)   Title (below image):

—

LOGAN
act one of three

3)   Credits:

Brian K. Vaughan & Eduardo Risso - Storytellers
_____ - Colorist
_____ - Letterer
Axel Alonso - Editor
Joe Quesada - Chief
Dan Buckley - Publisher

PAGE FIVE

Page Five, Panel One
Our flashback to 1945 begins. I picture this page being made up of four page-wide "letterbox" panels of the same size. This first one is entirely black.

No Copy

Page Five, Panel Two
This panel is a little brighter, and we can now see the blurry image of a MALE FIGURE standing over us.

1   Tailless Balloon: Flash?

Page Five, Panel Three
Similar framing, but now the blurry image becomes a little clearer.

    2)   <u>From Figure</u>: Flash!

Page Five, Panel Four
Same framing one last time, but now we can clearly see the face of LIEUTENANT WARREN, a 29-year-old American prisoner of war. He has blond hair and unshaven blond stubble. We'll eventually see that he's wearing a dirty old white shirt and short black pants (prison attire). He still has his glistening silver DOG TAGS around his neck. He's yelling down at "us" here.

    3) Warren: Flash, dammit!

    4) Warren: Answer me before I wring your damn neck!

PAGE SIX

Page Six, Panel One
Cut down to LOGAN (who looks slightly younger than when we saw him at the opening of our story). He's squinting up at us as he slowly regains consciousness.

    1)   Logan: My name ain't Flash, soldier.

    2)   Logan: It's Logan.

Page Six, Panel Two
Pull out to the largest panel of the page for a shot of both men. We can see that Logan is wearing the same kind of dirty old prison attire as Warren. They're alone inside of a dark, windowless PRISON CELL somewhere inside a Japanese military base. There are no bars, just stone walls and a solid iron door. A single bare bulb lights the scene. Logan looks annoyed with this brash American.

    3)   Warren: Flash is your challenge, smartass. So I know you're American, and not a Jap spy. Now what's the code reply?

    4)   Logan: How am I supposed to know?

    5)   Logan: I'm Canadian. First Parachute Battalion.

Page Six, Panel Three
Push in closer on the two, as Warren frowns at Logan.

      6)   Warren: Canuck, huh? Figures.

      7)   Warren: If you greenhorns had held Hong Kong in '41, this war would be going a lot better.

      8)   Logan: And if you boys hadn't waited until Pearl Harbor to get in the game, this war would be over.

Page Six, Panel Four
Warren smirks a bit, as he holds out a hand and HELPS Logan to his feet.

      9)   Warren: Yeah, you're Canadian all right.

      10)   Warren: I'm Lieutenant Warren. What rank are you?

      11)   Logan: P.O.W., from the looks of it. Where are we?

PAGE SEVEN

Page Seven, Panel One
This is just a close-up of Warren, looking tired and frustrated.

      1)   Warren: Military ((science??)) base somewhere on the Japanese mainland.

      2)   Warren: I spent the last three months in a hellhole labor camp just north of here… Mukaishima they called it.

Page Seven, Panel Two
Pull out to a shot of both men, as Logan silently listens to Warren's sad tale.

      3)   Warren: My squadron was supposed to sink the light cruiser Tone in Kure Harbor, but we had to ditch after taking fire from the shore batteries.

      4)   Warren: Half of my guys were K.I.A., me and the other six got pinched.

Page Seven, Panel Three
Push in close on Warren, as he tries to contain his rage over what the

Japanese did to his men.

5) Warren: Two died of starvation in the camp. Dysentery took another three.

6) Warren: And my navigator… my navigator hanged himself by his shirtsleeves. Guess he got tired of digging cesspools at bayonet point twenty hours a day.

Page Seven, Panel Four
This is just a shot of Logan, as he eyes the off-panel Warren suspiciously.

7) Logan: How'd you survive?

Page Seven, Panel Five
This is an ominous shot of Warren, as he stares at the off-panel Logan. Is this American hiding a secret? Is *he* a mutant like Logan?

8) Warren: Exact same way you lived this long, Logan.

9) Warren: Dumb luck

PAGE EIGHT

Page Eight, Panel One
Pull out to another shot of both men.

1) Warren: Anyway, they transferred me here last night.

2) Logan: Why?

3) Warren: Interrogation, probably. Torture. And presuming we keep our traps shut--

Page Eight, Panel Two
Push in closer on the two, as Logan motions for his cellmate to shut up. He's heard something with his heightened senses.

4) Logan: Speaking of which.

5) Logan: Three guards coming.

6) Warren: I… I don't hear anything.

Page Eight, Panel Three
Change angles on the two, as Logan cracks his knuckles.

7)   Logan: This is probably the only chance we're gonna get.

8)   Warren: What, to escape?

9)   Warren: Maybe you were out cold when they dragged you in here, but this place is a fortress.

Page Eight, Panel Four
Push in closer. Warren can't believe what he's hearing.

10)   Logan: I've busted out of worse.

11)   Warren: You're insane.

Page Eight, Panel Five
This is just a cool shot of the deadly serious Logan, as he looks at us and says:

12)   Logan: Do yourself a favor, bub.

13)   Logan: Stick to the shadows 'til I'm through.

PAGE NINE

Page Nine, Panel One
Cut outside this cell for a shot of a brightly lit hallway inside the Japanese military base, which has Japan's old imperial FLAG hanging on one of the walls.

There are some windows in this hallway, too, so we can see that it's late at night out.

Standing outside this cell are THREE JAPANESE IMPERIAL SOLDIERS. The first is unlocking the heavy iron door with an old key, while the other two soldiers keep their rifles and bayonets trained on the door.
The soldier with the keys can look like one of these guards.

1) <u>Head Guard</u>: <Keep your safeties on. The doctor says these are *kaiju*, that they're more valuable than-->

Page Nine, Panel Two
As the first soldier opens the door, Logan immediately comes POUNCING out of the cell like a wild animal, LEAPING onto the guard with the keys. (Eduardo, I'm suggesting fight choreography here, but please feel free to add/subtract panels, or to do something entirely different with the action. I trust you completely.)

      2)   <u>Logan</u>: RRRAHH!

Page Nine, Panel Three
Logan quickly and brutally SNAPS this guard's neck, as the two Japanese Infantry soldiers watch with stunned horror.

      3)   <u>SFX</u>: SSNAP

Page Nine, Panel Four
Finally coming to his senses, one of these soldiers STABS Logan in the back with the bayonet at the end of his rifle.

      4)   <u>Infantry Soldier #1</u>: HAAN!

PAGE TEN

Page Ten, Panel One
Cut into the dark cell, as Warren comes CHARGING out at us.

      1)   Warren: NO!

Page Ten, Panel Two
Pull out to the largest panel of the page, as Warren TACKLES the soldier who just stabbed Logan, knocking the bloody bayonet out of Logan's body.

      2)   Infantry Soldier #1: UHF!

Page Ten, Panel Three
Push in on Warren, as he angrily STRANGLES the guard he's just knocked to the ground.

      3)   <u>Warren</u>: Yellow scum!

Page Ten, Panel Four
Cut over to the other infantry soldier, who nervously aims his rifle at the off-panel American, and yells for him to "Stop!" in Japanese.

4)   Infantry Soldier #2: Yamai!

PAGE ELEVEN

Page Eleven, Panel One
Pull out, as the wounded Logan SPRINGS forward and GRABS the middle of this soldier's rifle with his left hand, pushing it upwards.

1)   Infantry Soldier #2: NAH!

Page Eleven, Panel Two
As Logan and the soldier WRESTLE for control of this rifle, Logan grabs the soldier's shirtfront with his free hand.

2)   Infantry Soldier #2: Nnnn…

Page Eleven, Panel Three
Similar framing, but as we hear a familiar sound effect, the soldier Logan is wrestling with suddenly CRINGES in pain. (Eduardo, with the hand grabbing this soldier's shirt, Logan has just plunged his sharp claws--which are still made of bone in this era, not Adamantium--into the soldier's chest, but this should be framed so that we *can't* see the claws at all, please.)

3)   SFX: SNIKT

Page Eleven, Panel Four
Push in close on the soldier, who looks stunned. What the hell just happened?

No Copy

Page Eleven, Panel Five
Exact same framing on the Japanese soldier, but now his eyes roll into the back of his head, as a little BLOOD leaks out of the side of his mouth. He's dead.

No Copy

PAGE TWELVE

Page Twelve, Panel One
Cut over to Lieutenant Warren, who is still on top of the first infantry soldier he just strangled to death. Warren's looking at the off-panel Logan with disbelief.

1)   Warren: What…what did you do to him?

Page Twelve, Panel Two
Pull out to the largest panel of the page for a group shot of this carnage, as Logan DROPS the limp soldier he just killed.

2   Logan: What I do best.

Page Twelve, Panel Three
Cut back to a grateful Warren, as he slowly gets to his feet.

3)   Warren: Well, ah, thanks.

4)   Warren: Wish I'd had a fighter like you at my side back in--

Page Twelve, Panel Four
Cut back to Logan, as he looks down at his kill.

5)   Logan: Yeah, yeah.

6)   Logan: Take whichever outfit's got the least bloodstains.

Page Twelve, Panel Five
This is just a dramatic shot of Logan, as he looks out a nearby WINDOW in this hallway at the silver moon outside.

7)   Logan: We ain't out of the woods yet.

PAGE THIRTEEN

Page Thirteen, Panel One
Smash cut to later that night (it's a late August evening) for this establishing shot of a dense area of TREES somewhere in Japan.

No Copy

Page Thirteen, Panel Two
Cut into the woods for this shot of several little wooden bridges, where two DARK FIGURES are walking. Eduardo, the bridges can look like the ones in this photo, but as always, feel free to use other reference you find, or your imagination:

Page Thirteen, Panel Three
Push in on the two dark figures, who we can now tell are Logan and Lieutenant Warren, carrying the rifles and wearing the uniforms of two of the soldiers they just killed. Dark-haired Logan isn't wearing a hat, but maybe Warren is covering up his blond locks with one of those old-fashioned Japanese military hats.

    1)   Warren: So, uh… how'd you end up in the Pacific Theater?

    2)   Logan: Theater? That what we're calling it now?

    3)   Logan: I was in Burma to blow up a train. Guess it went south, 'cause I woke up here.

PAGE FOURTEEN

Page Fourteen, Panel One
This is just a shot of the pissed-off Warren, as he fumes:

    1)   Warren: Goddamn animals.

    2)   Warren: The Japs won't stop until we've killed every last one of 'em.

Page Fourteen, Panel Two
Pull out to a shot of both men. Logan clearly doesn't have time for Warren's bull.

    3)   Warren: Wish I'd been in Normandy.

    4)   Warren: The Krauts may be bastards but at least they fight like men. These people… they're not even human. They're--

    5)   Logan: Why don't you save it until we're stowed away inside whatever cargo boat is gonna get us off this rock? We still--

Page Fourteen, Panel Three
Push in close on Logan, who's surprised to hear screaming coming from nearby.

6)   Atsuko (from off): Aiiee!

Page Fourteen, Panel Four
We're *behind* the two men for this largest panel of the page, a big shot of ATSUKO, a gorgeous, twenty-year-old Japanese farm girl wearing sandals and a stark white kimono.

Atsuko is standing on a bridge directly in front of Logan and Warren, and she covers her mouth in horror as she sees the two clearly Caucasian men. Even though she's terrified, we can tell that this young woman is heartbreakingly beautiful.

No Copy

PAGE FIFTEEN

Page Fifteen, Panel One
This is just a close-up of Logan, who looks stunned by the sudden appearance of this girl.

1)   Logan (small, a whisper): I… I didn't even catch her scent.

2)   Logan (small, a whisper): She's like a damn ghost.

Page Fifteen, Panel Two
Pull out to a shot of all three characters, as Warren raises his rifle and aims it at the frozen Atsuko, despite Logan's warning.

3)   Warren: If she's not yet, she will be.

4)   Logan: Stand down.

5)   Logan: She's just a civilian.

Page Fifteen, Panel Three
This is just a shot of Warren (who keeps his rifle trained on the off-panel Atsuko), as he shoots us a dirty look.

6)   Warren: There's no such thing as a Jap civilian.

7)   Warren: They're all spies and… and assassins for the Emperor!

Page Fifteen, Panel Four
Pull out to another shot of all three characters, as Logan begs his companion to lower his rifle.

8)   Warren: Besides, she looks just like the broad on that trawler that pulled me and my crew out of the drink.

9)   Warren: She's the one who turned us over to these monsters.

10)   Logan: Let it go. The girl's not a fisher, she's a farmer.

Page Fifteen, Panel Five
This is just a shot of Warren. We're looking down the barrel of his rifle, which he's aiming *right at us*.

11)   <u>Warren</u>: Then we might as well put her in the dirt where she belongs.

PAGE SIXTEEN

Page Sixteen, Panel One
Pull out to a shot of both men, as we reveal that Logan now has *his* rifle trained at Warren's head.

1)   <u>Logan</u>: You pull that trigger, you'll be joining her.

Page Sixteen, Panel Two
Pull out to another shot of all three characters. Atsuko is certain she's about to be executed.

2)   Warren: You forgetting who the enemy is here?

3)   Logan: Walk away, Warren.

4)   Logan: This is where you and me part ways.

Page Sixteen, Panel Three
This is just a shot of Warren, as he angrily lowers his rifle.

5)   Warren: You…you are a spy, aren't you? You're working for them!

6)   Warren: This is all some kinda setup!

Page Sixteen, Panel Four
And this is just a shot of Logan, as he gives a stern order.

      7)   Logan: Walk.

      8)   Logan: Away.

Page Sixteen, Panel Five
We're with Logan in the foreground of this shot, as he turns to watch Warren reluctantly retreat into the night.

No Copy

PAGE SEVENTEEN

Page Seventeen, Panel One
Change angles on Logan, as he looks down to discover that Atsuko is now KNEELING in front of him, bowing her head deeply in a sign of gratitude.

No Copy

Page Seventeen, Panel Two
Push in on Logan, who looks a little uncomfortable about this.

      1)   Logan: All right already.

      2)   Logan: On your feet, girly.

Page Seventeen, Panel Three
Pull out to reveal that Atsuko is still on her knees.

      3)   Logan: Come on.

      4)   Logan: Do-itashimashite and all that.

Page Seventeen, Panel Four
This is just a shot of the beautiful Atsuko, as she lifts up her head to look at us.

      5)   Atsuko: <You… you speak my tongue?>

PAGE EIGHTEEN

Page Eighteen, Panel One
Pull out to a shot of both characters, as Atsuko gets to her feet and takes Logan's hand.

    1)   Logan: <Some.>

    2)   Atsuko: <Please.>

    3)   Atsuko: <Follow me.>

Page Eighteen, Panel Two
Change angles on the two, as Atsuko begins PULLING a confused Logan after her.

    4)   Logan: Wait! What are you…?

    5)   Atsuko: <The sun will rise soon. You'll never make it to the harbor before morning. I can hide you until tomorrow's nightfall.>

Page Eighteen, Panel Three
Similar framing, but now Logan stops Atsuko in her tracks.

    6)   Logan: Stop.

    7)   Logan: If your people catch you with me, they'll kill us both.

Page Eighteen, Panel Four
This is just a shot of Atsuko from Logan's point of view, as she looks back at us over her shoulder with a seductive *smile*.

    8)   Caption: Did she smile because she didn't understand me…or because she didn't care?

Page Eighteen, Panel Five
We're in the shadowy woods with Lieutenant Warren in the foreground of this shot, as he watches Logan follow after Atsuko in the background.

    9)   Caption: Either way, I was hers.

PAGE NINETEEN

Page Nineteen, Panel One
Cut to later (the sun is just barely starting to rise in the distance) for this establishing shot of a modest farm somewhere in Hiroshima, perhaps something like this.

No Copy

Page Nineteen, Panel Two
Cut inside this small farm's old-fashioned kitchen, where Logan is kneeling in front of a small table, eating from a bowl of rice. Atsuko is reaching for something inside of an old chest, though we can't see what it is just yet. A small fire lights the scene. For some examples of old Japanese kitchens, check out the three websites:

No Copy

Page Nineteen, Panel Three
Push in close on Logan, as he struggles to find the words in Japanese to thank his hostess.

    1)   Logan: <I… I don't know how to repay you, um…>

Page Nineteen, Panel Four
Cut over to Atsuko, as she menacingly pulls out a glistening SAMURAI SWORD, which has a piece of cloth tied to its handle.

    2)   Atsuko: Atsuko.

Page Nineteen, Panel Five
This is just a shot of Logan, looking betrayed, *reflected* in the blade of the shining sword.

    3)   Atsuko (from just off): <My name is Atsuko.>

PAGE TWENTY

Page Twenty, Panel One
Pull out to a shot of both characters. As Atsuko approaches, Logan slowly puts down his bowl of rice.

    1)   Logan: If you want to hurt me, you're gonna need a sharper…

Page Twenty, Panel Two
Change angles on the two, as Atsuko bows a bit and PRESENTS the sword to Logan, handing it to him handle first.

No Copy

Page Twenty, Panel Three
Logan carefully TAKES the sword from the woman.
    2)   Logan: Hn.

Page Twenty, Panel Four
This shot of the sword can be from Logan's point of view, as he looks down to see a KAMIKAZE HEADBAND tied around the sword's handle.

    3)   Logan: Kamikaze.

Page Twenty, Panel Five
Pull out to another shot of both characters. Logan is still holding the sword, but Atsuko has just produced a small wooden box, which she's holding out here.

    4)   Logan: <Your… your father's?>

    5)   Atsuko: <He volunteered after mother was killed in the fire-bombings.>

    6)   Atsuko: <Before his final mission, father's wretched masters sent me that sword… and this.>

PAGE TWENTY-ONE

Page Twenty-one, Panel One
Push in on Logan, as he sets down the sword and takes the small box.

No Copy

Page Twenty-one, Panel Two
Again, this shot can be from Logan's point of view, as he looks down into the open box, which we can now see contains several FINGERNAIL CLIPPINGS.

    1)   Logan (from off): Fingernail clippings.

Page Twenty-one, Panel Three
Pull out to a shot of both characters, as Logan hands the box back to Atsuko.

> 2) Logan: <So you would have something to bury, right?>

> 3) Logan: <This… this is all you have left of him?>

Page Twenty-one, Panel Four
Change angles, as Atsuko sets aside the box, and takes Logan's hand with her free hand.

> 4) Atsuko: <No.>

> 5) Atsuko: <My father lives on…>

Page Twenty-one, Panel Five
Push in closer on the two, as Atsuko romantically PLACES Logan's hand over her heart.

> 6) Atsuko: <…here.>

PAGE TWENTY-TWO

Page Twenty-two, Panel One
Change angles, as a nervous Logan slowly pulls his hand away.

> 1) Logan: <Why did you help me?>

Page Twenty-two, Panel Two
This is just an alluring shot of Atsuko, as she begins to UNDO her kimono.

> 2) Atsuko: <I'm tired of war.>

Page Twenty-two, Panel Three
Change angles, as Atsuko REMOVES her clothing. Obviously, this isn't Vertigo, Eduardo, so please be discreet in how you suggest her nudity!

> 3) Atsuko: <And since it began, you're the first person I've met who seems at peace.>

Page Twenty-two, Panel Four
Pull out to a shot of both characters, as the naked Atsuko steps closer to

Logan, who looks away. He's trying his best not to give into temptation here.

> 4)   Logan: <That… that isn't necessary.>
>
> 5)   Logan: <You've done enough for me already.>
> 6)   Atsuko: Hai…

Page Twenty-two, Panel Five
Push in on the two. Logan closes his eyes as Atsuko begins to KISS his neck.

> 7)   Atsuko: <…and now it's time for you to do something for me.>

PAGE TWENTY-THREE

Page Twenty-three, Panel One
Change angles on the two, as Logan EMBRACES Atsuko.

> 1)   Logan: This is heaven, ain't it? I'm already dead, and now I'm in heaven.
>
> 2)   Atsuko: No… not heaven…
>
> 3)   Logan: Then what is this place? Where am I?

Page Twenty-three, Panel Two
This largest panel of the page (at least a half-SPLASH) is just a dramatic close-up of Atsuko from Logan's point of view, as she stares directly into our souls, and whispers a single word.

> 4)   Atsuko: Hiroshima.

Page Twenty-three, Panel Three
Finally, this is just an extreme close-up of Logan's emotionless eyes, clearly not realizing the horror that's on its way.

> 5)   Caption: It was just about the most beautiful word I'd ever heard.
>
> 6)   Closing Tag: To Be Continued…

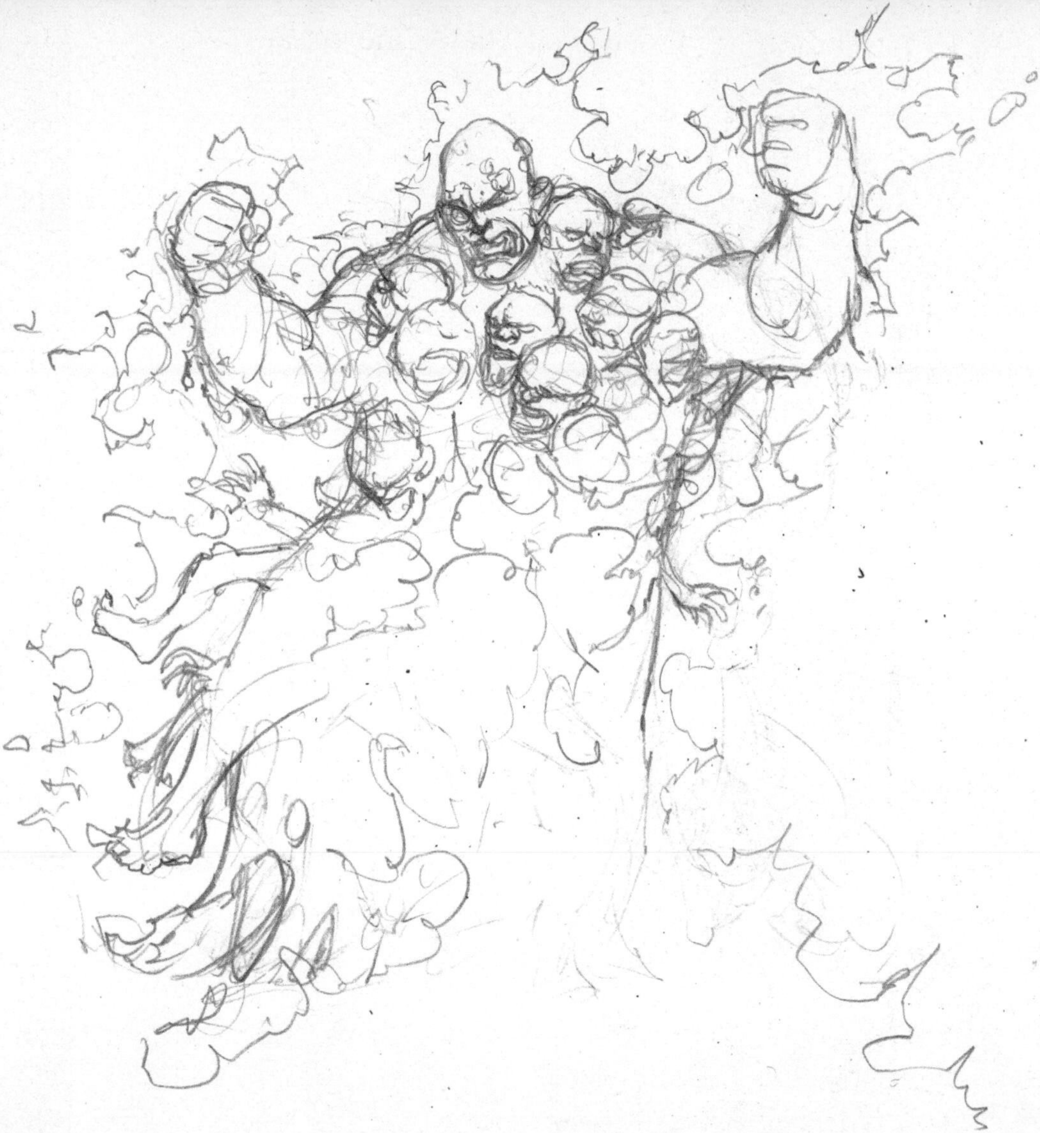

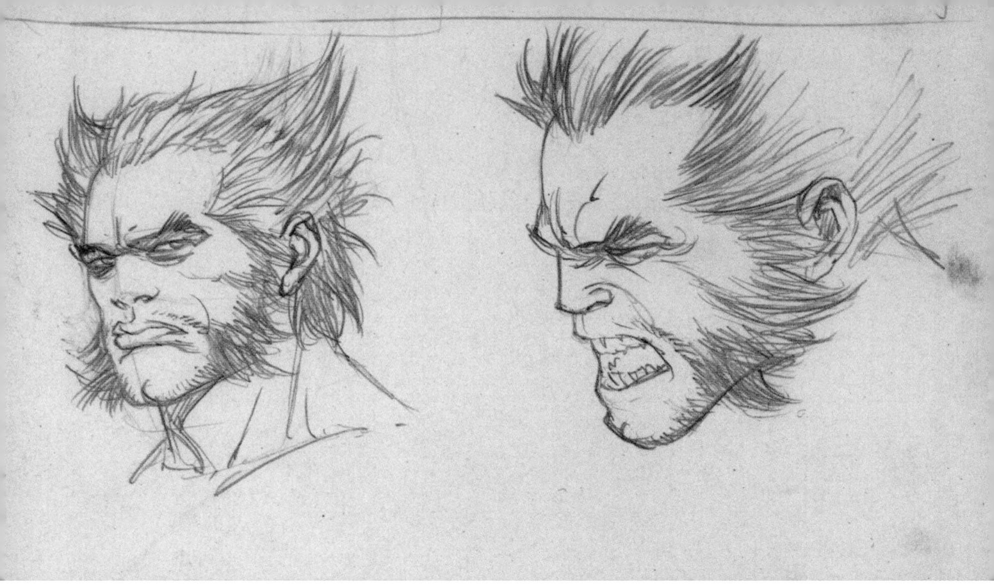

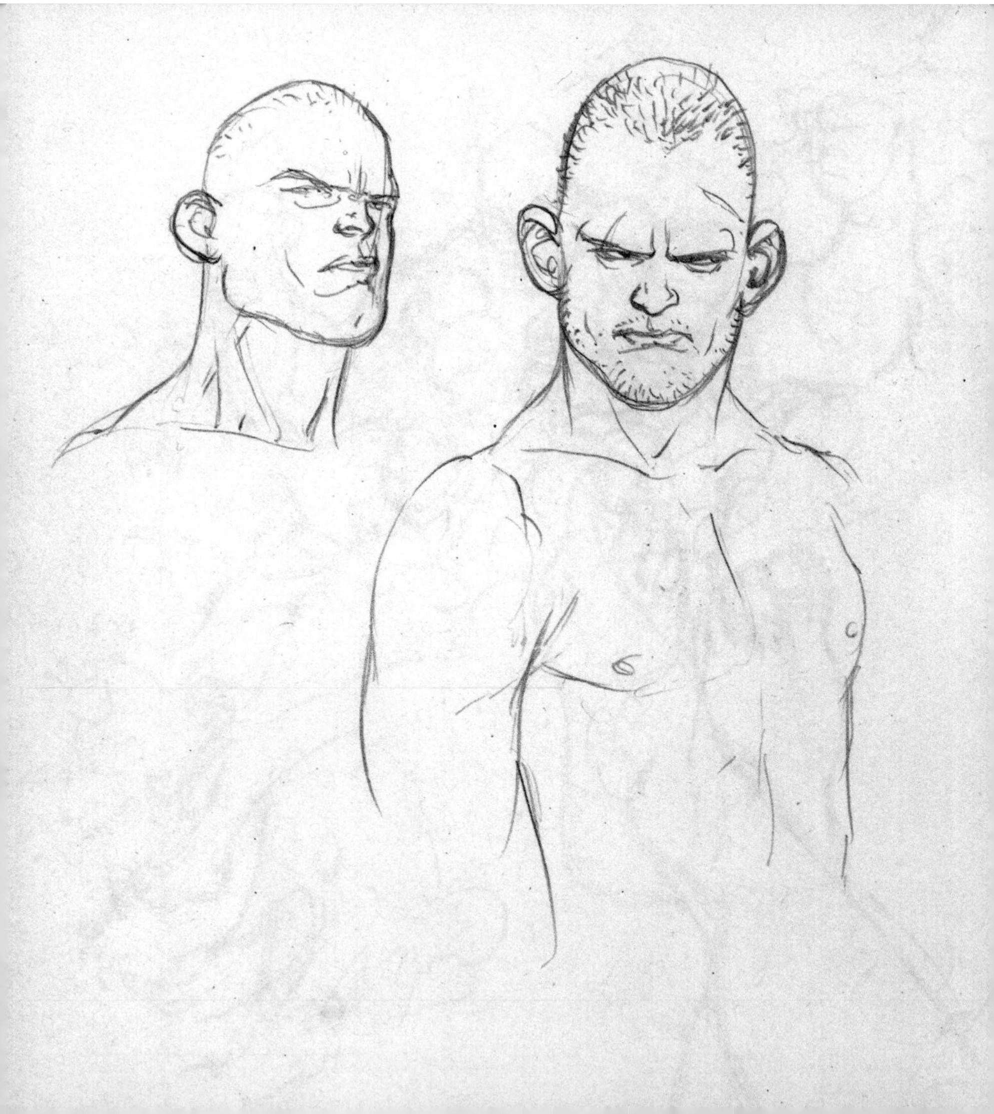

1

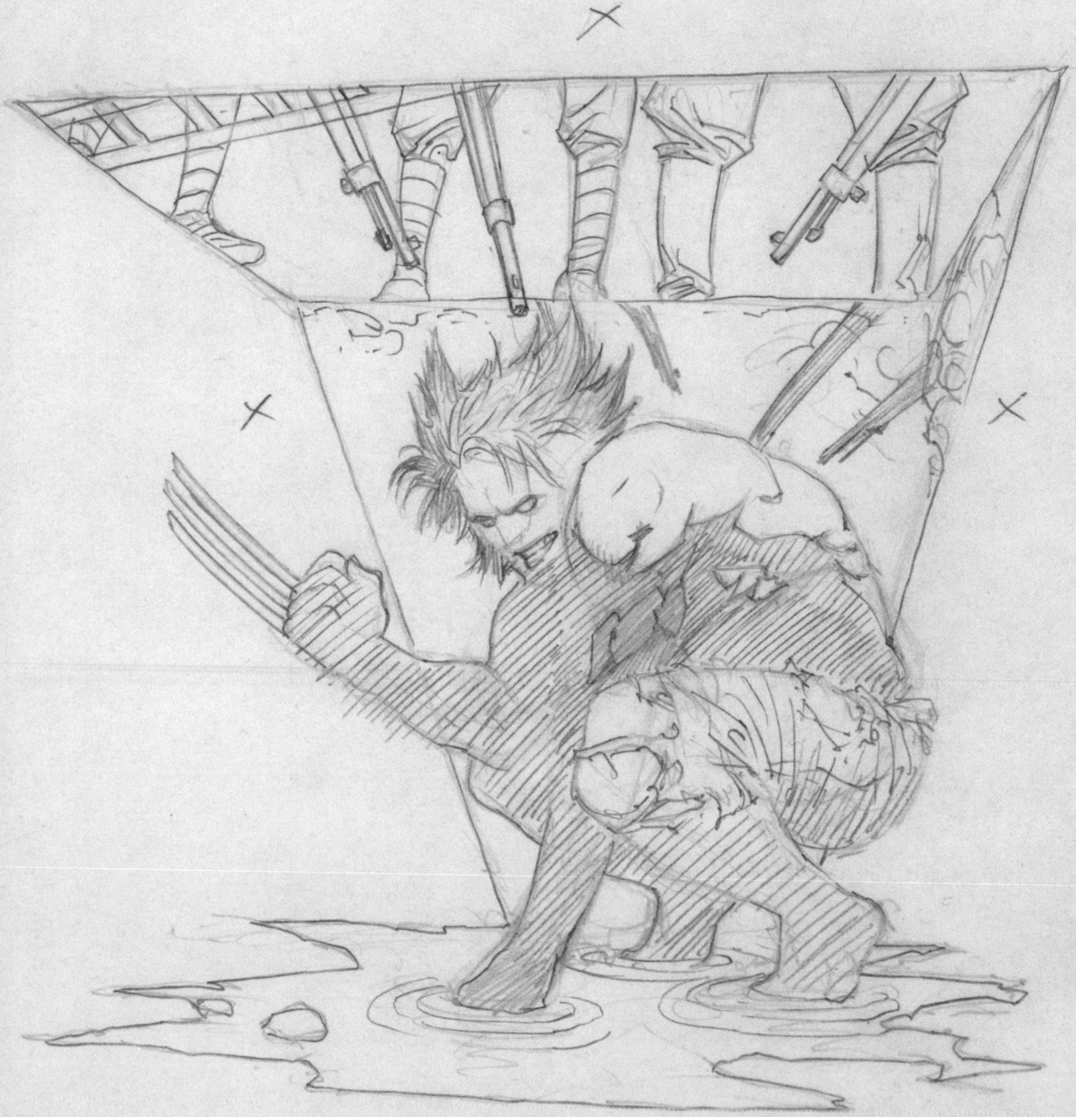

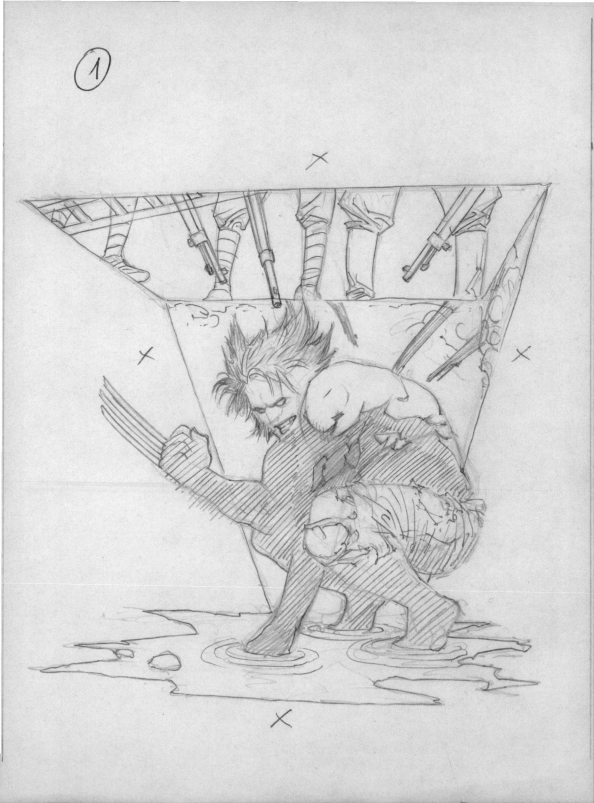

2

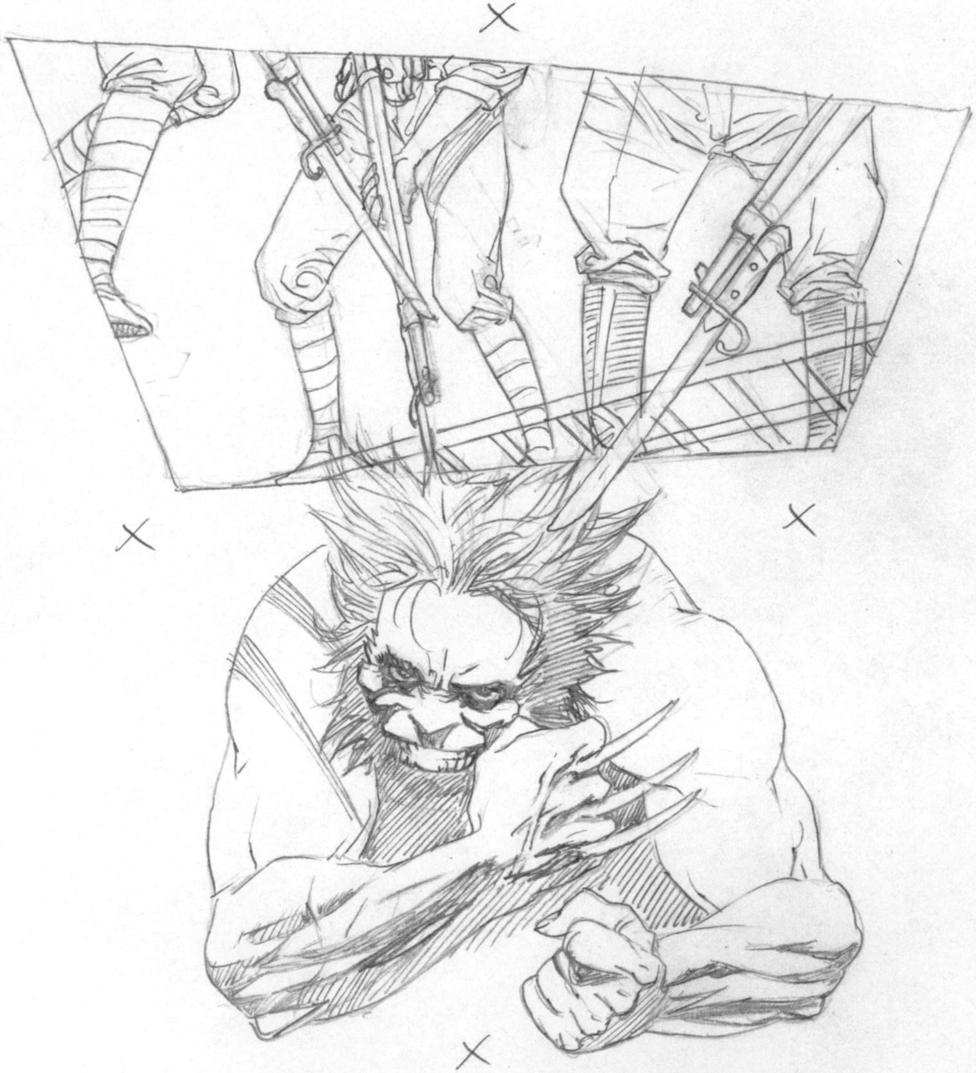

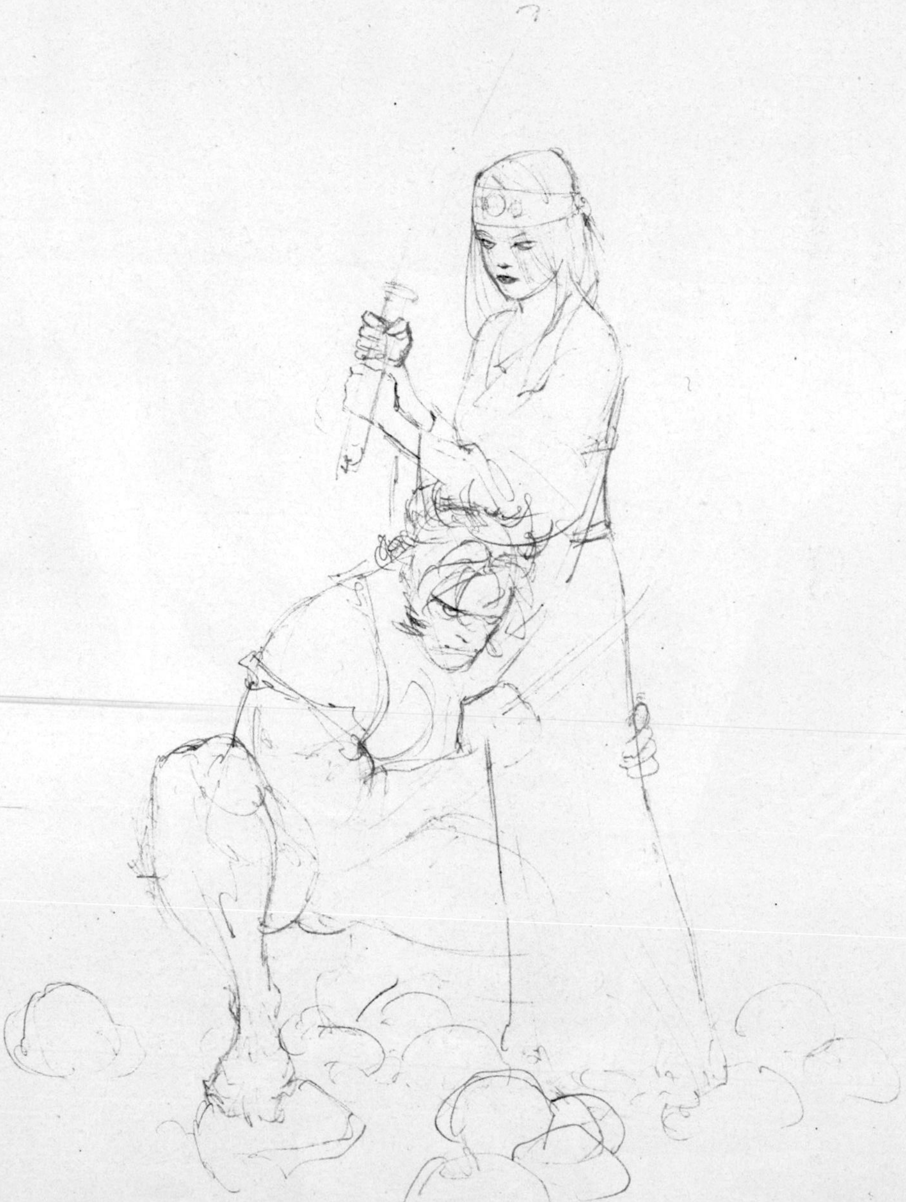

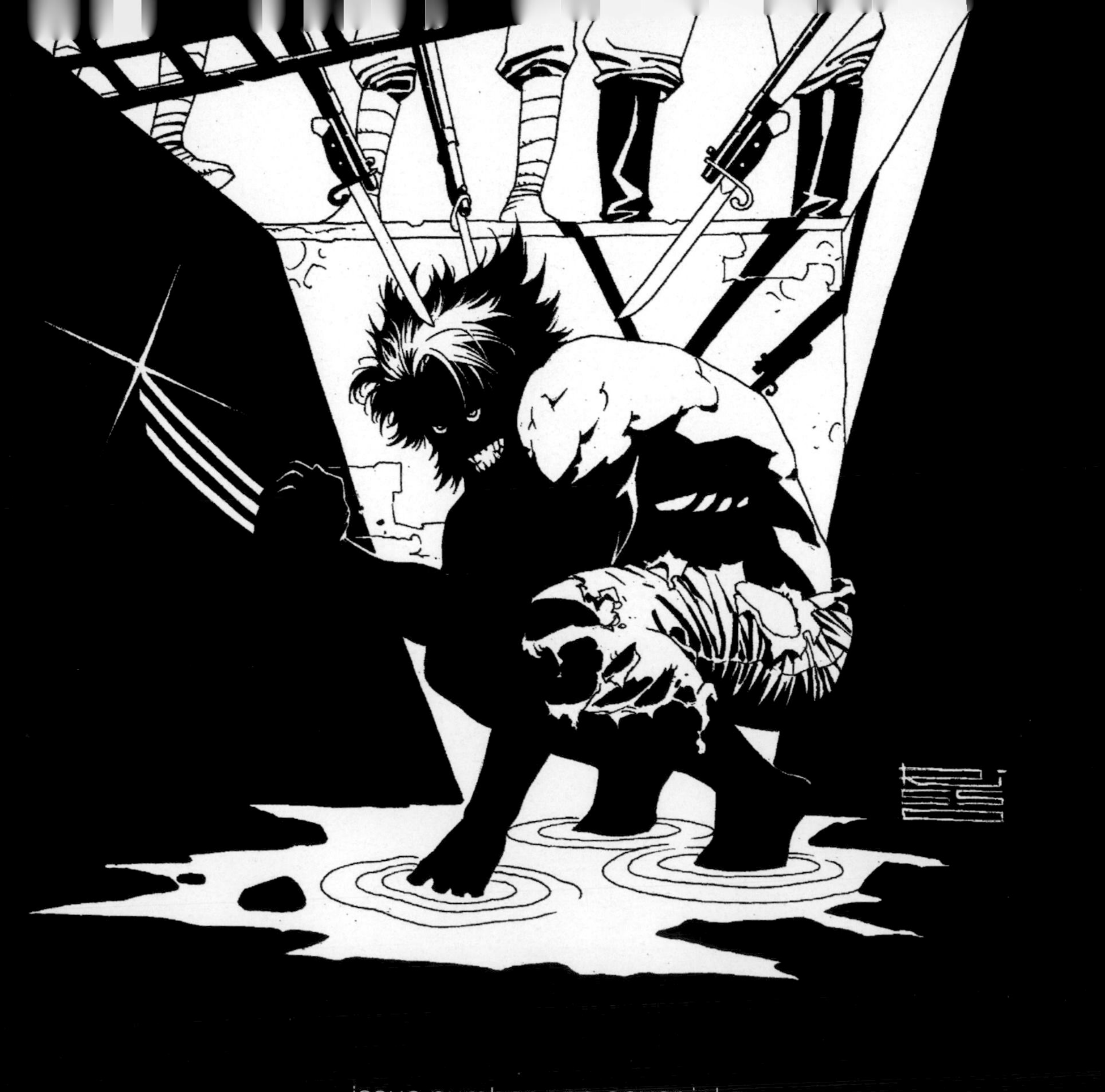

issue number one cover inks

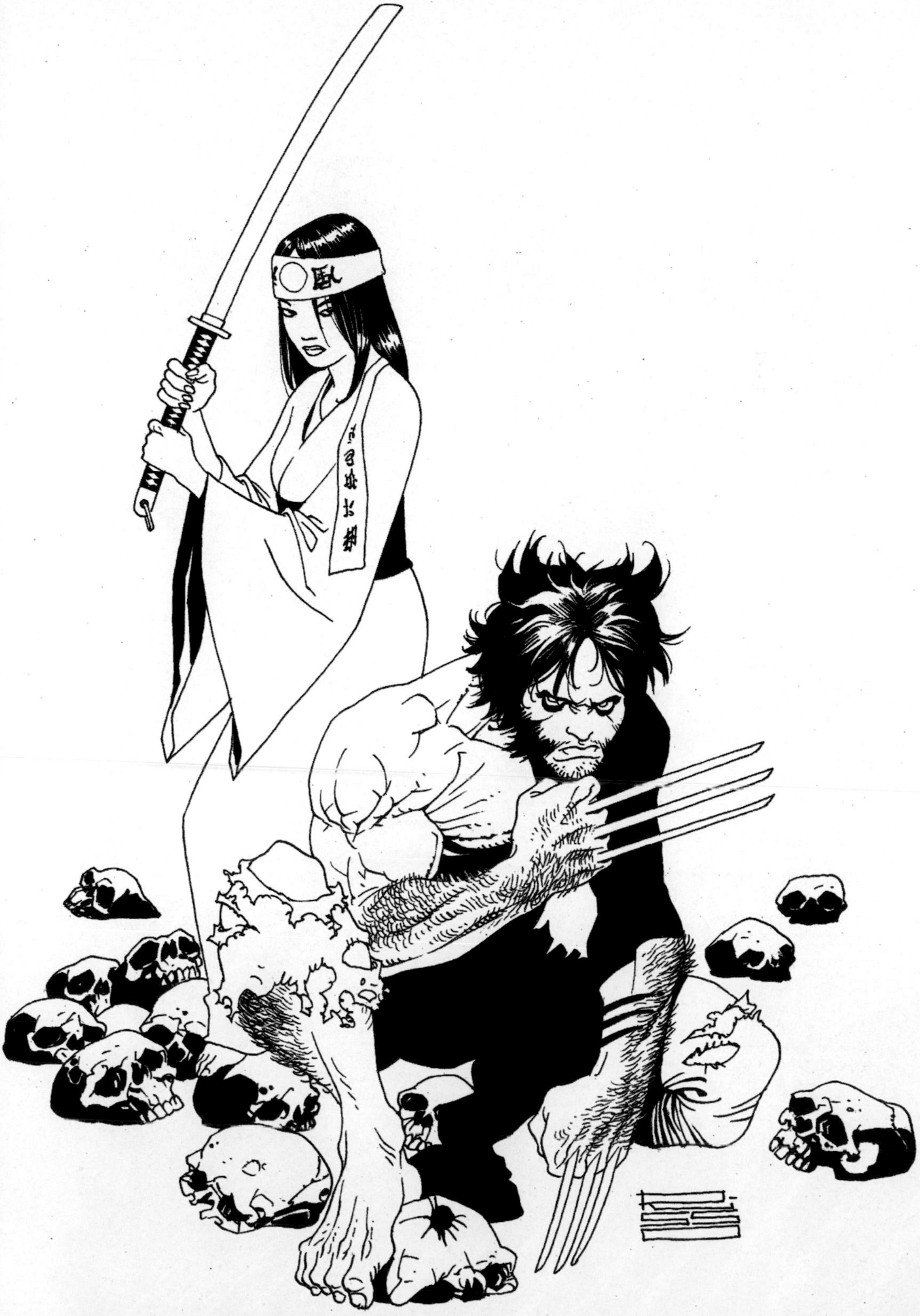

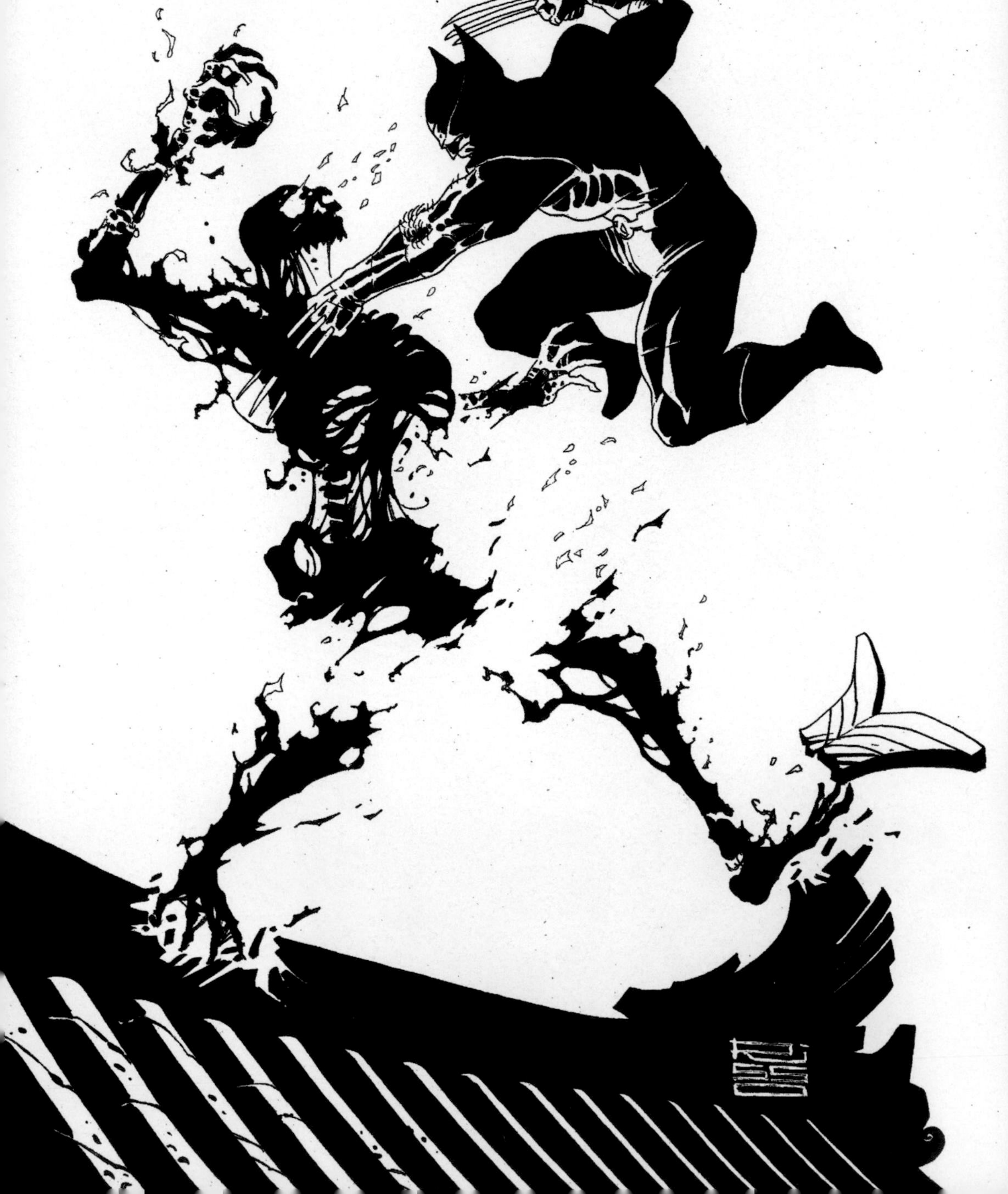

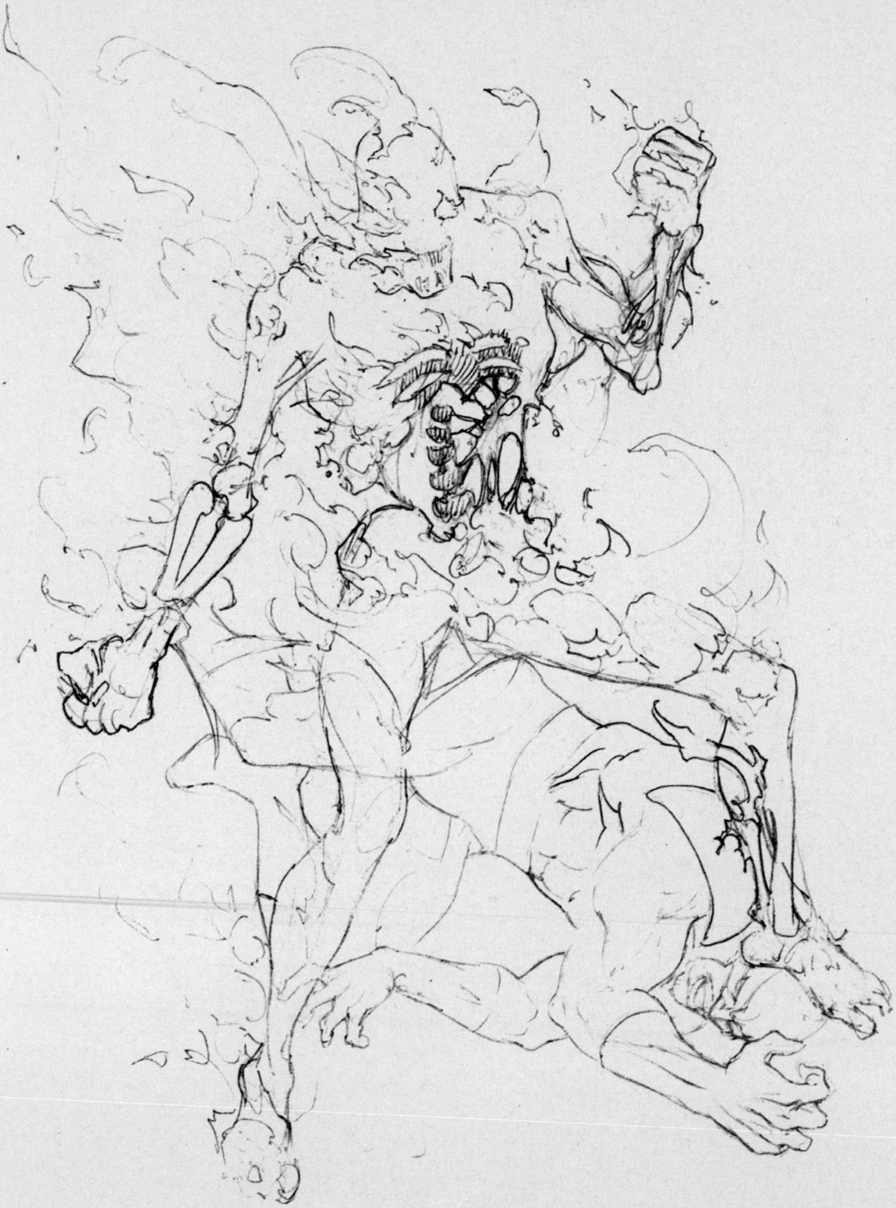

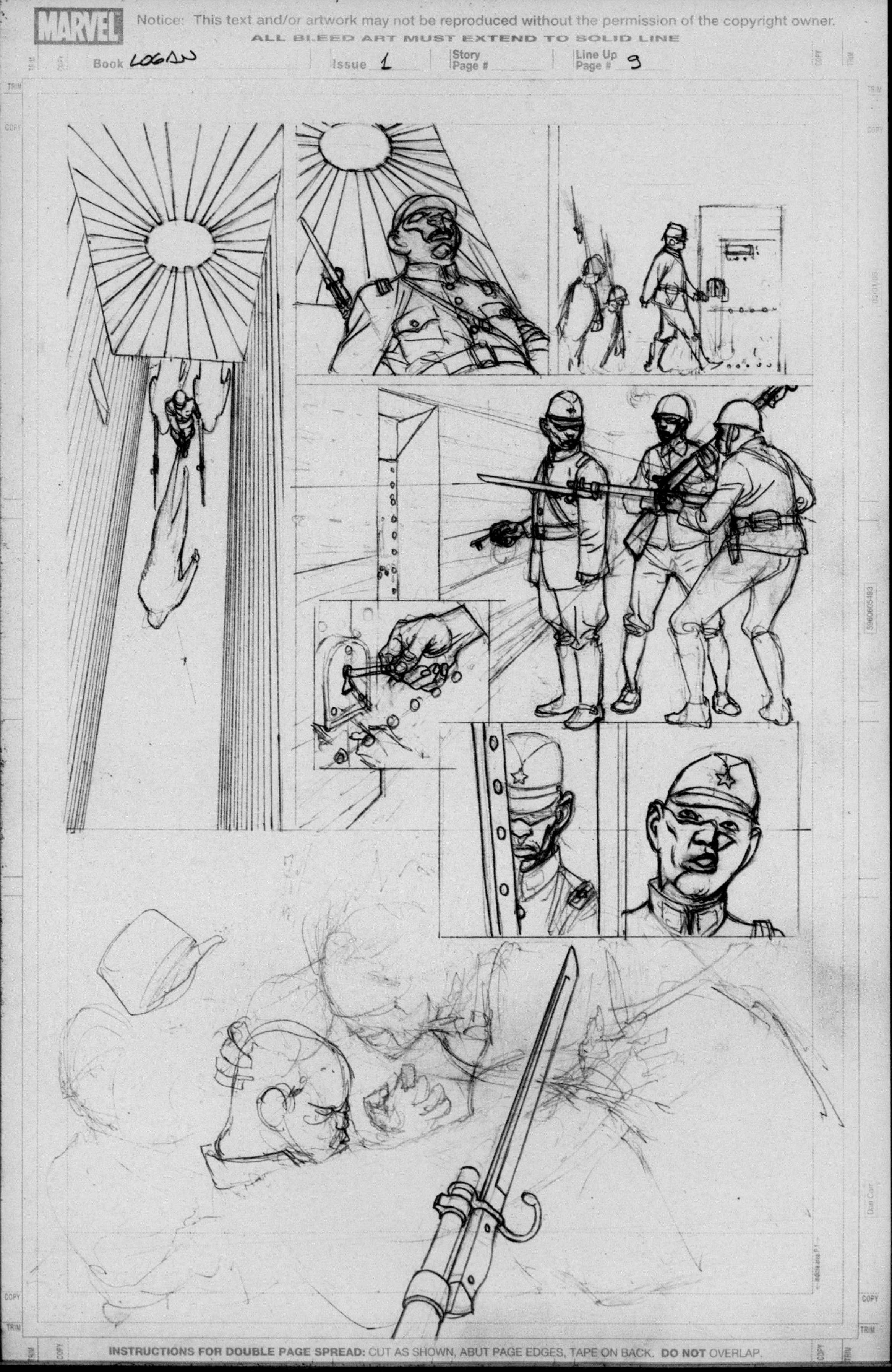
MARVEL
Notice: This text and/or artwork may not be reproduced without the permission of the copyright owner.
ALL BLEED ART MUST EXTEND TO SOLID LINE
Book LOGAN
Issue 1
Story Page #
Line Up Page # 9
INSTRUCTIONS FOR DOUBLE PAGE SPREAD: CUT AS SHOWN, ABUT PAGE EDGES, TAPE ON BACK. DO NOT OVERLAP.

unused pencils for issue number one, page nine

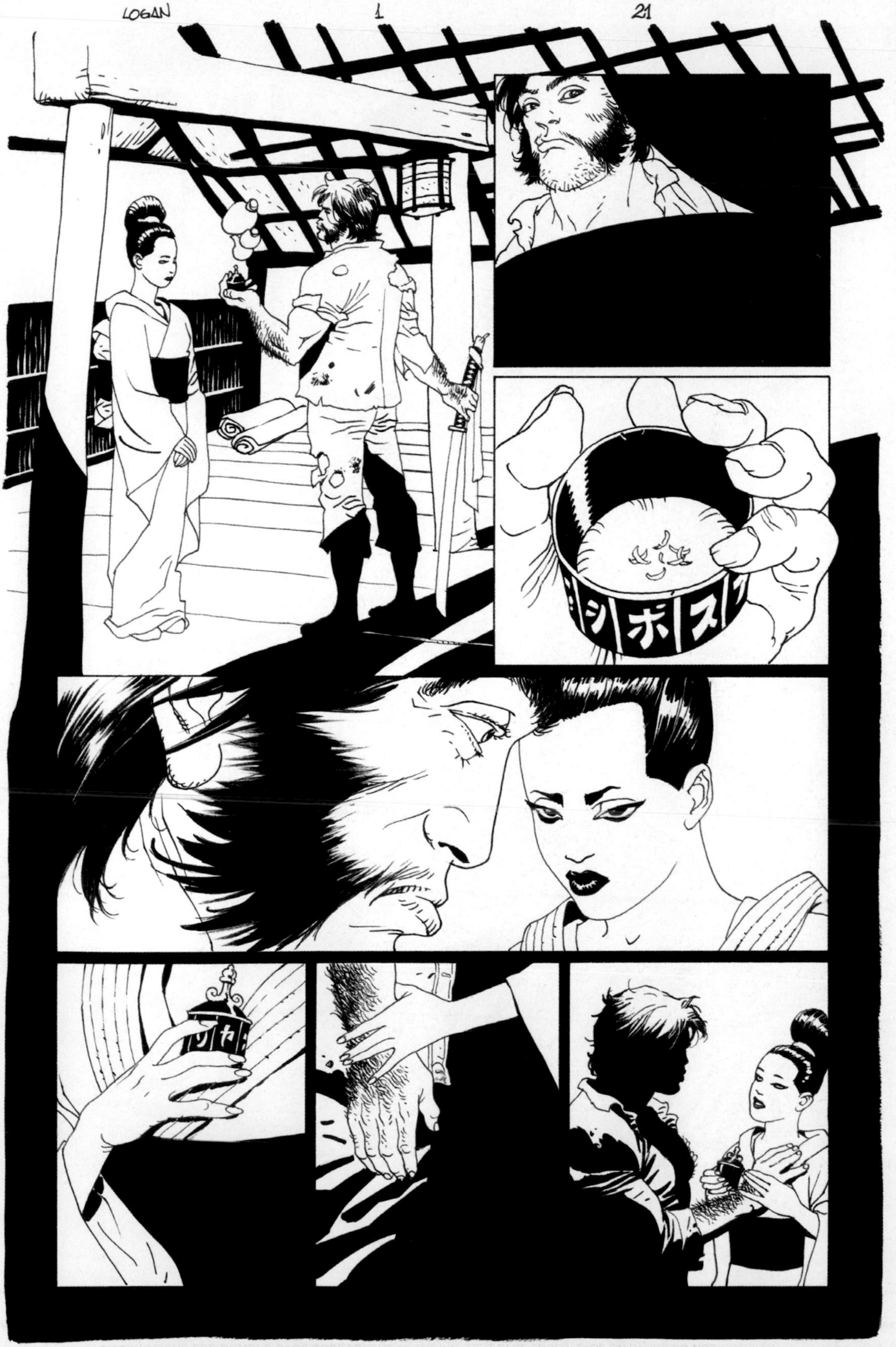
LOGAN
1
21

unused inks for issue number one, page twenty-one

INSTRUCTIONS FOR DOUBLE PAGE SPREAD: CUT AS SHOWN, ABUT PAGE EDGES, TAPE ON BACK. DO NOT OVERLAP.

unused inks for issue number two, page four

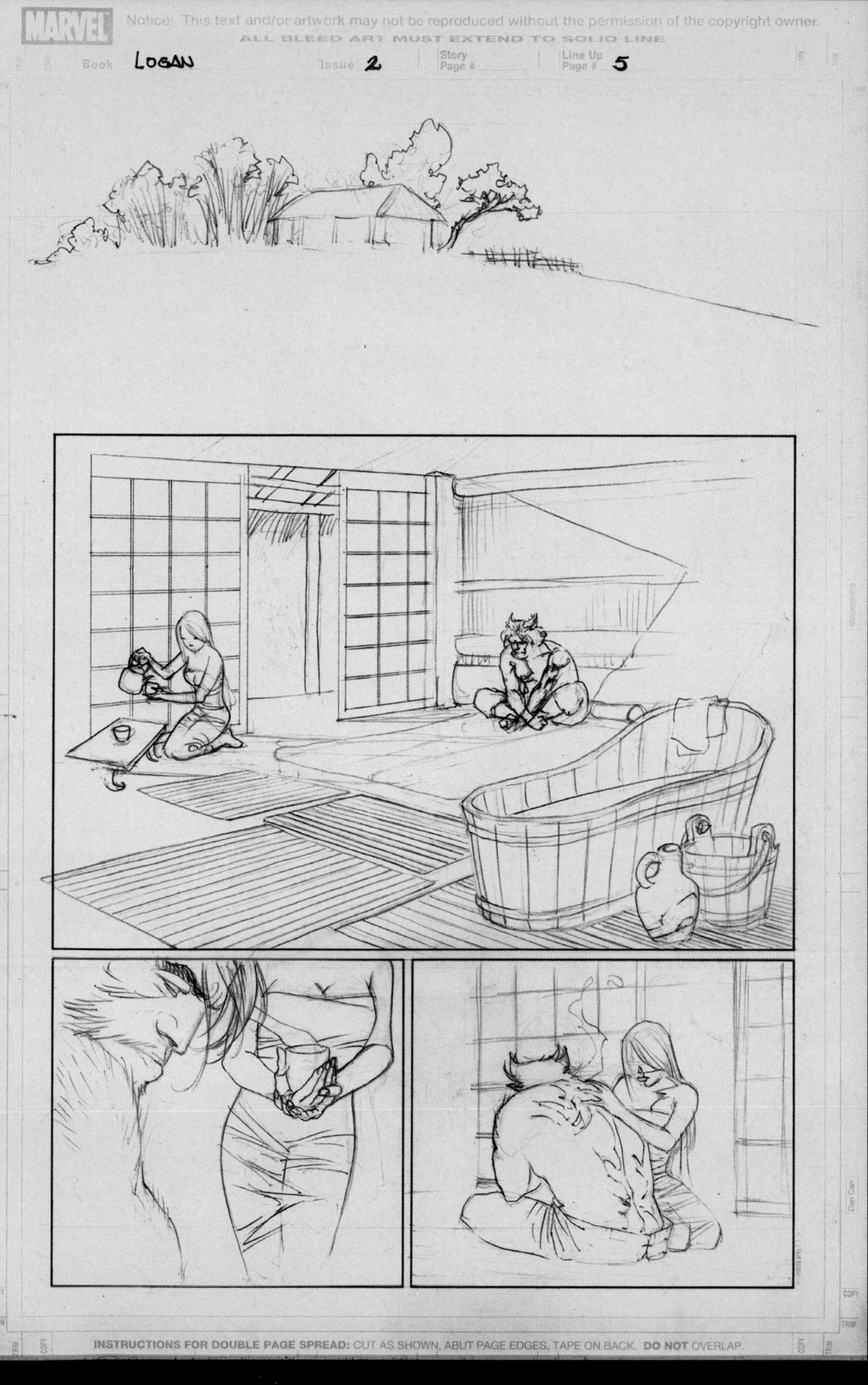

Book **LOGAN**   Issue **2**   Story Page # _____   Line Up Page # **5**

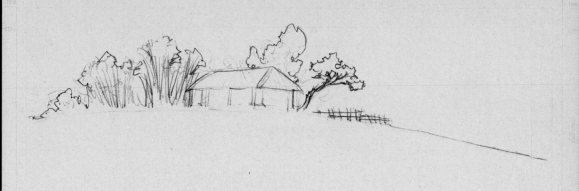

unused pencils for issue number two, page five

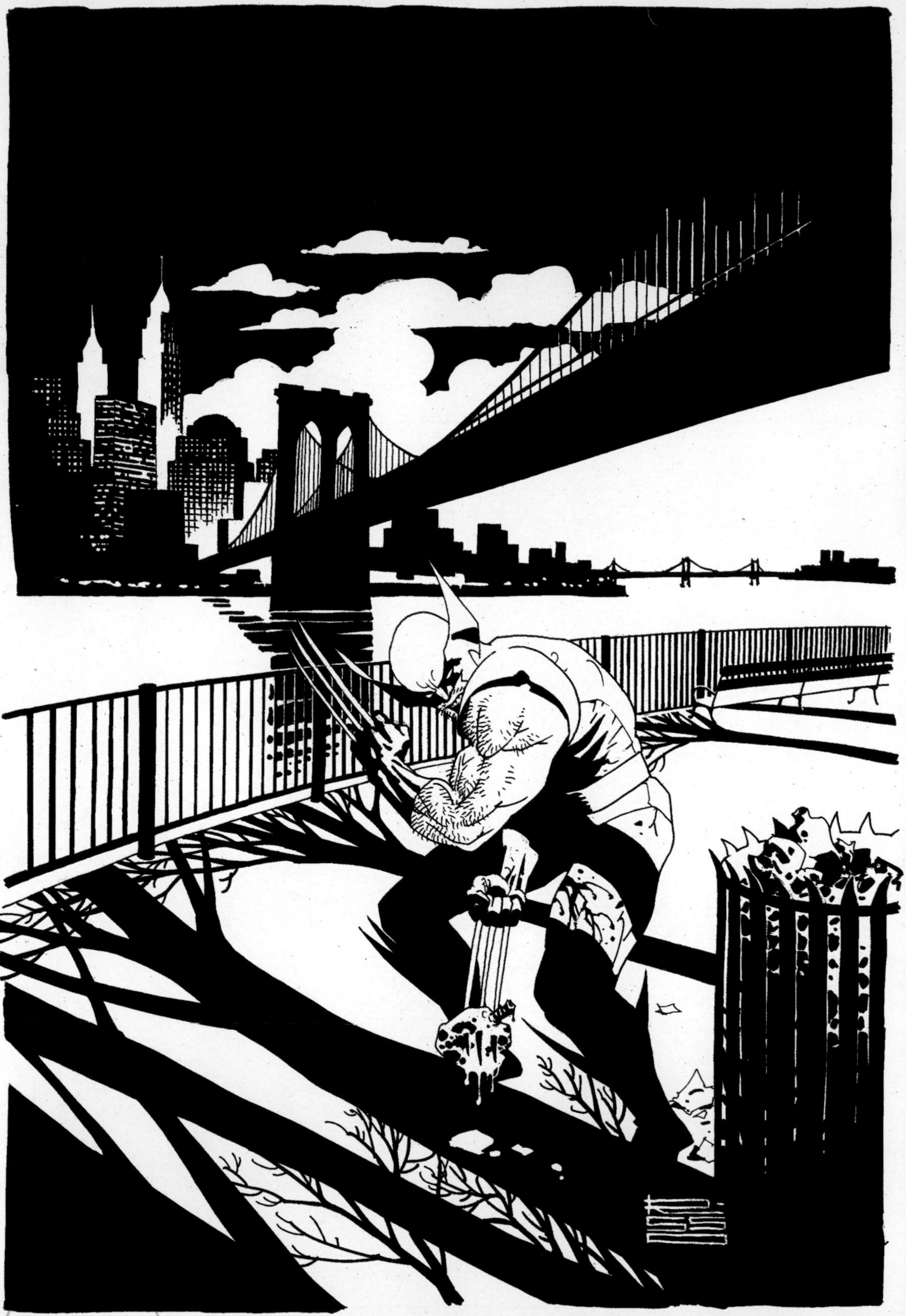

wolverine pin-up by eduardo risso .